FAKE CHURCH

THE SUBTLE DEFECTION

DAN SCHAEFFER

BARBOUR
PUBLISHING

Published by Barbour Publishing, Inc., P.O. Box 719, Uhrichsville, Ohio 44683, www.barbourbooks.com

Our mission is to publish and distribute inspirational products offering exceptional value and biblical encouragement to the masses.

Member of the
Evangelical Christian
Publishers Association

CONTENTS

Introduction 5

PART 1:
IDENTIFYING THE PROBLEM
  1. The Subtle Defection 9
  2. The Slippery Slope: The Process
     of Deception 25
  3. Naked and Unashamed: The Danger of
     Becoming Comfortable with Deception 45

PART 2:
IDENTIFYING ITS EXPRESSION
  4. Seeds of Defection 61
  5. Disconnected Defectors/Churchless
     Christians. 79
  6. Escape to the Virtual Church 100
  7. Friendship vs. Fellowship: What's the
     Big Difference?. 122
  8. Shepherd's Defection: Leading the
     Flock Astray. 138
  9. Plastic Evangelism 158
 10. What About Sin? 175

PART 3:
IDENTIFYING THE SOLUTION
 11. Coming Clean 197
 12. A Command Performance: Giving the
     Performance of Your Life 217
 13. Changing Course 236

INTRODUCTION

A writer is told time and again to "write what you know." It is with some chagrin, therefore, that I admit to being eminently qualified to write this book. In the past I have faked church. I still do, and I fear I always will. I do not feel lonely, however, since statistics indicate there are well over one hundred million of us in America alone. That's the bad news. The good news is that recovery is possible. It is possible, however, only to those who are able and willing to admit their condition. This book is dedicated to the brave souls who are willing to ask the hard questions and entertain the possibility that they have been, or presently are, faking church.

PART ONE

IDENTIFYING
THE PROBLEM

CHAPTER ONE

THE SUBTLE DEFECTION

FAKE—v.
*to practice deception
by pretending*

"We mold our faces to fit our masks."

JOHN ELDRIDGE

Ned sits down next to his wife, Tanya, in the church his family has called home for many years. He smiles, waves, jokes, and engages in friendly banter with everyone around him. He is a fixture in the church, having been involved in leadership for many years. Ned is well known, well liked, and deeply admired for his spiritual life. People continually stop and greet him. Frank, one of the men he has discipled, waves to him from across the church. Ned smiles and waves back. He spent several years sharing with Frank how to live the Christian life. Suddenly, he feels a pang of guilt.

Just this morning Ned blew up at Tanya, cursing and yelling at her. Unfortunately, this wasn't an aberration in his life; it was the norm. Ned hasn't read his Bible in months. His prayer life is haphazard and infrequent, and his temper can be titanic. Yet he has learned how to fake it in church. In church he prays glowing prayers and knows all the important spiritual phrases. His church background provided him a strong base of biblical knowledge that helped to thrust him into a teaching role. His leadership abilities were discovered and put to good use as well.

All those years growing up in church, learning how to talk and smile and be someone else—someone you wish you were—have paid off. He is considered spiritually mature and recognized as a spiritual leader. Ned likes the person he is at church, at least the person he portrays. He wishes he were the Ned everyone admires. Sometimes he even feels like he is that Ned. But then the real Ned comes out when he is safely away from church. Church is his whole life, his place of importance, the place he has made his mark in life. So he guards his secret carefully.

Betty has led a women's Bible study for several years and finds it the most fulfilling thing she has ever done in her life. She loves teaching. She loves being the source of information and the person all the women look up to. She is constantly held up as an example to the other women and secretly relishes that role. But recently she has become concerned. Sometimes it seems as if she loves her teaching role and the adulation that comes with it too much.

She knows that teaching about God is a good thing, but she can't help but wonder whether or not she is doing it for the right reason. Sometimes she feels guilty, secretly wondering about her true motivations. She thinks they might not all be sincerely spiritual, but she's pretty sure she doesn't want to find out. Everything is going smoothly, and there doesn't seem to be any reason to bring up problems. If no one is complaining at Bible study, why should she worry? Feeling better, she dismisses the disturbing thoughts.

Ralph and Jill decide to stay home again this Sunday morning. They've been doing it more and more lately. They used to be regular fixtures in the church. Ralph worked with the youth group, and Jill ran the nursery. But after their own children grew older and left for college, Ralph and Jill felt they had put in their time. Now they no longer sense any real need to be at church. It's time for them to enjoy themselves, to indulge in what they put off for so many years while they worked in the church. They believe it is time for others to do the job.

When people ask where they have been, they talk excitedly about their travel plans and visits with their grown children. But most of their Sundays are spent at home, sleeping in or going out to breakfast. They frequently have their old friends from church over and talk about the "good old days." Still revered as charter members of the church, Ralph and Jill feel they are good Christians—better than most. It's just that since their children grew up, church hasn't been quite as important anymore. They've heard just about every sermon you can hear, and Ralph says he's tired of "reruns." Besides, they have convinced themselves that they haven't left God; they are just leaving the church. After all, they *are* retired.

It happens slowly, subtly. Most Christians aren't even aware of it when it happens. It is easier to spot in others than in ourselves, and since it looks different in different people, it can be difficult to detect. The "it" is a spiritual defection. What others see of our faith and service to Christ has become distorted—inevitably in our favor. In others' eyes, and even in our own, our Christian faith is pure and strong, our motives unquestionable. Our reputation is pure and unsullied by any suspicion of improper motivation. But "it" has happened nonetheless. . .spiritual defection.

"It" has taken root.

You may have noticed it from time to time, that indelible stain upon your soul peeking out from behind your spiritual façade, but it seemed such a slight stain that it was acceptable. You aren't everything you are pretending to be, and you know it. Your godliness is often for public consumption only. Your patience can be plastic. Your public prayers are eloquent, your private prayers often nonexistent or anemic. You have begun the downward spiral of spiritual defection from sincere service to Christ and His church. But don't take this judgment too personally; you aren't the only one. I'm another. In fact, the church is filled with us. We come in all shapes, styles, and varieties.

You may read your Bible regularly, listen to Christian radio programs frequently, or watch Christian television religiously. You may read Christian books by the latest and most popular Christian authors, go to Promise Keepers or Women of Faith conferences faithfully. You may be a popular Christian "personality," a pastor, or a leader in your mission or denomination. You may even feel very spiritual at times. You are a fake. Sorry, but it's true.

The problem with us fakes is that we don't all look the same. We have the same problem, but we exhibit it differently. One fake does not look like another, the way one alcoholic doesn't look like another. Some alcoholics are obvious: staggering about disheveled on a lonely street at night in search of a drink. Other alcoholics dress in three-piece suits, drive expensive cars, live in expensive homes, and are never seen inebriated. They get drunk in luxurious privacy. Some alcoholics are very young; some are very old. Some have long hair, tattoos, and multiple body piercings. Some bake cookies and organize potlucks for 4-H.

Because we all look so different, you may not recognize yourself as a spiritual fake at first. The deception goes deep in some of us.

There are the happy involved fakers. Happy fakers don't even know yet that they are faking. They throw themselves into the "ministry" or service for all they've got. They teach the children, organize women's ministries, and lead the men's prayer meetings. They take the youth on outings or to concerts and help clean all the nursery equipment every week. They haven't missed a Sunday in years. What they don't know yet is that, despite all their feverish activity, they are often doing these wonderful things for the wrong reasons. They are well-intentioned, unwitting, and possibly even unintentional fakes—but fakes nonetheless.

Then there are the "service junkie" fakes. They serve faithfully and sacrificially: leading, serving, teaching, and organizing, seemingly always on the edge of spiritual burnout. No one would dare question his or her motivations. No one gives, or gives up, more than they do for church. They would never think of abandoning their spiritual posts. They are the first to arrive at church and the last to leave.

But, despite their impressive service record, much of their self-sacrificial service is not as self-sacrificing as it seems. They secretly crave the constant strokes and affirmation they receive the way a junkie craves drugs. They live to be needed, to be noticed. They do love God and truly do want to serve Him. But, unknown to many of them, it is a darker, less noble motivation that now drives them.

Some fakes are heavily involved (or even overinvolved) at church and frequently found in leadership; but, unlike the service junkie fake, their hearts are no longer in it. They are merely going through the motions, and they know it. They have secretly come to dread Sunday. It didn't used to be that way. What was once fun or fulfilling has slowly become a grind. They long for a reason to abandon their leadership roles. When they eventually find one, they fade away, leaving fellowship and service behind.

Then there are the patronizing fakers. For these fakers their defection from church and service is caused by a growing sense that spiritually they have grown beyond the church, beyond the silly squabbles over worship style and whether or not to recarpet the sanctuary. Petty jealousies and blatant hypocrisy make them look with disdain on this immature motley group.

The pastor's limited oratorical and homiletical skills leave them bored and critical. The smaller church's amateurish musical efforts and "folksy" up-front leadership cause them to roll their eyes. Larger churches with more polish and pizzazz strike them as plastic and glitzy—definitely unspiritual. Unfortunately, the one or two men whose spiritual insight and intelligence they could comfortably sit under died about fourteen hundred years ago. To them the church is an embarrassment. They used to feign respect for the pastor and leadership (in front of them), but it was an act. And the act grew thinner by the day, until finally it could no longer be tolerated. Their ultimate conclusion is that the church has nothing to offer them; they have grown beyond it. So they just gradually fade into the spiritual woodwork. At times they may even feel a twinge of sadness at the departure, but it is a patronizing sadness. They, too, are fakes.

There are many kinds of fakers. Maybe you recognized yourself; maybe you didn't. But deep down you know there's more truth in what I've said than you like, and it makes you feel uncomfortable. Join the crowd. You may have been faking it for a long time. You are the lucky one; at least you know you're faking. There are others who don't.

Fakers

One of the worst things anyone can be called is a fake. It is a word of contempt in our culture. Recently a very competent and respected college football coach landed a prestigious position at a prominent football powerhouse. Several days later he was forced to resign when it was discovered that he had embellished his résumé. Embellishing résumés is not simply a secular pursuit. It is the temptation of every Christian and a plague in the church.

Each of us knows at times that we seek to deceive people about the reality concerning us, especially when it comes to matters of spirituality. Maybe that's why you picked up this book. You wanted to see if you were a fake. You are. We all are. Oh, we're not all fakes all the time. In fact, we can spend a good deal of our time attempting to be truly genuine. But most of us would admit that the spiritual image others have of us isn't always accurate, in fact, at times it is nowhere near reality. And it is a fearful thing to let others in on the dark secret. We may be exposed as being. . .well, fakes!

When it comes to matters of spirituality, most of us throw up formidable defenses to any accusation that we might be in any way touching up our spiritual image. We shouldn't. Every one of us works from less-than-pure motives on a regular basis. Sin has so stained and infected our hearts that it is only through the grace of God and the power of His resurrection in us that we are capable of any truly sincere ministry and service for Christ.

In this book I am not going to deal with those who are not Christians but with what the Bible calls "wolves in sheep's clothing." In those people, there was never any sincerity, never any true seeking after Christ—only the deliberate attempt to use the façade of Christianity to further their personal ambitions (usually sexual or financial). Although these people certainly exist in churches today, it is my belief that they are rare. I will deal instead with the people who truly seek God, who don't mean to be fake but who realize that their spiritual appearance and reality don't match. People like me: easily deceived, easily deceiving, and wanting to change.

The problem, of course, is that deception is so ingrained in us that the deceit often becomes second nature—and not just in church. We wear baggy clothes to make us look thinner. We color our hair to make us look younger. We wear makeup to hide our blemishes. We drive cars we often can't afford to make us look more successful. Now, through cosmetic surgery, we can become more plastic than ever. We're so used to faking it that we can fake it without being aware that we are doing it. This is one of the reasons that it is so easy to fake it at church.

When I was in my early twenties, I was involved in a new church plant. I taught a group of children of various ages on Sunday morning. I was keenly aware of my spiritual image because I wanted desperately to move into church leadership. My goal was to be the pastor of my own church someday. This was one of my first ministry opportunities, and I was determined to make the best of it. This was also one of the hardest times in my life. Finances were tight, my business was struggling, and school was all consuming. I was lonely, tired, and often very frustrated at my lack of progress.

So when I came to church I put on the "happy face" and persona that I felt were requisite for leadership advancement.

Our Sunday school children, who were going through a particular study on the "Fruits of the Spirit," gave out awards one Sunday to the ones thought best typifying a particular fruit of the Spirit. I was given the "Joy" award. I was rewarded for being a good fake. I have a sneaking suspicion that I'm not the first. I didn't consciously seek to become a fake. It wasn't an ambition of mine, but one step leads to another.

Several years later I was making a ministry phone call to someone in our church. I had moved from children's ministries to being a small-group adult leader. My sister happened to be listening, and when I finished the call, she gave me an inquiring look and asked, "Why do you sound so different when you talk to people over the phone?" I told her I didn't know what she was talking about. "Well, you sound like you're all hyped up, all happy. It doesn't seem very real." I told her again that I didn't know what she was talking about. I did. I had even noticed it myself. I just thought that I needed to sound more spiritual as well as act more spiritual—the key words being *sound* and *act*.

I admit to these things only to help reinforce the truth that most of us are far more accustomed to "faking it" in church than we'd care to admit. There are many different ways to fake church. But it is essentially a subtle defection from the truth about our real spiritual condition and motivations and a corresponding attempt to mislead others as well as ourselves. If left untreated, it can eventually result in a physical defection from the church and service. It begins so small we barely notice it, but it can grow until most of what people see in us is false.

FINDING THE EXIT

A great deal of attention is being focused on reaching out to the unchurched. Yet, thousands are streaming out the back door while we are focused on the front door. In William Hendricks's timely book *Exit Interviews* (Moody 1993), he points out that fifty-three thousand people leave churches every week and *never* come back. Although there are a variety of reasons to explain this mass exodus, I believe that spiritual defection is certainly a strong contender in the lives of many.

The growing defection in the church of Christ today among those who had once proclaimed their loyalty to both Christ and Christian service is not a new phenomenon. It was present in the New Testament church as well. And, as we will see, spiritual defection is present among those seemingly most committed to regular attendance and participation in fellowship, not simply those who have chosen to walk away.

Peter, surely one of the pillars of the Christian faith, leaves an instructive legacy of the danger of self-deception. On the night Jesus was going to be arrested, our Lord enjoyed one last meal with His disciples. During this time Jesus turned to Peter and revealed to him that Satan was going to attack his faith and that he would come close to forsaking his Master (Luke 22:31–34). Later, at the Mount of Olives, Jesus prophesied that all of His disciples would fall away and forsake Him. Peter vehemently denied that this would happen to him (Matthew 26:31–35).

To Peter, defection from his Master was absolutely unthinkable. He was convinced he was incapable of such defection. Tragically, like us, his conviction was based on a faulty premise—that spiritually he was everything he imagined himself to be.

I believe with all my heart that Peter believed this about himself. I believe this because I, too, have experienced failure in faithfulness to my Lord that I never thought possible. My spiritual self-image was just as much a deception to me as to anyone else. Peter's experience is instructive to me and strangely comforting.

A physical defection from Christian service and fellowship is often only the final stages of a spiritual defection that began much earlier in our hearts. In fact, it is just as likely that those involved in spiritual defection will never leave the church. They will remain—cloaked and hidden. The terribly uncomfortable conclusion of Scripture and experience is that many Christians carry within them the seeds of defection.

Paul reminds us in 1 Corinthians 4:2–5, "Now it is required that those who have been given a trust must prove faithful. I care very little if I am judged by you or by any human court; indeed, I do not even judge myself. My conscience is clear, but that does not make me innocent. It is the Lord who judges me. Therefore judge nothing before the appointed time; wait till the Lord comes. He will bring to light what is hidden in darkness *and will expose the motives of men's hearts*. At that time each will receive his praise from God" (author emphasis added). This is a problem that is as old as the church itself. God is more interested in *why* we are doing something than in *what* we are doing.

Diluted Motives

Desires and motivations are hard to separate and identify. When you have a desire to serve Christ and a desire to be seen as important, which desire is the strongest? By which are you most motivated? If you have a desire to be a mature Christian and a desire to *appear* to be a mature Christian, which of these two motivations will ultimately prevail?

This is important, because a true desire to grow in our spiritual lives requires an honest assessment of where we really are. All spiritual pretense must be dropped, and all attempts at deception abandoned. However, if we allow the desire to have people think we are spiritually mature to prevail, deception rather than honesty is required.

We can feel free to mix genuine motivations with stealth motivations. We can create a spiritual persona through deception and then try to live up to the deception we've created. We can feel that since we know the real truth about ourselves and possibly have even confessed it to God, we can keep the deception in place.

If, by using the right words, hiding some of your less than spiritual desires, and working hard within the church, you develop a spiritual reputation that exceeds the spiritual reality, what do you do? People think you are the person you want to be, so what's the harm? Ultimately, you tell yourself, you will become that person anyway. It is a terribly humbling, difficult thing to truly and honestly assess your motivations for service. You are afraid that others will discover the truth about you, and then you will lose your spiritual reputation. It is not a pleasant discovery to realize one day that even though you do seek to serve God, you are faking much of your service and devotion to Christ.

I remember the day I was able to trace how one long and slow defection had been planted in my heart. I had become a Christian when I was only about fourteen years old. By that time I had already been in three broken homes and felt insecure about myself and my place in life.

I had been involved in a local church youth group where I found instant acceptance and friendships. My growth in the Lord was quick, as was my growing involvement in the group. It wasn't long before I found myself in leadership. I felt it was such an honor to be able to serve God in this way. After receiving many compliments on my leadership and teaching through the years, I graduated from high school and entered seminary.

Even though I firmly believe that I was called of God to go into pastoral ministry, I have to admit upon reflection that what drew me to this role was not *only* the leading of the Holy Spirit but also the example of my own pastor. He was a godly, well-respected man. Everyone admired him, which didn't escape my notice. To a young man who was as insecure about himself and his place in the world as I was, my pastor's job was very attractive. It would be nice to have people look at me the way they looked at him. It would be nice to be as respected by people as he was. I never verbalized that, but, though I didn't completely recognize it at the time, those feelings certainly played a large part in my decision. The seed was planted.

After graduating from seminary, I began a new church in southern California. For the first three years things went pretty well. Many people came to Christ and were built up in their faith. Certainly this was what I had gotten into ministry for. Or was it?

About the third year, the church began to experience some dissent. There were questions about my leadership and the church's direction and vision. I suddenly grew very fearful that I would lose the very thing I wanted most—my pastorate—and all the peripheral benefits I had coveted: purpose, respect, admiration, and authority. It finally got to the point where I felt that there was no saving the situation.

This was heartbreaking. My whole world was tied up in being a pastor. The pressure got so bad that I finally quit. I didn't submit my resignation to my elder board immediately because I still had a wife, three children, and a mortgage. But I remember the day I submitted my resignation to the Lord. It was a sad moment, but it forced me to ask myself, "What now?"

I realized with some chagrin that despite my dire premonitions, the sun would come out, the birds would sing, and God would still love me and have a plan for my life. Believe it or not, it was a very startling revelation. Since I was still at the church, I began to minister again but in a new way. Until then, I had not realized how much church service or "the Lord's work" had been about me and meeting my own needs. Since my humble beginnings of wanting to serve Christ, I had evolved into quite a self-centered, albeit much more theologically qualified, minister. The revelation of the extent of my spiritual defection was startling to me. How had this happened? The answer: slowly, gradually.

Church wasn't about me; it never had been. It was about Him, and it was about His children, whom I was there to shepherd. For years they had served as a wonderful audience. They had affirmed my self-worth; stroked my ego; and offered me respect, honor, and praise. I had been using God's precious sheep to meet my personal ego needs.

I truly did love Christ, and I truly did love this small church. But my motivation for service had become diluted, and I had never known how deeply. This failure brought it home. Ironically, as I began to minister freely, just biding my time until I could figure out where God wanted me, I began to fall back in love with ministry and the people God had called me to serve.

I eventually realized, with a sense of appreciation, that God had not called me out of ministry. He had merely needed to remind me whose ministry it was and what it was supposed to be all about. Ripping the plastic mask off of me had been terribly painful—exposing a festering spiritual sore—but necessary. Ironically, I am the only person who knew any of what was really taking place. It was a spiritual struggle for my soul, safely hidden behind "problems in the church."

The problems in the church gradually subsided, and I spent ten more of the best years of my life ministering to some of the greatest people in the kingdom of God. I have also learned that I am a "faker" the way an alcoholic is always an alcoholic. The temptation to deceive never leaves me. I am never far from temptation and only one moment away from defection. It has become clearer to me how often I have been guilty of faking church.

Perhaps a better way to say it is that our motives for service to Christ are diluted far more than we imagine. We often still serve for good scriptural reasons, but they are no longer the *primary* reasons we are serving.

Our own motivations for doing ministry are seldom examined. Indeed, many churches are so in need of help that the last thing they would do is question the motivations of anyone who volunteers to help in some way. It is simply taken for granted that someone who would volunteer to sacrifice his or her time, talent, and treasures for the cause of Christ must have spiritual reasons for doing it. Besides, beggars can't be choosy.

I do not believe that my ministry was in any way nullified or that the Spirit of God did not use me, even in my less than sincere moments. For I believe that a part of my heart truly wanted to serve Christ and His church in every single instance. What self-honesty provided me was His perspective on my service.

We can allow the slightest trace of sincerity to define our

motives. It is an easy and comfortable deception to approve of, and we usually do. If our consciences (or the Holy Spirit) bother us, we just give a slight nod to sincerity, and we instantly feel better.

The fact is that successful ministry, spiritual gifts and talents, or visible service for Christ can win you many accolades. At first we are surprised at these, don't feel worthy of them, and are frankly embarrassed at them. But, over time, we can begin to develop an appetite for them and begin to minister primarily to continue receiving these accolades. Service can become a means to an end and help create a false sense of spiritual maturity.

The hidden danger, the one I want to highlight in this book, is that if we don't consciously realize and adjust these motivations, a subtle defection will begin to develop even in the midst of our visible and effective ministries.

Gradually, the smallest of changes will take place in our hearts. We will begin to exchange the true joy of serving the Lord, who served us so humbly, for the more visible and tangible accolades that will inevitably come our way from those who can see only the worthiness of our activity or ministry, not the true motivation behind it. And one day, without even knowing that it has happened, we pass a threshold known only to God. We begin to minister, help, lead, organize, plan, bake, teach, preach, sing, visit, and give *primarily, though not exclusively,* for the accolades and self-affirmations we will receive for doing so, whether we deserve them or not. We begin to cultivate a spiritual reputation that does not reflect reality.

We have not lost our desire to serve Christ. We do not suddenly become fakes. We still love God and His church and service. But "it" has occurred nonetheless. We begin to serve ourselves just a little more than we serve Him. And over and over again the story of Ananias and Sapphira is reenacted.

THE ORIGINAL CHURCH FAKES

In Acts 5:1–10 we read the story of an infamous couple in the early church who, when they saw the generosity of other believers who gave up land and possessions to be sold to give to the poor, decided that was a great idea—in principle. What they were really attracted to was the increased spiritual standing that each of these people who so unselfishly gave received. They were held in high esteem among the brethren.

Ananias and Sapphira decided that they wanted a spiritual reputation like Barnabas and the others, but they wanted to fake it. Ananias and Sapphira are the original church fakers. Fortunately, their secret defection is illuminated by the Holy Spirit to serve as a warning to us.

They decided to sell a piece of land they owned, but they secretly gave only half the proceeds. This would have been fine, except that they clearly left the impression that they had sacrificially given *all* the proceeds for the poor. They wanted a spiritual reputation, but they didn't want to pay retail. They wanted the reputation of being great Christians for half the price.

We are taught to loathe their example, but I'm afraid we've often simply copied it, albeit to a lesser degree. I have discovered, with some shame, that there is a great deal more of Ananias and Sapphira in me than I care to admit. I'm not proud of it, but I can no longer deny it. If I have any consolation at all, it is that I know I'm not alone.

I remember when there was a great deal of talk about returning to New Testament Christianity. I fear that in at least one way we've succeeded beyond our wildest expectations. I have often received (and yes, even cultivated) a spiritual reputation that I did not deserve. Sound familiar?

It is instructive that at the end of the narrative of Ananias and Sapphira, we read, "Great fear seized the whole church and all who heard about these events" (Acts 5:11). What was everybody afraid of? They were afraid of the same thing happening to them, because there was a little Ananias and Sapphira in the best of them, too.

Ananias and Sapphira weren't the only fakers in the church,

and the Holy Spirit was stamping His loathing of this kind of activity upon the conscience of the church for all time. The worst part about this defection, this faking church, is that we give up a tremendously fulfilling activity for one that leaves us hungrier than we were before. Serving Christ unselfishly as our overriding and primary motivation brings a joy and sense of purpose that nothing else can. It is far more fulfilling than receiving or cultivating false praise.

It is my purpose in this book to help us examine our true motivations for doing service in the church of Jesus Christ. It will be a call to self-honesty; therefore, at times it will be difficult. It will be a call back into joyful and sincere service for Christ and fellowship in His body. I can attest that there is far more joy in sincere service than in embellishing a false spiritual résumé. . .or in faking it.

Yes, you are a fake. But you don't have to remain one.

CHAPTER TWO

THE SLIPPERY SLOPE:
The Process of Deception

DECEIVE—V.
to make [a person]
believe what is not true;
delude; mislead

> "It is an awful hour when
> the first necessity of hiding anything comes.
> The whole life is different thenceforth.
> When there are questions to be feared and eyes to be
> avoided and subjects that must not be touched,
> then the bloom of life is gone."

PHILLIPS BROOKS (1835–1893)

Before we go too far, it is necessary to struggle with how the process of self-deception begins. How does it happen? I say *struggle* because the whole issue of motivations is as complicated as human nature itself. Yet, at the risk of being overly simplistic, we need to wrestle with the issue.

One of the tragedies of deception is that it begins to remove what Brooks calls the "bloom of life." Our joy in the Lord, in life, and in fellowship can slowly begin to erode. When you see the problems it causes, you wonder why we ever began to deceive in the first place. Most of it began long ago.

When I was a little boy in elementary school, I had a classmate who one day informed the teacher and the class that he and his family were moving to another town. I remember the teacher's expression of sadness and how he became, for awhile, the center of attention. Everyone made a big fuss about his leaving, we had parties in his honor, and we gave him a grand send-off. Our fellow students all came up to him and told him how much we liked him and how much we were going to miss him. After awhile I couldn't help wishing that I were moving so that I could have that kind of attention lavished on me. It was a childish wish that grew in me.

The more I thought about it, the more I wondered how I could get that kind of attention. Then I had a brilliant (or at least it seemed brilliant at the time) idea. I would announce to the teacher and my class that I was moving as well. Then, at the appropriate time, I would simply tell them that we changed our minds and weren't moving. It seemed foolproof. I would get the attention I desired and yet still be able to justify my being at school (and my parents would be none the wiser). So one day I quietly took my teacher aside and told her my little lie as sincerely as a young child can do. As I expected, she was terribly sad to hear about this news. It was all I could do to keep from smiling with glee.

Soon she announced this news to my classmates, who did exactly what I hoped they would: They lavished attention on me. I was the man of the hour, the center of attention, and quite frankly I loved it. My mother and father never knew any of this; it was my little secret. Unfortunately, when you say you are going to leave, you have to tell the teacher when it is going to happen. I had made up a date, but as it drew near, I began to get worried. What would happen if they found out I was lying? What would happen if my mother found out? My plan had seemed so wonderful earlier, but I had immersed myself so deeply into this lie that I secretly began to wish that I could run away and fulfill my prediction.

On my "final day in school," my teacher and classmates were

especially kind to me. But it was becoming harder and harder to enjoy this little deception. What was I going to do? Would my little lie satisfy my teacher? Would she buy it? This was a lot of pressure on a boy who hadn't seen his eighth birthday yet. I hoped against hope that my parents would suddenly announce over the weekend that we were indeed moving. We didn't. And the next Monday I was on the same bus going to the same school.

I dreaded seeing my teacher. I dreaded seeing my classmates. I wasn't nearly as convinced now that my lie was going to work. When I showed up, I saw my teacher look at me quizzically.

"Danny, I thought you were moving away! What happened?" she asked in what I felt was a rather suspicious tone. This was it. The jig was up!

With all the sincerity I could muster, I casually said, "We changed our minds. We decided not to move after all!" I was hoping against hope that she would be just as excited that I *wasn't* moving and I would again be the center of attention. Hope springs eternal. But when I looked back at her, her look said it all: She wasn't buying it.

It was quite awhile before the teacher looked at me the same. It was one of my earliest attempts at full-scale deception. It had worked—for awhile. We learn early that we can deceive people and we spend a good deal of time trying to perfect the process. If we're honest, most of us will admit that we always wanted to be something we are not at some point in our lives. That is probably one of the reasons that the game of "pretend" is so attractive and fun for children. We can, for awhile, indulge our deepest desires to be something we are not. We can be pirates, action heroes, princesses, pop stars, actors or actresses, professional athletes, racecar drivers, and the list goes on. And since it is just a game, we can get away with it guilt free.

But one day we graduate from childhood yet realize with some chagrin that we still want to be something that we are not. The childish desires we had in our youth follow us into adulthood. A process of deception has begun, and we have learned that we can often make others believe that we are something we are not, and that often feels just as good. The seed of deception has become rooted in us though we hardly acknowledge it. Even those of us who have the courage to admit it are loath to admit how deeply we are affected (or infected) by it. Or maybe, more accurately, we have been practicing it for so long at this point that we are hardly aware of how much a part of our life it has become.

What is ironic is that few of us intentionally set out to become either self-deceived or deceivers of others. Deception is just that: deception. It is a sin that has power over us as well as a sin we have power over. Deception is not only a sin we choose, it is a sin we can fall into without always being aware it has happened. Even though we can at times carefully channel deception to nurture our egos, at other times we find that deception has the power to disconnect us from the truth and reality that keep us safe.

Deception is something that is so intricately connected to our sinful nature that, unless we choose to actively walk in the Spirit of God, we will never even recognize it. It is also something that we can consciously choose to use in full awareness of what we are doing.

SELF-DECEPTION

"The easiest person to deceive is one's own self," wrote Edward George Bulwer-Lytton. From the very beginning, in the Garden of Eden, we discovered that we could be deceived (Genesis 3:13). When God confronted Eve with her sin, her reply was, "The serpent deceived me, and I ate." We learn that we can be deceived by others, especially by the deceiver himself (Revelation 20:3), Satan. Yet, when we are tempted to cry that we are but innocent victims of someone else's deception, the Bible makes it clear that we can exercise a choice. In fact, we are warned against being the unwitting victims of deception.

In Galatians 6:7, Paul warns the Galatian church, "Do not be *deceived:* God cannot be mocked. A man reaps what he sows" (author emphasis added). Not all the ideas we have about God, others, and ourselves are true and reliable. Some need to be examined and rejected. But the important thing is that we understand that self-deception is easily rooted in us. Like a weed in a garden, it needs only the smallest encouragement to thrive.

Paul reminds us in Titus 3:3 that deception was a part of all our pasts and can easily remain an integral part of our present if we aren't careful. "At one time we too were foolish, disobedient, *deceived and enslaved* by all kinds of passions and pleasures" (author emphasis added). Those two words go together like bread and butter. One leads inexorably to the other. Sadly, if we think that becoming Christians places us beyond the reach of these twin destroyers, we are most vulnerable.

Jeremiah the prophet warned the children of Israel not to let themselves be deceived into a false hope. "This is what the LORD says: *Do not deceive yourselves,* thinking, 'The Babylonians will surely leave us. They will not!' " (Jeremiah 37:9, author emphasis added). Though the prophet had been faithfully telling the Hebrews that God intended to punish them through the Babylonians, they didn't want to believe it. It was comforting for the Hebrews to delude themselves into thinking that their greatest fear would not come about. But it was a delusion, a decision to believe that God was wrong and they were right. It was the ultimate self-deception.

In 1 Corinthians 3:18 Paul wrote, *"Do not deceive yourselves.* If any one of you thinks he is wise by the standards of this age, he should become a 'fool' so that he may become wise" (author emphasis added). As Christians, we are not immune from the temptation of self-deception. In fact, it may be the greatest temptation we face. Self-deception is quite possibly the most attractive of all delusions, for it dresses us up well, wishes us well, always speaks highly of us, and pads our résumé—airbrushing all our faults and blemishes so that they are no longer visible to us. It is intoxicating to live in the lure of self-deception. We can become whoever we want to be by the simple act of stretching the truth.

We are ripe for self-deception when we are unwilling to entertain truths about ourselves that are unflattering and negative. This was the condition we were in before we came to Christ. The apostle John reminds us, "If we say that we have no sin, *we are deceiving ourselves* and the truth is not in us" (1 John 1:8 NASB, author emphasis added). We are, like a victim of substance abuse, easily seduced by something toxic to our well-being: flattering self-deception.

The longer I have lived as a Christian, the more I have begun to understand how deeply my mind and heart have been stained with sin. In other words, some of my sins are easily visible to me; I can identify them rather quickly. But there are other sinful desires in myself, which it takes me years to identify. Thinking I have successfully resisted the sin of pride, one day I discover to my dismay that pride runs far deeper in my life than I ever thought it did; it is flowing freely in the subterranean caverns of my soul. It is not easy to identify until, like a geyser, it suddenly erupts with incredible power. I am equal parts surprised and disappointed.

This is the same for so many sins. The point is that just because we don't feel that we are deceiving ourselves, or being self-deceived, doesn't mean that it isn't happening.

THE FRIGHTENING QUESTION

As I originally shared the idea of this book with different people, someone raised a valid concern. They were afraid that Christians reading this book would find their service robbed of joy and spontaneity, as they would constantly be looking inwardly at their motives. The focus would turn on themselves instead of on the Lord, creating an unbearable load of guilt. Dare we question motivations—our own or anyone else's?

We seem to be terribly afraid these days to question anyone's motivations. Knowing that our knowledge is but partial and only God can know the heart, we are understandably hesitant. Yet, there are frequently signs that can be seen that point to our true motivations, and we are unwise to ignore them.

Once, I was part of a little church that was interviewing a candidate for a pastoral position. We were sorely in need of pastoral help, and our committee was very eager to hire someone. The man we were interviewing for the job seemed almost too good to be true. He was extremely talented, gifted, and definitely a leader. But something about him concerned me. I couldn't quite put my finger on it, so I kept quiet at first. When I was finally able to talk with him alone, we happened upon the subject of what motivated him. With a passion I can still recall, he looked at me and said boldly, "Dan, my greatest motivation is the fear of failure!" He said it with pride, not shame, and I was surprised by it. It dawned on me that he had said this with the intention of impressing me.

At the time, that idea struck me as dangerous at best. It put the motivation for his ministry not in shepherding the flock but in protecting his self-image. Even if we fear failure, should that be our greatest motivation? Paul urged us to be motivated by our love of Christ (2 Corinthians 5:14). It is undeniable, however, that a great deal of self-motivation is in this category. Although another committee member and I raised concerns, we did not push them, and the vote was unanimous to call this candidate. Tragically, several years later, his ministry crumbled under the load of hidden sin and self-deception. He had deceived us, but first he had deceived himself. He had tried to convince himself that his spiritual ambitions were good and right.

Is the ultimate goal in our Christian lives to feel good about ourselves and what we are doing or to honestly and genuinely serve Christ and His church from a pure heart? The mere attempt to examine our own motivations does not necessarily imply we will then feel guilty, because self-honesty is far more difficult than it appears on the surface. Self-honesty is a tremendous hurdle spiritually. In other words, not all who attempt to honestly assess their true motivations will be immediately successful.

Assessing our true motivations assumes we are equipped for

such a task. But are we? The Bible makes it clear that the basic direction of our hearts is against self-truth, not toward it (Genesis 8:21; Romans 3:10–12). As strange as it may sound, being truly and completely self-honest is one of the most unnatural exercises any of us can possibly perform. It can be accomplished only with the assistance of the Spirit of God combined with the Word of God, convicting our hearts of motivations we could not even identify apart from Him. It is like asking people who are tone deaf to sing with perfect pitch.

It can be a terribly fearful thing to even think about being completely self-honest. If you are like me, you just aren't that well practiced in it. I have walked with Christ now for over thirty years, and, as I have reflected on the point of my conversion, I marvel at the incredible grace of God. I had many different areas of weakness, including—but not limited to—pride, anger, jealousy, envy, lust, greed, and the list goes on. But, in God's tender mercy, He did not immediately reveal everything that was wrong with me. I am quite certain that if He had, I would never have recovered from it. The enormity of my sin would have been so overwhelming that I would have quit before I began.

So, as the Spirit of God applied the truths of God's Word to my heart and life, He began graciously and mercifully to take my façade, one piece at a time, and gently pull it back. This revealed the ugliness that lay beneath; but, at the same time, His Word encouraged me to change as His Spirit empowered my desires to be holier. Progress was slow but sure.

I say this to simply show that examining our motivations is not as simple as it sounds on the surface. We can't always just sit down in ten minutes and "do it." Furthermore, without the direct intervention of God, we can never accomplish it. We can no more hope to plumb the depths of our own motivations than we can hope to dig a hole all the way to China.

In fact, Paul writes in 1 Corinthians 4:3–4 (NASB), "But to me it is a very small thing that I may be examined by you, or by any human court; in fact, I do not even examine myself. For I am conscious of nothing against myself, yet I am not by this acquitted; but the one who examines me is the Lord." Paul is admitting that self-evaluation is at times unreliable because the examiner is blinded by personal bias. Yet Paul does not advocate that we never attempt to examine our motives.

Later in 1 Corinthians 11:28 (NASB), Paul urges every Christian who comes before the Lord's Table to "examine himself, and in so doing he is to eat of the bread and drink of the cup." Later, in 2 Corinthians 13:5 (NASB), Paul urges the Corinthians to "Test yourselves to see if you are in the faith; examine yourselves!"

Self-assessment and self-examination is no easy task; nor is it for the faint of heart. It will take more courage than we may feel we have at times. We marvel at the boldness of David in Psalm 26:1–2 (NASB) when he says, "Vindicate me, O LORD, for I have walked in my integrity, and I have trusted in the LORD without wavering. Examine me, O LORD, and try me; test my mind and my heart." He was willing to hold up his inner motivations to divine scrutiny.

Jeremiah knew that God was continually filtering all his words and actions so that any attempt at deception of God was useless. "But You know me, O LORD; You see me; and You examine my heart's attitude toward You" (Jeremiah 12:3 NASB).

SPIRITUAL SURGERY

The question must be asked: If we have been involved in self-deception, can we suddenly change course and begin identifying our true motivations? As one who has tried, I can attest to the fact that it is much harder than it appears. It requires a spiritual surgery we are unable to perform on ourselves. It requires a Divine Surgeon. That said, if we are not passive in the process, it is certainly not impossible. Even if we cannot provide the divine objectivity so desperately required for this operation, we can provide something equally important: the willingness to cooperate.

When people discover that they have a serious condition that requires radical invasive surgery, they have a choice. They can decide that their situation is not all that bad and they will get better without it, or they can check themselves into a hospital and allow a surgeon to do the surgery. Although they cannot do the surgery on themselves, the surgery cannot be performed without their consent. Furthermore, a patient who *desires* to get better has a *far* greater rate of success!

The truth is that we can and do resist this operation of the Spirit at times. Countless numbers of times I have been reading through the Bible when a particular passage will catch my attention. The reason it catches my attention is that the passage suddenly reveals a hidden motivation or sinful desire of my heart.

In that divinely orchestrated moment, God is peeling back another layer of my spiritual façade and giving me a glimpse of my hypocrisy, my ego, my jealousy, or some other resident sin that was ruining my heart and motivation. In that moment I have a choice: spend time allowing God's Spirit to apply His truths to my heart, painful though they may be, or immediately ignore them.

Sometimes it is simply because my blindness is so deep that I am unable yet to accept the truth. I am intrigued by this truth for some reason but can't make any connection yet. The Spirit is gently prodding me and will, I have discovered, eventually open my eyes. . .if I want them open.

The problem is that I am a lot like you. I hate to learn that I'm not nearly as good a person as I supposed myself to be. I don't like to learn that my motivations, which I always thought were beyond reproach, are not really all that noble. It hurts. I feel shame, guilt, remorse, and regret. Truth heals us, but at times it hurts before it heals.

In my high school days, I decided to learn to play the guitar—for two basic reasons. First, I enjoy music, especially the sound of an acoustical guitar. Second, I wanted to impress people. I wanted to be a great musician that the girls would swoon over and the guys would envy. At the time I *never* would have admitted that second motivation, but it was true.

A friend and I began to play together, writing music and

singing. We had several opportunities to go to Christian gatherings and play for them. It was exhilarating, intoxicating. There was a definite ministry in what we were doing, so I could justify all my feelings of excitement about "ministering through song." But I secretly enjoyed having people listen to us and tell us how good we were. (Although, in retrospect, maybe we weren't nearly as good as I remember!)

One day we were scheduled to do a miniconcert at our own home church along with some other people. But the day before we were to play, we were approached by a girl we both liked and respected. She came to tell us that most of our youth group was planning to intentionally skip the concert. We were stunned.

She gently told us that some of them had begun to feel that our egos had gotten out of control and that we were just trying to impress people. She assured us she didn't feel that way, but she wanted us to know so we'd be prepared. We did the concert and, sure enough, very few showed up. To this day I remember how deeply that hurt me. My hurt wasn't solely because of their absence but because someone dared to challenge my motivations for ministry. Didn't they know how much I loved God? Wasn't I a leader in the youth group? I made up all kinds of justifications to protect myself from the truth because deep down I suspected that at least a part of what they said was true. At the time that was the best I could do.

In retrospect, I fear that all they said was true. My ego had begun to run amuck and, although I had started off with good intentions, I had been seduced by impure motivations. It was crushing to suddenly discover that a blind spot in my life had gotten out of control. How did it happen?

There is a process of deception that we need to examine, because deception is never isolated only within ourselves. Deception is contagious, moving with microbial stealth from us to others—hidden, secret, destructive. Even though we will look at this process sequentially, it is doubtful that it works quite this way. Human nature is complicated and difficult to unravel. It is unlikely that we move from one stage to the next; deception probably enters our lives at all stages simultaneously. Yet, there are definite levels or stages of deception that we can recognize within ourselves. The first level of deception, of course, is personal.

PERSONAL DECEPTION

I am first and foremost self-deceived. I fool myself. I have failed to consciously examine my true spiritual condition or motivations, either through ignorance or a fear of inner honesty. I have found that it is usually unintentional, at least at first. We aren't trying to fool others; in fact, we are often unwittingly fooling ourselves.

This might be the hardest deception to expose. King David repented of his sin of immorality and murder for sinning with Bathsheba and having her husband, Uriah, killed (2 Samuel 11–12). In Psalm 51:6 David acknowledged to God an important lesson he learned, or relearned, through his tragic experience: "Behold, You desire truth in the innermost being" (NASB). How this truth must have convicted David's heart. David truly did love God, and he was a righteous man, but even righteous people who love God can be overtaken by sin, especially by the sin of self-deception. Self-deception helped to justify much more serious sins in David's life.

Not only was David deceiving his men, his kingdom, and Uriah about his true motivations, he was self-deceived into believing that he was justified in doing so. In some way David had justified his own sin to himself. He knew what had caused his problem: He had been lying to himself about his motives, desperately trying to put a good face on the evil he was involved in. What could have caused a great and godly man like King David to sin in such a bold and arrogant manner? He knew that adultery was wrong. He knew that murder was wrong. He knew the law of God; it was his joy (Psalm 19:7–8). Yet this law he professed to love expressly forbade both murder and adultery (Exodus

20:13–14). We tell ourselves lies to silence the gentle voice of conscience and God's Spirit within us.

David had both deceived and been deceived. Unless we begin to understand the tremendous power that sin has over our hearts and minds, we will be vulnerable. God's Spirit, however, can remove the scales from our eyes—even those we aren't aware of. As David wrote, "In the hidden part You will make me know wisdom" (Psalm 51:6 NASB). The hidden part, the part of us God sees, the person we truly are deep inside, that is the part of us that God can make to know wisdom, to reveal not only the truth about God but the truth about ourselves.

I have come to understand, like David, that I am easily self-deceived. There is on one hand the deception I am aware of. On the other hand, there's the deception within my heart that I don't yet see and comprehend. I may see a small part of the deception but not how deeply it is rooted in me. We often see only the tip of the iceberg, so we feel we can safely ignore it for the moment.

Faking church begins with personal deception. We must recognize that there is a power at work within us that would seek to keep us self-deceived. It is the power of sin, and we are both attracted to it by our old sin nature and repulsed by it with our new spiritual nature. However, once we have moved in the direction of self-deception, we are climbing down the slippery slope and will soon find ourselves tumbling headlong into the next deception.

INTERPERSONAL DECEPTION

I began a church when I was in my late twenties. Because of my youth and inexperience, I went to great lengths to leave the impression that at all times and in all situations I knew precisely what I was doing. I did this because I was afraid that if people knew I wasn't sure what I was doing, they would stop attending the church or following my leadership. I knew a great deal about theology and doctrine and was a fairly competent preacher. But my knowledge of running or beginning a church was not extensive. I had adequate seminary credentials but little actual experience in running a fledgling church.

I can remember church meetings in which I went out of my way to exude confidence and assurance to my elders and leaders that I did not feel. It was intentional. I justified it by telling myself that I was doing them a favor. They needed confidence in me, and I was giving it to them.

When issues would come up that I had little experience in, I faked it. Through tone of voice, body language, and other means, I portrayed a confidence and experience that was purely theatrical—Drama 101! I simply didn't have all the answers, and much of the time I wasn't quite sure what I was doing. How could I tell people that I was just "shooting from the hip" a lot of the time?

I did have some answers and some experience. I wasn't totally clueless, and I certainly knew the basics of church ministry and growth, but wherever and whenever I felt deficient, I reverted to smoke and mirrors. I was trying to portray a desired level of experience and spirituality that I simply didn't have. For what it is worth, the person I was trying to portray was the person I was, *at times*, or the person I wanted and intended one day to become. Yes, my deception was intentional, but it was regretfully intentional. When my conscience responded to the prompting of the Holy Spirit, I felt convicted.

I was working under the false assumption that I could create a false persona and then seek to live up to it. Maybe I could actually transition from fake to real. After all, if no one else but me could see this process, I might enjoy the benefits of a spiritual reputation before I actually deserved it. It was a credit card spirituality: buy now, pay later. Unfortunately, like credit card debt, we can soon find ourselves in deception so deep that we can no longer pay the bill.

The gap between reality and the façade can become so great that I am forced to either come clean or expend more and more energy in keeping the deception secret. Like those who have found themselves deeply in credit-card debt, those who owe a deep debt to honesty feel overwhelmed, guilty, ashamed, afraid, and increasingly removed from the true source of Christian joy and fellowship. Church becomes an increasingly unbearable burden and a danger because there is always the chance the secret might get out. Feeling bankrupt, many Christians can ultimately declare a spiritual Chapter 13 and just walk away. They can no longer keep up the "payments" on their spiritual reputation and are no longer motivated to try.

Bob has been leading a home Bible study for several years. Those in his study look to Bob as their spiritual example and leader. In his desire to encourage their spiritual growth he has, at times, shaded the truth about his own spiritual life. He has led the group to believe that he reads his Bible daily and prays constantly—something he knows should be true but hasn't been for a long time. He has lost the desire to read his Bible, and his prayer life is hit-and-miss. He desperately wishes he was the Bob he portrays himself to be.

These days he finds himself struggling with lust and thoughts of adultery. Knowing the effect this revelation would have on his group, he keeps it quiet. He tells himself he is doing it for them. He doesn't want to be a fake, but he knows he is. He also feels trapped. To reveal the truth might harm some people's faith; to keep it a secret only prolongs a lie. What will Bob do?

Gene became an elder in the church two years ago. He is known as a spiritual leader, Sunday school teacher, and gifted evangelist. Everyone looks up to Gene. His wife, Gladys, leads the women's ministry and is also a gifted soloist. They are considered to be the "perfect Christian couple." Gene and Gladys love the church and the people they are working with. If the truth were known, they also love the reputation and respect they have received.

Unfortunately, Gene and Gladys have historically had trouble with their marriage. Recently, however, things have taken a turn for the worse. The tension and animosity between Gene and Gladys is so bad that they are finding it difficult to be in each other's presence. Yet, Gene and Gladys sit next to each other every Sunday, faking it. While they are together, it is virtually impossible to know that anything is wrong between them. Their cover-up is polished.

They didn't start out intending to deceive people. They were both afraid that their marital failures might hurt those they had ministered to and would damage the reputation of Christ. They kept telling themselves that they would get their marriage back on track before anyone found out there was a problem. Most of all, they are ashamed that their own faith has not enabled them to overcome these problems. They are embarrassed. What will people think? How will they react? Soon, they realize, they will no longer be able to keep it a secret. What will they do? Will they leave church? Will they just slowly fade away to minimize the shame and avoid the questions?

Dusty comes to church every Sunday and is a part of the young-married class. He and his wife, Michelle, are an attractive and popular couple. They are funny, outgoing, successful, and intelligent. They attend all the functions and plan many of them. But they also have a secret: Dusty has a substance abuse problem. Michelle has to deal not only with the problem but also the family deception. Dusty denies he has a problem and insists that Michelle keep the issue quiet. Keeping the deception alive takes an incredible amount of energy and also keeps anyone from being able to help either of them. What will eventually come of their deception?

Harold comes to church every Sunday; he has for forty years. He is now retired and devotes himself to working at the church. He sits on several boards, including the elder board. A number of years ago the pastor did something that offended Harold. Harold never told the pastor how he felt, but ever since then a deep and abiding resentment has grown unchecked in Harold. Without ever showing any outward aggression or letting on that he has any personal vendetta, he has managed to find many ways to thwart the pastor's goals and plans. His bitterness is safely hidden behind a smiling, grandfatherly persona; in fact, to most people he is very kind and considerate. Harold's motivations may never be discovered. What will this deception cost Harold spiritually? What will it cost the church? What will it cost the pastor?

Many of these deceptions seem major, but there are innumerable amounts of seemingly less serious deceptions. We sing our songs of worship on Sunday morning, when our minds are a million miles away. Our expressions make it seem as if we are being very spiritual. We know they do, which is why we do it. The truth is we're faking it. We gossip about someone we dislike, choosing our words carefully so that our motives can't be questioned. Yet we know that we are seeking to disparage them in others' eyes. These are only the deceptions we are aware of. What about the others?

We deceive others to cover our mistakes, our failures, and our shortcomings. You do it; I do it; we all do it. Ironically, since we all do it, we have almost decided that it's okay. But it's not. Because if we keep faking it, we can never become the people we so desperately want to become. Bob's secret will prevent him from taking the steps he needs to repent, change, and make progress. Gene and Gladys can't find the help they need because that would threaten their deception, their fake spiritual façade. Dusty and Michelle's deception keeps Dusty from ever getting any help and Michelle from understanding how to truly love her husband. Harold's deception keeps him from ever reconciling with the pastor or even allowing the pastor to apologize. It also endangers the health of not only a pastor but also an entire church.

Faking spirituality takes an inordinate amount of energy. It's like trying to plug a leak in a dam with your finger. You can plug the hole at one place, but the built-up pressure will simply find another place of escape. Soon the number of places where water is escaping will overwhelm your ability to stop it.

When we begin to deceive ourselves, we have given ourselves permission to deceive others as well. The precedent has been set, albeit reluctantly. Unfortunately, the deception does not even stop here. There is one more part of the devolution of honesty. There is self-deception, the deception of others, and finally the attempt to deceive God.

THE ULTIMATE DECEPTION

"Lies can be so furbished and disguised in gorgeous wrappings that not a soul would recognize their skinny carcasses," wrote Henrik Ibsen.[1] Yes, as strange as it sounds, we can try to deceive God. Not consciously, of course, because we know that God cannot be deceived; but, don't forget, we can. Whenever there is the potential for self-deception, it only follows that we will project our self-deception to God. If we have convinced ourselves that we are better, purer, and nobler than we really are, we can begin to believe that God sees us this way also. We may even nurture this belief. Thomas à Kempis wrote, "Man sees your actions, but God your motives."[2]

If you doubt this, just remember the Pharisees and Sadducees. They were the religious rulers of Jesus' day. Under the impression that their lives were totally pleasing to God, they must have been surprised and angered when Jesus attacked their piety.

In Matthew 23:25–28 (NASB), Jesus proclaimed, "Woe to you, scribes and Pharisees, hypocrites! For you clean the outside of the cup and of the dish, but inside they are full of robbery and self-indulgence. You blind Pharisee, first clean the inside of the cup and of the dish, so that the outside of it may become clean also. Woe to you, scribes and Pharisees, hypocrites! For you are like whitewashed tombs which on the outside appear beautiful, but inside they are full of dead men's bones and all uncleanness. So you, too, outwardly appear righteous to men, but inwardly you are full of hypocrisy and lawlessness." Jesus made it clear that He could see, as Henrik Ibsen calls it, "their skinny carcasses."

And who can forget the parable of the tax collector and the sinner? Interestingly, this parable was told by Jesus "to some people who trusted in themselves that they were righteous, and viewed others with contempt" (Luke 18:9 NASB). The prayer of the Pharisee in the temple is instructive. He stands in the temple and prays inwardly, "God, I thank You that I am not like other people: swindlers, unjust, adulterers, or even like this tax collector. I fast twice a week; I pay tithes of all that I get" (Luke 18:11–12 NASB).

We need to understand that this Pharisee was first self-deceived. He truly thought he was as good as he was saying he was. Secondly, he had easily managed to fool most people who could only see his outward piety. But his self-deception was then projected upon God. He was sure that God saw him the way he saw himself. Was the Pharisee serious about his relationship with God? Yes! He was in the temple and praying to a God that he was sure was listening to him. Was he also involved in trying to deceive God? Yes.

Can we blame someone for not being truthful when they are self-deceived? Yes, we can, because God will continually attempt to break through our self-deception—through conscience, other people, His Spirit, and His Word. We have to intentionally ignore these attempts to remain ignorant. It is a lack of willingness to seek truth in the innermost being. Pride, a desire to be seen as something better than we are, can create blinders. Not blind*ness*, but blind*ers*. It's not simply that we are unable to see our deception but rather that at some point we refuse to see it.

When we fake church, we create a persona, craft it carefully, and come to enjoy it, and even to need it. We focus on what we choose and ignore what we choose. The blinders are not of ignorance, or blindness, but of our choosing. For whatever reason, we feel we are entitled to keep our reputations, however they were achieved. It is not that God has not tried to reveal our deception but that at each and every point we have refused to entertain the thought.

If deception were something we had no control over, no decision in, then this discussion would be totally unnecessary. But the fact is, we do. Yes, deception is part of our sin nature that has a powerful effect on us, but we also choose to go along with it. The more we do so, the more we lose the power (or will) to challenge the deception. Like Bob, Gene and Gladys, Dusty and Michelle, and Harold, the more we allow ourselves to indulge a forbidden desire, the more power the desire gains over us.

A deception is pleasant, at least at first. Whether we are deceiving ourselves, others, or God, it makes us feel good about ourselves and makes us look good in the eyes of others; and for many of us, that is more important at the moment than truth. On the other hand, truth can be painful, difficult, and frightening. This is the predicament that Bob, Gene and Gladys, Dusty and Michelle, and Harold are in. The right choice is not an intellectually hard one for them to make, but the ramifications of the choice can be extremely difficult. We do not often struggle with what is right or wrong but with the price tag associated with doing what is right or wrong.

What will they do? Will they maintain their deception and interpersonal deception, or will they choose to begin the process of seeking truth in the innermost parts? They often know what they should do. The issue is, will they do it? They have started down the slippery slope, but there is still time to make a change. The ever downward spiral of deception can be reversed.

CHAPTER THREE

NAKED AND UNASHAMED:
The Danger of Becoming Comfortable with Deception

NAKED—ADJ.
completely unclothed; bare; nude
b) uncovered; exposed

> "Faces we see, hearts we know not."
>
> SPANISH PROVERB

Author and pastor Calvin Miller prays, "Dear Christ, make one that which we are and that which we appear to be. Be Lord of naked faces."[3] Years ago, when I was a little boy, there was on the advertisement pages of my favorite comic books something amazing you could order called X-ray glasses. You may remember them. They were advertised as having the ability to allow you to see through clothing. It was a questionable claim (and since I never purchased them, I'll never know if it was true!). It would certainly be disconcerting if it were true.

Fortunately the power of those X-ray glasses is mythical. We don't want people seeing anything other than what we want them to see about us, do we? If you're like me, you like to tightly control what others see of you, what they see you doing, what they hear you saying, what they notice you involved in. Regardless of all our protestations to the contrary, we do care deeply what others think about us. It is what makes it so easy for us to be lured into deception—both self-deception and deception of and by others. It is why we so carefully guard our images, especially at church.

THE EMPEROR'S NEW CLOTHES

I am reminded of the famous fairy tale by Hans Christian Anderson, *The Emperor's New Clothes*. In many ways this famous fairy tale has much to say to those of us who struggle with appearances and work so hard on our spiritual images. It is also a timely message for the church.

The emperor is a vain ruler, living only to buy and wear new clothes. Vanity makes him susceptible to several enterprising charlatans who come to town one day, advertising themselves as expert weavers. The claim is believed that their cloth is not only the most beautiful to be found but also has magical powers. Their cloth is totally invisible to any person who is stupid or unfit for office. Naturally, as the charlatans pretend to be working, the emperor's messengers who go to check on their progress see nothing. The messengers are left with the idea that they must be either stupid or unfit for their high office. Unwilling to risk their jobs or reputations, they all return with glowing reports of the weaver's progress and the beautiful clothes.

Finally, when the emperor views the new "air" clothes, he is also faced with either admitting he can't see the material or lying and keeping up the charade. Deciding the better part of wisdom is lying, he finally models his new clothes for his subjects by walking through the city naked. At first all his subjects pretend to see the emperor's clothes, which delights the king. But finally one little child, unaware of the magic cloth's special features, shouts out honestly, "But the emperor has no clothes on!" Soon everyone, spurred on by this truthful revelation, begins to shout out the truth. The emperor indeed is naked; he is wearing nothing but his self-deception.

It is difficult to miss the analogy. We are desperately afraid that somehow others will see parts of our spiritual nakedness. None of us is truly and fully clothed. Positionally, before God, each believer wears the righteousness of Christ. As Paul says, "For you died, and your life is now hidden with Christ in God" (Colossians 3:3). God credits Christ's righteousness to our account. Yet, in our lives the tangible evidence of practical human righteousness is often missing.

The jealousy we know is wrong still resides in us. Anger, greed, malice, covetousness, and a host of other sins are resident in each of us in differing concentrations. We know these are unacceptable, so we all seek to hide these spiritual blemishes with the "magic cloth" of deception. Like the emperor, the church today seems to be attempting to walk naked with great dignity—an awkward experience at best. Perhaps we're not fooling as many people as we think we are.

We may struggle with being truly holy, but we don't struggle nearly as much with appearing holy. Our private life with God may be anemic, but our public façade is robust. And yet, like all those deceived by the claims of the "magic cloth," we are inherently uncomfortable with the deception. We are often relieved when one weary, honest soul finally admits, "I'm not all I appear to be."

I have done a number of small-group discipleship programs over the years, and at each one I've literally experienced people who have let their façade drop in the presence of others whom they have grown to trust. Tentatively, they exposed how they had been faking some aspect of their Christian lives or ministries. That one confession opened the floodgates for the others, like the voice of the innocent child in the story who dared to speak the obvious about the emperor.

When we think about it, the emperor believed that he was fully clothed and regally attired, but what led him to the ultimate deception was not the swindlers; it was his own personal vanity. We are reminded in James 1:13–16 of the inner pull that leads us toward sin; it is part of our fallen nature. These inner desires make us vulnerable to any temptation that caters to those desires.

I feel for the poor prime minister and courtier in the story. There were times when I wondered whether the discovery of my true spiritual condition and motivations would render me "unfit for office." What a horrible revelation! What would they do? What would they tell the king? What would they tell others?

WHY BURST THEIR BUBBLE?

You and I know exactly what they would do, because each of us has been in exactly the same situation. Few of us are brave enough to challenge someone's exalted opinion of us with the truth. Oh, we may indulge ourselves in what we evangelicals call "being vulnerable," yet usually we choose carefully what we will be vulnerable about; and, more often than not, we play it safe. We admit to generic and general weaknesses but nothing too close to the naked truth.

Revealing that there are times when I lose my temper in my marriage will get me a reputation of being "honest and vulnerable." Confessing that I am less than a perfect father will give me nods of approval from others, as long as I'm not too specific. After all, I am just being transparent.

On the other hand, admitting that at times we may yell or curse loudly at our spouses or children in titanic fury is another thing. How cruel we might choose to become or how we might specifically demean each of our children is also safely avoided. To admit to a struggle with impure thoughts is safe; however, revealing a weakness for pornography is something else again. It can be easy to subtly deceive others about our true spiritual condition and motivations.

We will eventually come to believe that it is much safer to conceal than to reveal. Too much is at stake to tell the truth.

And since many people develop their attitudes and thoughts about us without any direct input from us, we feel we have done nothing wrong.

COMFORTABLE WITH DECEPTION

Perhaps our greatest fear is that becoming truly self-honest will necessitate revealing to every person in church our deepest sins, our most putrid thoughts, or our most vile motivations. After all, isn't that the goal of this book? Hardly! I am not advocating a kind of talk show exposé.

Like the emperor, the main problem we have is self-deception. His inflated view of himself led to his utter humiliation. This is the origin of the problem I am addressing.

The church today finds itself in the same condition as the kingdom did in the fairy tale. Deception has become commonplace, accepted, and even normal. Since each of us knows we all do it, we find it easier to perpetuate status quo than to challenge it.

Sure, maybe at times our motivations for ministry are suspect, but aren't we still doing ministry? Aren't people actually being taught? Okay, so we fudge a little about our true spiritual condition, but doesn't our masquerade actually make us more effective at times? We realize that we still have much to offer, and there is still a lot we can do for Christ, even if our motivations are not always pure. Aren't we still leading people to Jesus Christ? Isn't our worship and music still ministering to many? Doesn't our teaching encourage many?

In the process of becoming comfortable with deception, we also insulate ourselves from any feelings of real danger. Each year millions of people cheat on their taxes. Because it is so widespread, many feel little danger. But people do get audited, penalized, and thrown into jail. Each year millions of people drink too much alcohol and then drive. Most of them arrive safely at home, and because nothing bad happened, they convince themselves there was no great danger.

But you and I know what happens when those feelings of overconfidence are perpetuated. The overconfident play with fire many times without getting burned. But one day tragedy occurs, and they are faced with the consequences of a dangerous idea that was never confronted and challenged. They had always been in great danger and were a danger to others, but they didn't face that reality.

Only recently a U.S. congressman who had a terrible driving record finally killed a motorcyclist by running a stop sign—one he had run before. He had been spotted running that same stop sign by a witness years before. He had driven recklessly so many times without anything serious occurring that he had come to believe he was in no great danger or was placing anyone else in danger. He had lost his fear of consequences for dangerous behavior. It was only a matter of time.

INCREASING THE RESISTANCE

When we fail to engage in the necessary exercise of self-examination, being honest with ourselves about ourselves, as David said, desiring "truth in the inner parts" (Psalm 51:6), we will then fail to appreciate the danger we are in. When we begin to believe the lies we have told ourselves, a serious defection has begun. At that point, we aren't in danger of being deceived; we are already deceived. When we begin to resist one truth about ourselves or our motivations, we can easily begin to resist other truths as well.

When we replace form with substance in one area, can we then limit that behavior everywhere else? Personal self-deception about our true spiritual condition and motivations for service is the beginning of a slow defection that, if left unchecked, could ultimately result in a literal defection one day in the future.

When I was in seminary, I remember a chapel when a very popular local pastor with a national radio ministry came to speak.

He was warm, engaging, charismatic, and persuasive. He had been invited to speak on the subject of "Lordship Salvation," a favorite topic of his. The basic premise of his talk was that unless there was a visible, tangible demonstration of conversion and change, one couldn't really claim to be a Christian.

Despite a claim to have accepted Christ, if people have not made Christ Lord of their lives and if that isn't instantly visible in their changed lives, then they have not really been converted. This explains, he said, why so many who claim to be Christians, who profess to have "accepted Jesus as their personal Savior," never seem to exhibit true Christian fruit and character. We spent some delightful time debating this issue with this pastor in the student lounge later. (Not all of us agreed with his ideas.)

Several years later I was stunned to learn that this same pastor had fallen into immorality. What was even more disconcerting to me was to learn that it had been a long-term immoral situation. I thought back to when he had been preaching so eloquently and persuasively in chapel. While he was trying to convince us that salvation can only be true and genuine when people are submitting themselves entirely to the Lordship of Christ in a visible manner, he had been actively engaged in and concealing his own flagrant sin.

I have never forgotten that. Even though what this man did was wrong and he was rightly removed, I can see now how easily someone could fall prey to self-deception. As strange as it seems, I do believe this man probably loved Jesus Christ and wanted to serve Him. He was a phenomenal leader, communicator, and pastor, with a charisma that drew people to him. But he also had a secret. Things were not all they seemed in his life. I can't pretend to guess where the self-deception began, but it isn't hard to see why he began to fake it.

A pastor is supposed to be a man of God, a man of prayer, and a man of unquestioned moral integrity. Of course, he is allowed to struggle with temptation, but we always assume that he is eventually going to be victorious in his struggles. But what if he's not? The lies will begin within his own heart, and he must justify his sin at some point or guilt will overwhelm him.

Does he privately blame his wife for his difficulties or when he failed to resist the opportunities for sexual sin that eventually presented themselves? Does he simply confess his sins to God and pretend to himself that he will never fail again? He probably has no true idea how warped his own heart has become. Do you see the problem? When he lies to himself about his true spiritual condition, it can have devastating impact later on—not only on his life but also on many more lives.

I truly understand, being a pastor myself, the intense pressure to keep up the façade of being an always-victorious, always-holy, always-growing man of God. I don't want to ruin that image others have of me, because frankly I like the image and I can use it. It is flattering to my spiritual ego and personal vanity.

Furthermore, I have witnessed the expressions and attitudes of people when they accidentally discover one of my flaws. They never view me quite the same way again. They have seen a side of me that many others haven't. I'm not all I appear to be, and now someone besides me, my wife, and the immediate family knows. I feel like I've been unmasked, because I have. It is an unpleasant experience that I will try hard to avoid repeating if at all possible, which is precisely the problem. I don't like being seen "naked," without my spiritual makeup in place.

The real problem is not merely my deception being revealed, but how my service will now be affected. Or, perhaps to put it a better way, I am being allowed to see for the first time what some of my real motivations are. Like the fallen pastor, I truly want a strong spiritual reputation, and perhaps I feel I still deserve it, despite several lapses in integrity or less-than-sincere motivations for service.

Is my concern the reputation of Jesus Christ in the world or His church? Chances are that my motivations have become seriously diluted. My personal, unaddressed sins have made me feel that, like my original forefathers, Adam and Eve, I need to hide— both from God and from man. There are certain parts of my life that require covering up.

THE DANGER IS REAL

Just because we have less than pure motivations at times doesn't mean that we will experience the cataclysmic results this pastor and other high-profile leaders had when their masks were removed. But we cannot hope to isolate and ignore our deceptions in the belief that nothing will ever come of them. More importantly, when we begin to involve ourselves in self-deception and then actively begin to deceive others, however slightly, it is not a small thing. Something fundamental is going to change about us, and it is serious. We have entered a tributary of sin that will send us careening at great speed toward a great fall, unless we change course.

A very wise man named Solomon once wrote words I have since committed to memory and have called upon numerous times to guard me from internal deception and sin.

"Watch over your heart with all diligence, for from it flow the springs of life" (Proverbs 4:23 NASB). The NIV translation says, "Above all else, guard your heart, for it is the wellspring of life."

In the ancient East, a spring was the source of life, for in it could be found the clean, fresh water that sustained life. It was necessary for both livestock and agriculture. Lives depended on finding a source of clean, fresh water. If the well was polluted in any way, all the water drawn from that well would be polluted.

In the same way, deception pollutes our hearts—the source of all our feelings, thoughts, and actions. When we have polluted our hearts with deception, all of our thoughts and ideas about the importance of honesty and integrity are challenged or, at the least, diluted. When one red sock is put in with a white load of laundry, the entire load ends up pink. Deception has the same kind of effect on our hearts.

When we think of self-deception, or of deceiving others about something seemingly as tame as whether we're quite as spiritual as we make ourselves out to be, it is hard to be too concerned about it. After all, we tell ourselves, we're not embezzling, we're not committing adultery, we're not killing anyone. In fact, when all is said and done, we're still very good Christians. Better than many, that's for sure. In other words, we don't see this as a very serious defection from Christ or His service, which is precisely where the danger lies.

When we begin to deceive ourselves and then others about our true spiritual condition and motivations for service, we have made a serious defection. The problem is that it doesn't *feel* that way. We can still minister, teach, sing, serve, and appear to be great Christian examples. There are no external warning signs of danger. We are the only ones who hear the gentle voice of God's Spirit convicting us of sin. Unfortunately, we can change the subject, drown out that voice, or ignore the prompting. We will not look any different to anyone else or be treated any differently. In fact, in the midst of some of our most serious deception, we may garner some of our most lavish praise from others.

Philip Yancey, in his book *Reaching for the Invisible God*, quotes popular pastor and author Gordon MacDonald, who spoke to the issue of self-deception. "The most costly sins I have committed came at a time when I briefly suspended my reverence for God. In such a moment I quietly (and insanely) concluded that God didn't care and most likely wouldn't intervene were I to risk the violation of one of His commandments."[4]

When we begin to deceive, we begin receiving conflicted messages. On the one hand, the Holy Spirit, through the medium of God's Word, tells us that we are not truly what we are portraying ourselves to be. And it is easy to simply quiet those voices by closing our Bibles and limiting our prayers to certain "safe" items. On the other hand, we are receiving messages from others that we are just fine—even better than fine. So, given the choice, what voice do we listen to? I don't know about you, but I know which one I'm most tempted to listen to.

SEISMIC SHIFTS

At the moment it seems such a slight thing, such a minor deviation.

We may even assure ourselves that we will correct the situation sometime. But the main issue is that we decide to continue the deception.

We may speak blithely about our "personal relationship with Jesus," when we are actually walking in darkness rather than light. He bids us come one way, but we go in the opposite direction. When our service and hearts are no longer sincere, can our relationship with the Lord be healthy and strong? Each of us must first defect from fellowship with Jesus before we defect from fellowship with His church. The church is not Jesus' company or a human institution; it is His body, His beloved. It is not an optional extra in the life of believers; it is the very body the Holy Spirit of God baptized us into. We will speak more of that in a later chapter, but we need to recognize that sincerity and truth are the hallmarks of true Spirit-filled living.

Tragically, our ministry and service can look almost exactly the same whether sincerity or deception motivates it. While all looks well, our Lord sees the defection, our relationship and fellowship with Him are affected, and we have grieved the Spirit of God. If this all sounds very serious, it is. That's precisely the point. Something fundamental to our spiritual growth and health has been severely weakened.

Unknown to anyone else, a seismic shift has just occurred within our hearts. Motivations, which once sprang from love for Christ and a desire to serve Him, have now been infected by other less noble motivations. Each now competes for our allegiance. We can still choose to serve God from pure hearts and sincere motivations and see ourselves in proper perspective, but we can also choose to serve the new motivations.

This situation is neither permanent nor irreversible. It is, in fact, eminently correctable—if we see it, recognize it, and stop it. We do not have to wear the "magic clothes" we are so tempted to put on. But it is far easier to fake it than to be real.

Self-honesty is hard work; deception requires less pain and discomfort. Committing ourselves to fundamental changes in our lives and attitudes will require close attention, increased energy, and some discomfort as we address some ugly truths about ourselves. The longer we have been involved in deception, the deeper its roots are in us, and more work will be required to root it out. On the other hand, maintaining status quo is always easier.

When we talk about being "naked," we are primarily thinking in terms of how others might perceive us. But we need to begin thinking of what God sees. Most of our deception is aimed at those in our world who cannot see all our weaknesses, who cannot penetrate our sophisticated façades, or who cannot perfectly and instantly dissect our motivations. Because we focus on those whom we can deceive, we lose our appreciation and reverence for God.

Years ago I was told a (probably apocryphal) story by a pastoral friend about a baptism at his church. A particular baptismal candidate was undressing behind a curtain that shielded him from the congregation, preparing to don his baptismal robe. He accidentally leaned forward and knocked the curtain down. He was instantly exposed in front of everyone. Realizing his predicament, the man knew he could either cover his face, disguising his identity, or cover his body, revealing his face. He chose to cover his face and run off the stage. I guess he figured that as long as no one saw his face, he was safe—even though they saw the rest of him!

I can't help but think that's what I often do to God. I spend an inordinate amount of time and energy covering my true spiritual condition before others while parading about naked and unashamed before my Father.

This is perhaps the greatest danger of choosing to deceive others and myself; I lose my reverence and concern for how I look before God. Again, it is not intentional; I have simply shifted my focus spiritually from a heavenly audience to an earthly one.

We speak casually at times of our "service to Christ" and being involved in "His ministry," when our service has often become targeted more for human consumption than for divine approval. It has been sobering for me, at times, to look back on much of my "service for Christ" and realize that much of that service was diluted with selfish motivation.

I do not regret the service; nor do I feel it was a waste. No service for God can be performed in perfection, since none of us is perfect in deed, thought, or heart. It did have an impact, and God did use my service—and He uses yours, no matter how diluted the motivations may be. But I desperately wish I hadn't treated my loving heavenly Father that way. We forget that faking church is an offense against God first. Remember Ananias and Sapphira?

I never realized how much I had moved away from the proper and true motivations for service, worship, and ministry: gratitude to the One who saved me and gave me His name, His inheritance, and His abiding love and grace.

We can go to church every Sunday, attend every Bible study, sing in the choir, give generously, teach powerfully, lead effectively, serve tirelessly, and be the epitome of a model Christian—all the while parading naked before our God with our true intentions completely exposed to His divine eyes. Worse, we can be totally clueless that there is a serious problem.

In the graciousness of our God, He keeps calling us back to truth, back to reality, back to Him. As our risen and glorified Lord said in the Revelation, "Here I am! I stand at the door and knock. If anyone hears my voice and opens the door, I will come in and eat with him, and he with me" (Revelation 3:20). (This verse, usually used as an evangelism text, actually refers to backsliding believers who need to return to fellowship with Him.) We do hear His voice at times, and we are concerned, but we never feel quite as naked as we truly are. The price of deception is a loss of perspective, a sense of God's holiness and presence.

God sees right through our façades and into our naked hearts, and yet He loves us. In our fake, plastic, airbrushed condition, we are still the eternal objects of His amazing love, mercy, and grace. It is truly amazing—and one of the reasons I am able to admit my true condition.

I hope I have begun to awaken a sense of the awareness that

deception has within it the seeds of potential danger. It blinds us to what God sees, and we lose a very important sense of reverence for God when we choose to deceive. Whenever we fake church, we are faking it before God, as well as before others. Maybe you, like I, have felt like the emperor and suddenly realized that all you assumed was safely covered is rather well exposed.

It is not a truth most of us are unaware of, of course. We aren't in the least surprised that God sees all and knows all. But we often intentionally, or unintentionally, insulate ourselves from those truths that might make us feel uncomfortable, ashamed, guilty, or sad. Facing such revelation, we often seek to simply change the subject.

But I encourage you not to. It is not a vengeful, angry God who calls to us; it is One who took the penalty of these sins and bore them on the cross. He has seen all our nakedness; He is not surprised by it. He also knows that we do truly want to serve Him with genuine and sincere hearts but that we struggle with a sinful nature that can only do this with great effort and intentionality—and then only imperfectly.

Faking church is first an internal issue, but eventually it will express itself externally in a number of different ways. We will find that an internal defection can often lead to a literal physical defection from church and fellowship.

In Part 2 of this book we will move from identifying the internal problem of deception and faking church to identifying its external expression and some of the external factors that conspire to encourage our defection.

PART TWO

IDENTIFYING
ITS EXPRESSION

CHAPTER FOUR

SEEDS OF DEFECTION

DEFECTION—N.
abandonment of loyalty,
duty, or principle; desertion

> "Half the work that is done in the world
> is to make things appear what they are not."

E. R. BEADLE (1812–1879)

To understand why we slowly defect from sincere service to Christ and, at times, even from church itself, we need to take a much deeper look at why we signed on in the first place. The real reasons we became involved are seldom articulated. Perhaps that is because our motives were mixed. Our entry into Christ's service may be prompted by a number of motivations—not just one. Angelus Silesius, an ancient church father, once wrote, "God does not care what good you did, but why you did it. He does not grade the fruit, but probes the core and tests the root."[5] We also need to probe the root of our motivations.

When we were born again and entered the kingdom of God, the Lord put the desire to minister in our hearts. The Holy Spirit gifts and fits each person into the body of Christ. We'll talk more about that later. It is probably fair to say, and some encouragement to us, that most service begins with the leading and prompting of the Holy Spirit in our hearts. He calls us to take our places in the body, to serve alongside the other members of His body. It is not just a human desire.

However, other motivations—some we aren't even well aware of—soon come into play. These do not originate with God; they come from within us or from others, or both. So let me start by saying that I believe that as true children of God, no matter how deeply we may have defected spiritually, we heard God's call into service. That was our first and true motivation and perhaps, to our mind at the time, our only motivation. We do not truly know ourselves as well as we think we do.

Veteran Volunteers

In short, our spiritual defection does not have its roots in our new spiritual nature. But we all have another experience as well. In our world there are groups to join, clubs to be a part of, sororities to enter, neighborhoods to move into, schools to enroll in, and jobs to take. For varied reasons we have joined or become involved with all these different groups as well. We become experienced and veteran volunteers.

The reason we tend to volunteer for these things is what we need to discuss, because they often become our motivations for service to Christ and His church. These reasons are not usually bad in and of themselves; in fact, some of them are actually quite good. But even though they may be worthwhile reasons for serving in all of these other areas, they are not necessarily good reasons for serving in God's kingdom.

In addition, we often aren't aware at the moment we are asked or volunteer to serve what our exact motivations are. It is the rare church that has clearly articulated the true spiritual motivation for serving in Christ's church to people before they begin their service. Even if an attempt is made to do so, it is rarer still for them to be challenged to truly consider what other motivation might be prompting their service.

Churches large and small are often so desperate for help in different areas that they are guided more by the need to put a warm breathing body into place than by a desire to help that person truly understand the nature of genuine service for Christ. Churches have often spent time in training of volunteers and helpers without spending specific time in helping them to understand what the true motivation for service should be.

WHY WORRY?

You may wonder why it is necessary to try and search for the source or seeds of our defection. Why can't we just admit that it is true, since the Holy Spirit and our consciences bear witness to this truth, confess it, and move on?

Just being aware that we may have defected does not tell us how it took place. If we are unaware of what prompts our defection, how can we stop it from happening again? How can we even effectively address it now? Besides, there is rarely just one source of defection; life is seldom that neat and clean. Even when faced with the true source of our defection, we can remain ignorant. Unless the Holy Spirit opens our eyes and we seek to cooperate, we can remain in blissful ignorance indefinitely.

We will need to cooperate with God as He leads us down paths we'd rather not travel and exposes motivations we'd rather leave covered up. As we look at some of these motivations, keep in mind that one, or several of these, might be one of the main reasons that we entered service ourselves or why we continue to serve. Here we may begin to discern the seeds of our own defection.

SERVING BECAUSE WE ARE ASKED

I distinctly remember, as a pastor, wanting to begin or further enhance ministries within our church. I would conscientiously go through our church roster, thinking about how certain people might fit into the new ministry ideas I had. On numerous occasions, I or other members of our church staff would ask someone to accept a particular service or ministry opportunity. This may be the exact way you entered Christ's service in your church, denomination, or mission.

It is not a complicated motivation. Many of us feel (and rightly so, I might add) that when we encounter a need that we can meet, we should try to meet it. It's likely we cannot meet all the needs we are made aware of, but the concept has been lodged in us that, if at all possible, we should seek to help when help is needed.

On the surface, this appears to be a noble reason. If someone asks us to help in some way because there is a genuine need and we agree to help, that is a good thing, isn't it? It certainly can be.

This is often how the Holy Spirit of God leads us into various ministries. In fact, we have a recorded instance in the New Testament of this very thing happening. In Acts 16:9–10, we read: "During the night Paul had a vision of a man of Macedonia standing and begging him, 'Come over to Macedonia and help us.' After Paul had seen the vision, we got ready at once to leave for Macedonia, concluding that God had called us to preach the gospel to them." It is clear that responding to a genuine need with a genuine spirit of service is laudable. We don't usually get such a supernatural call to service, but the Holy Spirit certainly uses others in the church to help us find our places of service.

To be truthful, we all probably have been asked to do something we didn't want to do. Often one of our greatest motivations for doing some service is our inability to say "no." So with our plastic smiles etched on our faces, we show up for service, even though our hearts are not in it. If we are not gifted for this particular service, we may not be very good at it either, which adds to our growing frustration.

When we are asked to serve where we really don't want to, our motivations often can be less than sincere. But, if we want to please a pastor or leader in the church or want to display a spiritual fervor for service that doesn't truly exist, we might agree to serve. Let me hasten to add that just because we *might* have less than pure motives doesn't mean that we do. It is just that we need to begin to ask ourselves hard questions—questions we are willing to be honest about. It may even take some time to go back to our initial service and try to remember why we said yes.

The goal is to try and find where a seed of defection might have been planted.

SERVING OUT OF OBLIGATION

Maybe the pastor, denomination, or mission has ministered to us in some way, and when a cry for help comes, we feel we owe someone something. This sense of obligation needs to be kept distinct from the obligation that God places in our hearts and lives. This motivation is not prompted by the Holy Spirit but by an inner feeling that we really ought to do something because we are in some way indebted to individual people, groups, or churches.

Again, this isn't necessarily a bad motivation. When people do kind things for us, it is only natural to want to return the favors. When I was going to seminary full time, I worked full time and worked at church many hours a week. Schedulewise I had a very full plate but moneywise a very meager plate. I lived in an apartment and made approximately eighty dollars less a month than it cost me to live. One of the things that had to occasionally be cut was food.

There were many times when I was hungry. I was hardly starving, but three square meals a day was not in the budget. My sister and brother-in-law lived downstairs and, if they had known of the situation, would have gladly helped me. But, along with my full schedule, I had full-blown pride. I didn't want to admit that I needed help just feeding myself. I remember driving to church in my little blue '69 Volkswagen Beetle and going out to that little car after the service to find it filled with grocery bags of food.

Somehow my friends at church had figured out that I needed help. Their generosity overwhelmed me. As a result, I took every opportunity to serve that I could. This seemed a wonderful way to say, "Thanks!" After all, I owed them something. That was the problem. Owing someone something, no matter how important that feeling may be, is not a true motivation for serving Christ and His church.

I don't like the feeling of being indebted. It was simply another form of my pride. From the outside, the service looked good and noble. But inwardly, a large part of my motivation was stubborn and unyielding pride. I believed in "paying my way."

SERVING OUT OF GUILT

I shudder to think of how much goes on in the name of serving the Lord that has its roots in guilt. I shudder because I recall using this method more than once to get unwilling people to become willing servants. I was a fake, helping to create more fakes. Tragically, it was often very effective because guilt is a powerful motivation. Few things work more effectively.

"Betty, if we don't get someone to sign up to plan the annual church barbecue, which we've had every year since we started, it just isn't going to happen this year. I've asked everyone else, and they've all declined. There's no one else to ask. So how about it?" Poor Betty is faced with the idea that her failure to "volunteer" could bring an important church tradition to a halt. Is that really true? Hardly. Is it really fair to ask that way? Not at all. Is it usually effective? You have no idea.

"Tom, this is Frank at church. I'm on the Sunday school board. I'm just calling all the parents of our third- and fourth-grade Sunday school students. As you may know, our teacher had to move, and we can't find a replacement. No one has volunteered. Now I know that you and Sue are busy, but so is everyone else and, besides, you do have a

child in the class. It seems only natural that you would be
interested in the spiritual welfare of your own child. Can we
count on you both to help our children learn more about God?"

How many parents are willing to say no and leave the impression they don't care about the spiritual welfare of their own children? So they often reluctantly volunteer. They may actually enjoy their service after awhile and be glad they were asked. Furthermore, God may use them in a great way. But what originally prompted their service? Part of the reason, at times a major part, is guilt.

I remember hearing a story regarding a large church in California that had thousands of members. They had advertised the ever popular and widely avoided "Church Workday!" On the scheduled workday, out of thousands who attended the church, only a handful showed up to help. The next Sunday the righteously angry pastor recounted the incident and left the clear impression that everyone ought to be ashamed of themselves. He also pointed out that they scheduled another church workday for the next week. The clear message was that the faithful, true servants would be there. Hundreds showed up.

I won't presume to judge the actions of the pastor. Frankly, I don't blame him. I'll also admit that the church needed to hear that not-so-gentle rebuke. And I'm equally sure that many who showed up did so for the right reason. But you can be sure that there were many there directly as a result of guilty consciences.

Now you may say, "So what's wrong with that? They needed to have guilty consciences; they were guilty!" The problem surrounds motivation for service. The church, contrary to the way we often act, is not an organization; it is a divine organism, the body of Christ on earth. When we serve at church, we are supposed to be primarily serving Christ out of love for Him, as we serve one another (2 Corinthians 5:14).

Using guilt as a tool to manipulate our actions appeals to the lowest and basest of motivations: protecting self-image. Although it was not wrong to point out the sin of laziness or to challenge someone to enter Christ's service, and even if the pastor's anger was justified, in this case guilt could become merely an appeal to protect our spiritual reputations. It is concerned primarily with our reputations among others. It is, therefore, ultimately self-serving. The idea is that we will redeem our reputations in others' eyes by showing up or volunteering, even when we'd rather not. Then we are not primarily serving Christ; we are primarily protecting our own reputations.

The fact is that there are scores of people in churches with terribly tender consciences. It is very easy to take advantage of them, and it is tempting for the leaders who need something done. They are people pleasers, terrified of the thought that someone might think they are in some way shirking their spiritual responsibilities. They can't stand to let anyone down, so they don't. They are also usually the ones who are already pulling their own weight at church. Ironically, most pleas using guilt snag the same people over and over again, having little to no effect on the less sensitive and often far less involved majority in the church.

There are times when guilt is a reasonable and appropriate response to something we have done, but it is an improper motivation for service to Christ. When it becomes a part of our motivation to serve, the seed of defection has been planted.

SERVING TO FIND FRIENDSHIPS

One of the lessons experience teaches us is that the best way to get to know a person in any organization is to get involved. You simply get to know people better when you work with them. It is no accident that many people's closest friendships are developed with coworkers they had never met before they began to work together.

Working with others on a common goal is an important social tool. Becoming involved in service at church is a wonderful way to meet and get to know people. When we recently moved three hours away from where we used to live, I immediately got us involved in a local church. Within a month we had met many friends as a result of working together on different ministry projects.

Is this wrong? Of course not, as long as our primary motivation is serving our Lord. However, when social interaction is really the primary motivation for volunteering for service, we are serving ourselves more than Him.

How can you tell if this is your primary motivation? One indication is that you begin asking whom you will be working with or who else is going to be involved in this project before you say yes. If so, your social goal actually becomes more important to you than the ministry itself.

I have seen people lose all enthusiasm for their ministry when close friends who were helping them quit. Only then did it become clear why they were primarily serving. I don't mean to imply that they had no interest in serving Christ; they certainly did. But subtly, over time, their *primary* motivation had become social rather than a genuine desire to serve their Lord. We have all witnessed and even been a part of cliques in church who do everything together or not at all. They are willing to serve as long as "so-and-so" is doing it as well.

Later in the book I will deal with the issue of the difference between friendships at church and Christian fellowship, which are often confused. But in the meantime we all need to ask probing questions. Are we primarily seeking to serve our Lord in our tasks and ministries? Do we make decisions on service opportunities based on who will or will not be involved? Are we willing to serve without the fun and social rewards? Are we only willing to serve with certain people and not with others?

Do you see how a very good thing, such as Christian friendships, can subtly begin to dilute your motivations for service? Externally it is almost impossible to distinguish, because you are happy in your service and you are performing a valuable ministry to the body of Christ. Only God knows your heart.

The answer of course is not to break off your friendships or resign your service. It is also not to beat yourself up over this. For the time being, it is enough that you begin to recognize that your

motivations might need to be scrutinized. Some of your per-
ceived spirituality, as evidenced by your involvement, may be less
than it appears.

SERVING TO HAVE OUR SAY

On numerous occasions I have heard different Christians take the
position that we should not be allowed to criticize a particular ministry until we have been involved in it. The idea is simple and logi-
cal. If we criticize the way something is done, it's probably because
we have no real idea of the pressures and struggles the task entails.
Criticism without experiential knowledge is largely unwelcome.

So it is not unusual for us to get involved in a particular ministry or service with a secret agenda. One way we can have our say
and, more importantly, have it carry some weight is to get deeply
involved. How, you ask?

- Don't like the Sunday school curriculum being used?
  Join the Sunday school board!
- Don't like the direction the church is going? Become
  a deacon or an elder!
- Skeptical of the youth program? Become a youth
  sponsor and you can keep an eye on it!
- Want more say in financial matters? Join the finance
  committee!
- Was the last church social a dud? Join the activities
  committee!

I could go on and on, but you get the idea. By volunteering, you can
begin to make significant changes in the way things are being
done. Many of us have a desire to be leaders, decision-makers, and
policy influencers. We may even have a genuine administrative gift
from the Holy Spirit. But it is entirely possible to use a spiritual gift
in a self-seeking way and to a self-seeking end (1 Timothy 1:3–7;
2 Peter 2:1–3).

If our ideas are not accepted, are we still willing to serve humbly and joyfully? Is our service truly Christ serving, or is it merely self-serving? Is a desire to please Him our primary and continual motivation, or is that just a line we use? Do we exhibit the fruit of the Spirit (Galatians 5:22–23) even when our ideas are not accepted? The value of any service in God's eyes is the love for Him that prompted it and continues to power it. Many seeds of defection have been planted in this area.

SERVING TO SHOWCASE OUR GIFTS AND TALENTS

This may be one of the most difficult motivations to admit. We all know beyond a shadow of a doubt that this is a very prevalent motivation for service within churches. It is also the one we are most loath to admit may power much of our service. To admit to being a fake in general is relatively easy; perhaps we all mislead others to some extent about our true spiritual condition. But to admit, even to yourself, that the desire to showcase your gifts or talents to gain human praise motivates your service can be loathsome. This motivation is not unusual, though; the New Testament apostles had to deal with it constantly (2 Corinthians 2:17, 10:12).

This is one of the church's secret sins that everybody knows about, gossips about, and sees in others but rarely admits to personally. The fact remains, however, that ministry and church are convenient vehicles for musicians, teachers, leaders, and others involved in public up-front ministry to showcase their gifts and talents.

Musicians and singers must be vigilant regarding their true motivation for service. If you don't get asked to do a solo, are you bent out of shape? If you are not asked to be part of a special ensemble, are you offended? Do you have a strong desire to perform? The seed of defection is planted so easily. The old adage that when Satan fell from heaven, he landed in the choir loft often doesn't seem that improbable.

This doesn't mean that those who struggle with this don't also love God; it's just that their ministry might become so diluted by personal ambition that it ceases to be primarily for Christ. It is easy to pretend that all they do is for Him. The limelight is still the limelight, even if it is located in a church.

Teaching ministries also struggle greatly with this same issue. Teachers and leaders are influential, visible, and frequently admired. Jealousies are easy to develop. If a Sunday school teacher finds his or her class dwindling because another teacher is more popular and becomes jealous or envious, true motivations often are revealed.

Or, if someone else is given the teaching ministry you were hoping for and you grow resentful, your true motivations become obvious.

I was once in a church in which a new and exciting ministry was opening up. I was hoping to be chosen to lead the ministry because I felt I was the best qualified, and I was sure I would be chosen. I wasn't. I was frustrated, angry, and jealous. Of course, I didn't show it. Instead of getting the cream teaching position, I was chosen instead to teach the high school ministry. Only one problem: We had no high school ministry or any high school students to put in one. I was encouraged to start one.

So one Sunday I showed up and found that we had some visitors to our church: three siblings, all in high school. For about three weeks I taught them, at which point they decided to go to another church. For some odd reason a youth group consisting entirely and exclusively of their siblings did not excite them. Go figure.

All of a sudden, I was back to zero. The position I had hoped to occupy was doing very well under someone else's leadership. I had what I was sure was an amazing teaching gift and no place to let it shine. At that point, I seriously thought about leaving the church. It wasn't that I thought there would never be another position in the church; it's that I wanted to show what I could do!

Later, I was able to use my teaching gifts extensively at this church. More importantly, God was working to dislodge a destructive attitude that would threaten to destroy any true and sincere ministry I might attempt. The more I taught, the more proficient I became at using my gifts. The more proficient I became, the more

I was able to reach greater heights. I wanted greater and greater platforms for displaying my gifts. I had forgotten that my gifts were not given me for this purpose; they had been given to glorify Jesus and to strengthen His church.

When you represent God so vocally, such as with a teaching gift, it can be nearly impossible for anyone to detect you are a fake. You are saying great things about God, urging everyone to seek Him, and doing all the right things. Outwardly you appear to be the picture of sincerity. If you don't do self-examination, no one may ever know. Except for God. Seeds of defection can grow deep roots in your soul, even as your ministry reputation expands. I have observed that your spiritual gifts can often take you much further and faster than your spiritual maturity can keep up with.

SERVING BECAUSE OUR CHILDREN ARE INVOLVED

In a day and age in which children's activities are given such pro-minence—it is not unexpected that more than a few parents have volunteered for service primarily because their children are in-volved in some way. When our children become involved in ex-tracurricular sports activities, or 4-H, or dance, or scouting, or any other type of activity, we are expected to be involved in some way. It is usually required.

So when it comes to our children being involved in the min-istries of the local church, it is only natural that we would volun-teer to help there. When our children are babies, we might help in the nursery or lead that department. As they graduate into Sun-day school, we might decide to help by becoming teachers or teachers' helpers or sponsors. If our children are involved in the junior- and senior-high youth ministries of the church, we might become sponsors or drivers or host a group in our homes. You can often chart the level of people's involvement in church by the ages and involvement of their children.

There is certainly nothing wrong with this; in fact, it is only to be expected. It is natural for parents to want to be involved in some way in the Christian education of their children at church. You not only get to help your own child, but many others as well.

Please don't misunderstand me. It is important for us to be involved in encouraging and participating in our children's growth in the Lord. It is a good and proper motivation for service. The danger is that it may not be our *primary* motivation for service. It is tempting to get Machiavellian and simply declare that the ends justify the means. But Scripture makes it quite clear that God is just as concerned about our motivations as He is with our actions (James 3:1–3; 1 Timothy 1:5; 2 Timothy 2:22). Sadly, it is not uncommon to gradually lose interest in church and ministry when our children graduate from Sunday school or the youth ministry.

I have spoken with a number of adults who recount the "good old days" when they ran the youth group or taught the third-grade class for many years. Yet, they are no longer involved; in fact, some of them have quit coming to church altogether. Of course, there can be a variety of reasons why someone loses interest in church and service, but a real possibility is that they saw their service primarily through their role as parents. As parents they felt it was their duty (and yes their delight) to be involved with their children.

But are we to view our service in the body of Christ primarily through our role as parents or, rather, our role as members of the body of Christ? Were we called into service by virtue of becoming parents or by virtue of becoming a member of the body of Christ? Is it our love for Christ or love for our children that motivates our service? Of course, the best answer is *both!* The reality is that often our love for Christ and understanding our place in the body of Christ is immature, but our understanding of our parental responsibilities and love for our children is mature.

A good thing can potentially plant seeds of defection within us. So even if we are happily involved in ministering in some aspect of Christian education in our church, if we aren't careful, we may be slowly planting seeds that will bloom into future defection. And our service for Christ may be less than sincere.

Serving to Receive Affirmation

Some of the people most heavily involved in Christian service and ministry have no idea how questionable their motivation for service really is.

Linda is asked to lead a Bible study. She has never done this before, and she is insecure and tentative, not knowing how she will do. Yet, to her great relief (and genuine surprise), she discovers that she is having a powerful impact on the women in her study. She is growing greatly in her own relationship with God as well. Soon she begins to hear things she never expected to hear.

"You don't know how your teaching has helped me grow in the Lord!"

"I respect you so much."

"I wish I could be more like you."

"You are such a special lady."

In no time at all, she is being asked for her advice on any number of issues. As her ministry is confirmed to her, she finds a fulfillment and joy in this ministry she never knew she could experience. She suddenly feels important, needed, appreciated, and respected. Never in her life has she had such feelings. Her ministry becomes her life.

Sally reluctantly accepts the job of leading women's ministries in her church. There isn't really much to lead up: The ministry has been floundering for years. But Sally has some innovative ideas, and soon she begins a number of programs that generate enthusiasm. She discovers she has an administrational and leadership gift. Others rally around her, want to work for her, and ask her to help lead them.

Soon all eyes are on Sally. She has become an acknowledged leader. Though her secular job is unsatisfying and her marriage marginal, here she finds a place where she shines. She throws herself into the ministry, heart and soul. She begins to hear wonderful words of affirmation, which are like water to her parched soul.

"Without you, there wouldn't be a women's ministry!"

"You have revolutionized our church!"

"You are so organized."

"You have no idea how badly we needed you!"

And slowly her ministry becomes her greatest source of self-affirmation. She sees herself in a whole new way. Horizons open up for her that she never could have imagined.

John is an accomplished musician. He isn't very excited about the Sunday worship style; but he's not alone. One day he is approached by the pastor, who asks if he would be willing to lead the worship on Sunday evening for several months—to try a newer, more casual and contemporary service. John, who has never led worship before, feels tentative.

But with some encouragement, he agrees to give it a try. The first night only a handful of people attends, which is fine with John. But after the service, he is inundated with compliments and praise. People who had barely spoken to him before are shaking his hand and smiling at him. The pastor is ecstatic. Worship had never been this good. Each week more people show up, until finally the evening service is the most popular service in the church, primarily due to John's leading the worship. He begins to hear things.

"Before you, I didn't know what worship was."

"You are so talented."

"God has obviously given you a great gift!"

"Every time you sing I feel heaven open up."

Never in his life has John received such encouragement and praise. Leading worship is now his life, and he throws himself into it with all his heart.

Each of these people found powerful ministries and discovered the incredible joy of using their spiritual gifts to affect others. Affirmation is a strong tonic to an insecure soul, and it can feel spiritual and wholesome. It may all be true as well. Indeed you may be especially gifted and have had a powerful influence in others' lives. This may be the first time that God has used you in a powerful way, and you are humbled and excited.

However, if Linda, Sally, and John aren't careful, a seed of defection can be planted even in the midst of their great joy and effectiveness. When Jesus sent out His disciples on their first mission, they came back and exclaimed with great excitement, "Lord, even the demons submit to us in your name" (Luke 10:17). He encouraged them but later warned them: "However, do not rejoice that the spirits submit to you, but rejoice that your names are written in heaven" (Luke 10:20). We need to be vigilant that we celebrate the right things in ministry.

Although Linda, Sally, and John still serve Christ, slowly they may unexpectedly be drawn more to the tokens of affirmation, the compliments, and the personal praise. Feeling needed, respected, wanted, and significant can begin to be as great a motivation in their ministry as their love for Christ. And if they aren't careful, one day their love of the affirmation that their ministry brings them might become the biggest motivation to their service.

Because so much good is still occurring in their ministries, they may never notice that their love for Christ is no longer the primary reason they minister. The seed will have taken root.

Surely there are other reasons people sign up for service as well. A.W. Tozer once wrote, "Many a solo is sung to show off; many a sermon is preached as an exhibition of talent; many a church is founded as a slap to some other church. Even missionary activity may become competitive and soul winning may degenerate into a sort of brush-salesman project to satisfy the flesh."[6]

I remember sitting in Talbot Chapel while I was in seminary, listening to the great preacher Chuck Swindoll. We idolized him—a popular speaker, effective pastor, and successful author. Maybe that's why I have never forgotten something he said to us, who so desperately wanted to be like him. Some of us would one day be gifted and talented enough to become very effective in ministry and, hence, very popular, he pointed out. But then he warned us,

"When that happens, don't start believing your own press releases." I have never forgotten that wise advice.

Even though each of these motivations for entering ministry can lead to spiritual defection, that doesn't mean it's inevitable. In each and every situation, the Holy Spirit's gentle warning can help us make instant adjustments in motivation. Sadly, we can also ignore those warnings.

If we are serious about no longer faking church, if we sincerely want to address the issue of defection, we need to begin with where the seed was planted in our sinful natures and allowed to grow. It may take some time and thought, but it will be worth the effort.

CHAPTER FIVE

DISCONNECTED DEFECTORS/CHURCHLESS CHRISTIANS

DISAPPOINT—V.
to fail to satisfy the hopes
or expectations of;
leave unsatisfied

> "A large measure of disappointment with God stems from disillusionment with other Christians."
>
> PHILIP YANCEY

Precious few people storm out the doors of the church announcing, "I'm never coming back!" Instead, most seem to just slowly fade away, reluctantly—perhaps even sadly. As church attendance has surged in North America, there has been a corresponding, but little noticed, exodus of the faithful. The church in America has been very successful recently in wooing the unchurched in the front door, but there has been a corresponding failure to keep many of the churched from exiting the back door, as noted earlier in William D. Hendricks's book *Exit Interviews.*

Of the dozens of what he calls "dropouts" across the country,

Hendricks interviewed only one who rejected God outright. People are not necessarily consciously abandoning their faith, but they are consciously abandoning their churches.

Allan Jamieson, pastor, sociologist, and author of *A Churchless Faith* (Society for Promoting Christian Knowledge, August 2002), agrees and points out a new trend: Christians who decide to go their faith alone instead of being part of a local church. He dubs these people "postcongregational Christians." What is most amazing about his findings is that those exiting the church are not the nominal Christians who were never really committed in the first place. Jamieson found that 94 percent had been leaders—deacons, elders, Sunday school teachers. And 32 percent had been full-time ministers!

Pollster George Barna supports these findings as well in *Grow Your Church from the Outside*. "Relatively few unchurched people are atheists. Most of them call themselves Christian and have had a *serious dose of church life* in the past."[7]

David Barrett, author of the *World Christian Encyclopedia* (Oxford University Press, 2001), estimates there are about 112 million "churchless Christians" worldwide, about 5 percent of all adherents, and he projects that number will double by 2025.

What is interesting is that many Christians who leave the church say they do so not because they lost their faith but because they say they want to save it. Jeanette Gardner Littleton wrote, "They feel they'll grow better spiritually on their own than confined by the problems that sometimes plague congregations."[8]

If you've spent any time in church over the years, you didn't need to hear these statistics; you can cite stories of your own. Countless times I have been speaking with Christian friends who ask, "Say, what happened to _____ and _____? Why don't they come to church anymore?" At times we simply explained away their absence by assuming they were "afraid of commitment" or were "backsliders." This was the only explanation we could imagine or perhaps the only one we were ready to accept. But, more often than not, we were off the mark.

The seed of defection is watered within us by our own inner weaknesses, as we have seen, but there are other factors that affect us as well: *external* factors. When these demotivational experiences are teamed with our inner struggles with self-honesty, the ensuing result can become a literal physical defection. The sad truth is that many Christians have been hurt and disillusioned by experiences within their churches or ministries. Unfortunately, these hurts are often camouflaged so that often we never find out what prompted their defection.

One of the fascinating headlines that can make news is the defection from a communist or totalitarian regime of a famous leader, politician, or athlete. The reason it is so intriguing is that defection is not an easy task in these environments. You can't simply announce you are going to do it or even give the appearance you are contemplating it. You would find yourself jailed or worse if the authorities suspected your true feelings. To be able to effectively defect, you have to learn how to live two different lives—one on the outside that others see and the other a hidden secret life known only to yourself and maybe close family or friends.

I can only imagine how agonizing it must be to constantly have to live a lie, to pretend to be going along with the program when everything inside of you is screaming to escape. Sadly, there are many Christians in churches that feel some of these same emotions. The loyalty or feelings they once enjoyed with churches or ministries have changed significantly. They have been going through the motions while wondering how they could leave or escape the current situation gracefully, without answering a lot of uncomfortable questions.

Maybe you have felt these emotions in the past or are experiencing them now. Afraid to reveal the extent of your disillusionment, pain, or disappointment, you keep going through the motions, hoping you will feel differently soon. Instead of facing and dealing with your feelings, you may be tempted to just pretend that all is well.

This is especially true of those who are insecure or immature in their faith and the understanding of their places in the church. Surely the reason they feel the way they do is due to some deficiency they feel within themselves, something they feel should be kept secret.

Each of us will struggle with things that no one knows about. Whether we are ashamed of these struggles or feel that no one would understand or care, we cover our feelings with masks. The danger is that now no one can see our pain, confusion, fatigue, boredom, hurt, or other feelings, creating a gulf between us and others that grows wider with time, making us feel more disenfranchised than ever.

There are five common demotivators that, if not dealt with properly, can prompt people to seriously consider leaving church and service. What they all have in common is that they are usually hidden from plain view. People frequently struggle with them in silence. You will likely find that you have experienced at least several, if not all, of these demotivators at one time or another if you have spent any time in church. But if one of these demotivating experiences is strong enough and left unaddressed long enough, defection is a very real possibility.

DISCOURAGING EXPERIENCES WITHIN THE CHURCH

You've been hurt. Admit it. It is simply impossible for people to live and work for any length of time around others without conflict or misunderstanding. Years ago, when I was working at a small church, I was approached by a man I had always had a good relationship with and had always respected. With a friendly face, he handed me an envelope containing a letter and asked me to read it when I got home. I had been recently nominated to be an elder within the church, and he mentioned that he had given a copy to the other elders as well. Assuming only the best, I thanked him and took the envelope.

Later I went home and read the letter. This individual proceeded to question almost everything I had ever done in the church, casting a negative and accusatory slant on many of my recent activities. I was baffled as much by surprise as by the accusations themselves, because many of the accusations were so patently absurd that I laughed aloud. He was terribly uninformed. I had my flaws, to be sure, but not the ones listed. It wasn't funny, and it hurt deeply. If this person had taken the time to approach me on any of the issues he was concerned about, he would have learned the truth, but he didn't bother. Worse, I never had any reason to believe that he had any problem whatsoever with me. I tried in vain several times to speak to him about the letter. What hurt more deeply is that I was honestly innocent of his accusations.

Every Sunday I saw this individual and his family. I treated them as if nothing had ever happened and pretended to still be on friendly terms. Every Sunday I had to deal with feelings of hurt, confusion, and anger. Furthermore, aside from my wife and the other recipients of the letter, I had no one who knew what I was going through. There were times when my pain and anger were so intense, I was tempted to just walk away.

In every group of Christians who gather together for fellowship in local churches, ministries, organizations, or denominations, there will be inevitable conflict. Everyone is not mature and filled with the Spirit at all times, regardless of the positions they hold or notoriety they have attained. Dwight L. Moody, the famous evangelist of the last century, was once asked if he was filled with the Spirit. "Yes," he replied, "but I leak." I'm afraid that is a common experience.

The love of God is not always flowing through every Christian as they interact with other believers. Oh, that it were so. My story was not the only time I was hurt by someone at church, and it won't be the last. My experience has probably prompted a memory of a time when you were hurt by someone in a church. It might be recent or it might have happened long ago, but if I'm right, you can still feel the pain.

You aren't alone. Each of us carries a pain from someone in a church or ministry who hurt us, and part of our pain is the source of the attack or cruelty. We learn, to our chagrin, that Christians can be just as cruel, ugly, or malicious as any nonbeliever when their old sin nature is being satisfied at our expense. We also learn how bitter and spiteful we could become if we gave in to our desires to strike back in kind. And we *are* tempted. It is in our desire to be spiritual and forgiving that we often internalize our experience. We know we need to forgive, and we often feel the most effective way to do that is just to pretend nothing ever happened. Internalizing the pain, we are walking wounded and no one knows.

All of our experiences are different, and there may be hundreds of them, but you may recognize some of the following.

- The choir is dissolved.
- You are active in the choir and have a talent for singing, but you are never asked to sing a solo.
- Your child wanders away from the faith, and the youth pastor doesn't seem to do enough about it.
- They stop singing your favorite songs in church in favor of more contemporary songs.
- A beloved clergy member is caught in immorality.
- The Christian education department asks you to stay in Sunday school to help deal with your unruly child.
- Your good idea is ignored.
- You have been sick for a month, and no one at church even called or noticed you were gone.
- The church promises to reimburse you for expenditures but never does.
- You have marital problems, and it seems like no one seems to be comfortable around you anymore.
- You get divorced, and it seems like people are treating you differently now.
- Kids are cruel to your children at church.

The sad thing is that we have often drawn the wrong conclusion from our experiences about the church in general and people in specific; but, because it is a private, hidden hurt, those conclusions can't be challenged. And when we begin to perceive people in a certain way, we become suspicious of them, often assuming the worst of their words and actions, even when the worst wasn't intended.

When these kinds of experiences occur, we can begin to wish we were somewhere else, starting off with a brand-new slate, a new batch of friends, and a "better" church or, as is often the case, no church at all. If we never challenge these feelings and thoughts, it is a small step toward walking out the door and never coming back. An entire process has occurred in our minds and hearts, completely hidden from view—a process that concluded that we are far better off leaving than staying.

FEELINGS OF DISENCHANTMENT

You've been disillusioned! I remember sitting across the table from someone at a pastor's conference who had been involved in a church plant with a former acquaintance and fellow student of mine. He was recounting what it was like every Sunday for several years in their young church plant. If attendance was up that week, the pastor's mood was up and everyone was excited; but if attendance was down, he was downcast and depressed, and so were all the others in leadership. The church fellowship seemed to swing from emotional extreme to emotional extreme. He began to dread Sunday mornings because attendance was not always steadily increasing. The excitement they had begun this ministry with began to ebb as they realized the incredible results they had envisioned might be a long time in coming—if ever. This wasn't what they had hoped for at all.

Disillusionment begins to set in when our expectations are not being realized, whether that is in interpersonal relationships within the church, the leadership, the worship style, the organization, the passion, the aesthetics, or any number of other issues that matter to us. It becomes worse when we have had better experiences in these areas in the past.

Being a church planter, I have had discussions with other church planters. When people sign up for some new ministry or some new thrust within an older or dying ministry, they often do so with an unspoken expectation. They are expecting within a fairly short time to be a part of some dynamic and exciting church growth.

However, when the church appears not to be growing as hoped or even begins to enter decline, some get disillusioned. Their connection with the church was directly related to specific expectations of growth and productivity. When it begins to appear to them that they are a part of a sinking ship, they seek to bail out. To them, the only real church is a vibrant, dynamic place, and anything less is not acceptable. It is not the church or what the church is going through that is the issue; it is their expectations of what the church should be. Disenchantment with a lack of progress or quick results causes some people to leave.

We might have been involved in a church in our past in which we had many close friends. But in this new town and church we don't have those kinds of relationships, so we become disillusioned. We might have come from a church that had a dynamic music program; our present church, by contrast, is woefully inadequate—even an embarrassment. Our former church might have been large and impressive; our new one is small and amateurish. Or perhaps our former church was small and comfortable; our new one is large and impersonal. Our former pastor was dynamic and charismatic; our new pastor is quiet and rather ordinary in the pulpit.

In my seminary's alumni magazine one year, a former student opened up and confessed his own attitude of disillusionment at church and the real source of the disillusionment.

Nothing like starting out a sermon with a video clip (sigh). . . Oh great, a statistical analysis of Scripture. Does the fact that money is mentioned 2,000 times in the New Testament versus a combined 500 for faith and prayer really

*make money more important?. . . The widow gave more
than any of us at church today? How does the pastor know
how much the people in the pews have given? Some time
ago, I found myself in a nondenominational church with
these thoughts floating through my head. After years of the
highest caliber training at Biola, a return to my home church
yielded, not learning, but frustration at shaky exegesis and
offensive rhetoric.*

*Then, in a glimmer of grace, it came to me. I realized
that the pastor's message, though not flawlessly executed, was
at least coherent, applicable, and appropriately frank. Though
the pastor's words clung loosely to the Scripture cited, timeless
truth was held in them. The problem was not in the message,
but rather my heart. I began to actually listen, and the sermon
was no longer lost on me. I believe this frustration and scorn
for the church is quite common among those who have attended robust Christian universities. I fear that, in our efforts
to gain wisdom and understanding with the intent of serving
and edifying our churches, we often gain instead a tendency to
despise them. We begin seeing ourselves as superior, shaking
our heads in smug disapproval or shaking our sides in outright mockery.*

*Those who have attended Biola are especially at risk.
Four years (or more) of a rigorous Bible curriculum, regular
doses of eminent chapel speakers and the occasional overdose
of those annoying elements of Christian culture all serve to
prime educated Christians for cynicism toward our churches
and their people.*[9]

Disillusionment isn't limited to church performance or com-
parison. There are an almost unlimited amount of things that can
lead a person into disillusionment and ultimate defection.

A single mother in the midst of a church of predominantly
married couples can silently feel out of place, disillusioned that
there doesn't seem to be any place where she fits.

A single or divorced man can feel that his very presence threatens the married men in the church when he talks with their wives. It might be easier just to stop coming.

Teenagers who wear their hair differently than all the other kids at church, like different music, and have different hobbies and interests can feel like they don't belong or aren't wanted.

People who have been recently separated from their spouses or been divorced can feel alienated, disenfranchised from the church. The couples' class they used to attend doesn't seem to fit them anymore. The friends they had don't know how to relate easily to their situation.

Those of another color or race can easily feel slighted or unwelcome if they find they are definitely in the minority and no one seems interested in reaching out to them.

People who don't hold what they feel are the same political views as others in church can wonder whether they are really welcome.

Years ago a lady, new to our church, requested an appointment with me. When she came into my office, she looked uncomfortable. She was obviously hesitant to ask me the question she had. After encouragement, she opened up. She wanted to know if she had to be pro-life to be a part of our church. She had noticed some stickers on the cars in the parking lot and had recently sat through our Sanctity of Life sermon. For a moment I was stunned. I had never been asked that question before.

Probably sensing my confusion and surprise, she then explained her predicament. She worked in law enforcement and regularly saw the terrible things that neglectful or abusive parents can do to their own children. It had just broken her heart and, even though she had never before believed in abortion, she couldn't help wondering if some children might be better off being aborted than having to live the kind of lives she had seen children subjected to. It is easy to paint with a broad brush everyone who believes differently than we do. She was not in the least advocating abortion for convenience, and she detested the idea of killing babies. She was one of the most compassionate women I ever met. She was just conflicted with the reality she had to face daily and the culture she encountered at church.

Because she was able to articulate her feelings, a strong disillusionment with our church and policy was avoided as I was able to empathize with her situation. Though we never changed our policy, I was able to explain in nonemotionally charged terms why we believed as we did, and she was able to understand it. She had heard our words before but not our hearts. Because she was wise, we were able to derail a potential disillusionment before it happened. Tragically, this is the exception, not the rule.

Christians who struggle with moral sins and are too ashamed to admit them and get help to overcome them feel that the church is simply not the place for them. There is no way they can live up to the requirements of the church or try to pretend to be as holy and righteous as the other people they see at church. Though they are desperate to change, they feel they are on the outside looking in. Their silent agony is disillusioning to them, and they choose the path of least resistance and leave.

Christians with hidden sinful pasts or experiences—sexual immorality, abortion, homosexuality, drug or alcohol abuse, crime, imprisonment, divorce, or some other taint—can feel terribly disillusioned if they attend a church where all these vices are continually thundered against. Feeling that they really don't belong with these people who haven't experienced any kind of serious weakness or failure in their lives, they can become disillusioned with church.

Someone once confessed to me that she felt uncomfortable in our church because no one in the church had any real problems. All our members came in looking so clean, holy, and perfect. Their families were perfect; their marriages were perfect; their lives were perfect. Of course, I knew this wasn't true, but I also knew I would not dislodge this idea by my words alone.

One Sunday not long after this, I did an interview on Sunday morning instead of a sermon. I asked a number of our church leaders, both male and female—the very ones my friend had felt were so perfect—to share their testimonies. One after another, they shared their often sordid and unholy pasts. The message got through. They had come into the church broken and hurting, and the church had accepted and encouraged them. Their present conditions (although not nearly as holy as the person imagined) were the result of time, the work of God, and wonderful Christian fellowship.

A potential disillusionment was averted. But, sadly, this is the exception and not the rule. I was fortunate because some expressed their disillusionment, and I was able to address it. More often than not, the disillusionment is not adequately verbalized; it is instead internalized. An unchallenged perception is given free reign in our minds and hearts. Given enough time, it will often lead to a disconnection, a defection from the church we once called home.

Spiritual Fatigue

You've been neglected. One of the most tragically disillusioning experiences, and all too common, is that of the faithful who have become disillusioned through a lack of attention to their spiritual condition. There are literally millions of Christians who are showing up for church and service every Sunday who are spiritually exhausted and on the verge of spiritual bankruptcy.

Unfortunately, although physical fatigue often has visible symptoms, spiritual fatigue can be far more difficult to detect. What does someone look like who has become spiritually hungry and underfed? What happens when Sunday school teachers' spiritual expenditures exceed their spiritual resources? Do they start frothing at the mouth? Do they fall to the floor in wild convulsions? Do they start sweating profusely or bleeding suddenly? No, actually they often pack up their Sunday school materials, get doughnuts and coffee at the snack table, make small talk, and then go home. They will very likely be back again next week, looking and acting about the same.

What do spiritually fatigued ushers, helpers, or teachers look like when they are overtaxed? About the same as they do the rest of the time. How do spiritually exhausted elders or deacons act when they know their spiritual lives are anemic? Do they go running from the room at some point in time screaming hysterically? Hardly. It would almost be better if they did. At least then we'd know and we could intervene.

Unfortunately, because we are such skilled deceivers at times, we can easily mask this serious malady. Service for Christ in the church is an emotionally and spiritually taxing exercise. Yet, in the same way that we can appear physically healthy for awhile, even with a diet of junk food, we can appear spiritually healthy while neglecting to partake of spiritual nourishment and rest. We can be spiritually starving, and no one might ever guess.

Do you begin to see the tremendous danger of deception? When we fake church, when we pretend a spirituality that does not reflect reality, we are the victims. We are shooting ourselves in the foot. A healthy, growing relationship with God is not a given. Nor is it the experience of many Christians. I've talked with scores of people who everyone assumed were growing spiritually but who later confided to me they were burnt out spiritually.

Did God or ministry do this to them? No. Did the church do this to them? No, but it might have helped. All of us make assumptions; that's how we get along in life. We assume that a smile means all is okay, a laugh indicates a good attitude, and someone's presence means they are spiritually healthy.

Tina has been teaching the third graders for ten years. She loves the children and they love her. Yet no one knows that at times it is all Tina can do to get to church. She used to look forward to teaching and working with the children. But slowly her attitude changed, and she is ashamed of it. At one point she used to read her Bible regularly and pray faithfully, but the busyness of life gradually squeezed out that spiritual habit. Now she relaxes with TV, a good novel, and soothing music. The Word of God no longer nourishes Tina's soul and provides her the wisdom to counter her feelings of futility or discouragement. The passion she once enjoyed for her ministry has waned. She no longer remembers to ask God to change her heart and strengthen her. She no longer reflects on spiritual truths. Tina is going through spiritual starvation but does not recognize the symptoms.

I have done a number of discipleships with men over the years. One of my priorities is to get the men involved again in spiritual disciplines—not simply to fulfill some spiritual duty but to help them become reacquainted with the God who loves them and is waiting to nurture them and encourage them every single moment of every day. Almost to a man, the men I have discipled were failing to regularly feed themselves spiritually; almost to a man, they were so very grateful that someone was taking the time to help them.

I wish I could say I was the model of perfection on this issue, but I'm not. Over the years I have learned the importance of periodically checking people's spiritual health, because so often I've had them leave, desert their post, or just collapse in discouragement. Had I been more attentive to their spiritual condition, instead of just being happy they were taking care of an urgent ministry need, I would have been more insistent. But I wasn't. I suspect I'm in good company.

Without regular spiritual discipline in your life—constantly being fed spiritually, being nourished through the Word of God and prayer, and being built up and encouraged by other believers whom God has put in your life for your edification—you *will* become spiritually fatigued. It is not a matter of "if," only of "when." The major problem is that you will not identify the seriousness of the situation, and eventually you will gradually succumb to spiritual numbness and apathy, a result of ministry without power.

SPIRITUAL DOUBTS

You've been conflicted! A serious problem within the church is the condition of those who are struggling with spiritual doubts but who are afraid or embarrassed to mention them to anyone. At times we may come across a truth or verse in the Bible that we desperately wish was true, but our own experiences seem to dictate the opposite. We simply can't reconcile the feelings we have or the thoughts we think with the truths we are supposed to believe.

We are told that God has a wonderful plan for our lives; but, when a child dies, we lose our jobs, or our marriages are in turmoil, we have trouble reconciling these experiences with the wonderful plan of God. Yet, as we listen to others, it truly seems that God indeed has a wonderful plan for *their* lives. It must just be us. Somehow we are different. It sure feels that way. When we try to pray the prayer of Jabez, we can't seem to get a divine dial tone. Somehow our spiritual wiring must be bad.

I just recently received an E-mail from a wonderful Christian couple. The husband had lost his job of thirty years due to downsizing and was unemployed for a long period. Life was difficult, money tight, the outlook bleak. Then, miraculously he landed a job nearby. Now, only several months into the job, they have learned that the company he works for is being investigated for false advertising. Though he had no part in this, he wonders if he will again be unemployed.

We are often surprised when trials come our way, even though Scriptures tell us not to be (James 1:2; 1 Peter 1:6; 2 Peter 2:9). Without God's Word to provide balance, we can easily succumb to the idea that we are simply spiritually cursed in some way. A form of spiritual superstition begins to be formed in us as we seek to "read the signs" in our lives.

When we are told that God answers prayers and our prayers seem to go unanswered, when we are told that God provides and we are going deeply in debt every month, when we hear about the "abundant life" that God wants His children to have and the only abundance we know is abundant confusion and pain, we inevitably struggle with doubt. We do indeed hear the biblical messages that everyone else hears, but we also hear something else: doubts, confusion, and conflicting messages. Others don't struggle with these issues like we do. We almost feel cursed. If the truth were known, we have more doubts than faith. We do believe and desperately wish we didn't have our doubts, but we do. We can feel a sense of abandonment by God and think it a strange thing. But it isn't as strange or unusual a feeling as we may think. Popular author Philip Yancey talks about just such moments in his own life.

> *Any relationship involves times of closeness and times of distance, and in a relationship with God, no matter how intimate, the pendulum will swing from one side to another. I experienced the sense of abandonment just as I was making progress spiritually, advancing beyond childish faith to the point where I could help others. Suddenly, the darkness descended. For an entire year my prayers seemed to go nowhere; I had no confidence God was listening. . . . My prayers seemed lost, my hymns dead in the vast silence. . . . I now look back upon that period of absence as an important growth time, for in some ways I had pursued God more earnestly than ever before. I came away with renewed faith and an appreciation of God's presence as gift rather than entitlement. . . . In the Bible I see that God's absence may represent a time of testing from which Jesus Himself was not exempt ("My God, My God, why hast Thou forsaken Me?"). It may, on the other hand, represent a phase of relationship with no great underlying significance. I am not the first to experience dark times and will not be the last.*[10]

Sadly, when we try to articulate our feelings to others, it can sound like we have no faith at all. We feel like we are outsiders, somehow strange and unlike everyone else. When we see suffering that we can't explain, we question. We do want to believe, but trusting is hard, and the questions keep gnawing at us. We'd love to get answers, but we realize that our very questions make us sound suspect to others who don't share our doubts and confusions. In fact, in some churches, articulating doubts and confusion is unacceptable.

Only victory is allowed, only overcoming, only conquering. It doesn't take long before we feel like fish on dry land, completely out of our element.

So we keep our doubts and confusion safely hidden behind clichés and trite sayings we know are acceptable. It doesn't take a genius to realize that it won't be long before the energy of living a charade will take its toll on us.

In Gary R. Habermas's book *The Thomas Factor: Using Your Doubts to Draw Closer to God,* he writes:

> *In my experience, the two most difficult points in the entire process of dealing with emotional doubt are discovering the falsehoods we tell ourselves and implementing God's truth. It seems especially tough to do the latter precisely during the time in which we are most in need. . . . Given that even believers ignore God's teaching and disobey Him, why, more specifically, might a Christian fail to apply God's directives concerning their emotional doubt, when they are so obviously hurting and obedience might render relief? One reason is that it is difficult to pinpoint our own unedifying thoughts. After all, why would we ever want to lie to ourselves? Yet, God has forewarned us that it is very difficult to know our own hearts, and why we do the things we do (Jeremiah 17:9). It would seem that we are all candidates for unintentionally misdirecting ourselves.*

Habermas points out later that:

> *When partial truth is mixed in with untruth, the doubting individual is often tempted to wonder if our biblical procedure for relief really works at all. This sort of case is more difficult to work through, specifically because the person is less likely to see that they are still repeating untruths. . . . In other words, the chief obstacle with half-true statements is that the false portion will work on us, frequently causing anxious*

doubt. Like an undetected physical sickness, the lie stays hidden behind the partial truth until it is strong enough to produce some harm. By then, it is much more troublesome to remove.[11]

Many Christians experience a seeming inability to lead the victorious Christian life that is so frequently advertised. Instead of feeling victorious and faithful, they feel just the opposite. They struggle with:

- Doubts about their true salvation
- Doubts about their relationship with God
- Doubts about certain key doctrines
- Doubts about the effectiveness of prayer
- Doubts about God's love for them
- Doubts about the Bible

There are answers to these doubts; however, they are not trite, easy, or quick. They will require attention, prayer, and help from others. Having doubts doesn't mean you can't exercise faith or trust God or believe in prayer. Having doubts doesn't mean you aren't really saved or that you don't really have a relationship with God. Having doubts about key doctrines doesn't mean you reject them—only that you have unanswered questions that need to be dealt with before you can assimilate them as wholeheartedly as others. Having doubts about God's love for you certainly doesn't mean God doesn't love you; it just means that at times you have trouble identifying what His love is like.

I remember a woman from my church who appeared on my doorstep one evening. She apologized profusely for interrupting me at night, and when I invited her in, she politely declined. It was obvious she wanted to tell me something, and it was hard and slightly embarrassing. She finally shared, quietly and graciously, "You know, Pastor Dan, you are a good speaker, and I learn a lot from your messages. You have good illustrations and stories. . .

but. . .sometimes what I need to hear more than anything else is just that Jesus loves me." I'll never forget that. She was letting me in on a compelling need of her heart. And she was right. I was so busy trying to be a good speaker that I was forgetting at times that we simply need to hear again that Jesus loves us very much.

Unknowingly, she had a great impact on my life and preaching. But she was one of the brave souls who was able to share her weakness. Her life was difficult in many ways, and I began to realize how doubts about God's love for her could easily overwhelm her. There are many more who will harbor real doubts—doubts they would do anything to remove if they could. But it is their secret alone.

If everyone were able to articulate his or her deepest doubts, confusions, and concerns to others, the problem could be addressed and probably would be. Alas, such is not often the case. Doctors, nurses, and bleeding and sick patients walk blindly by each other every Sunday, oblivious to the presence of the others. Jesus created His church to be the healing balm to doubts, confusions, and concerns. We will talk more about that in a future chapter. But for the time being it is enough to know that unaddressed spiritual doubts can lead to feelings of disenfranchisement in people. If the issues are not ultimately addressed, chances are good we will slowly fade away from church itself, feeling we never really fit anyway.

PERSONAL PROBLEMS

You've been distracted! When I took a pastoral counseling class in seminary, I was told about the problem of "internal noise" when you are counseling someone. If, while listening to your counselee's problem, you suddenly find yourself identifying with those same feelings, you are hearing "internal noise." You can't help but begin to focus on your own inadequacies and fail to be able to truly focus on the needs of the one you are counseling. At times we are ashamed of the issues we struggle with, such as lust, greed, envy, jealousy, and anger. The problem is, of course, that if no one knows the real struggle, no real solution can be offered. Furthermore, a deep gulf is created between us and others we feel aren't like us. You are not strange if you identify with what I am writing; in fact, you are quite normal.

Maybe you suffer from:

- Depression
- Loneliness
- Fear
- Confusion
- Job-related issues
- Unanswered questions
- Guilt or shame about sins
- Financial stress
- Marriage or parenting problems
- Feelings of hypocrisy

These and others are quite common. We might even want to tell someone about our struggles, but we're not sure whom to talk to—not to mention that we feel embarrassed and ashamed. If we feel that we should not be having these feelings, we hide them all the more. "Good Christians shouldn't suffer from depression; they should always have joy in the Lord." That's what we often hear. That's not the case, of course, but that is the message people often receive at church. The biblical account is quite different.

Elijah the prophet, after an amazing act of spiritual faith, soon found himself so despondent and depressed he wanted only to die (1 Kings 18, 19:4). The prophet Jonah, after finally obeying God and prophesying to the city of Nineveh, became so depressed at God's decision not to judge the Ninevites that he, too, wanted to die (Jonah 3:10–4:3). These men were greatly used of God, yet they were also struggling with powerful negative emotions. David, in many of the psalms, also uses language that describes feelings of depression.

Feelings of depression, loneliness, fear, and confusion can be terribly strong and powerful feelings in our lives. In fact, at times, these feelings can be deafening, drowning out everything else. But many Christians are afraid to admit that they have such weaknesses because they are afraid they will be labeled weaklings.

So many times when I would follow up on people who had drifted away from fellowship, I would find substantial issues in their lives that had been neglected and caused them to pull away from others. It might be marital issues they were ashamed to acknowledge, or a feeling of unworthiness, or a substance abuse issue, or a struggle with feelings they felt they should not be having as Christians.

Once they had felt that they fit in the church, but they no longer did. Their issues caused a separation in their minds between them and the other "normal" Christians in church. Since they obviously struggled with issues that others didn't, since they couldn't seem to fix their lives the way other Christians could, since prayer and reading their Bible hadn't changed them the way it obviously changed everyone else, they assumed that there must just be something wrong with them. None of these conclusions is right. But, they had gone unchallenged. The fact is, they are actually quite normal and others are faced with the same or similar issues.

Because we have a desire to protect our self-images, we can decide it is better to leave without disclosing the real truth. We can make up many excuses to cover our trails, and, in the absence of any information to the contrary, they will be accepted.

There are undoubtedly other ways that we can become disconnected from the church and fellowship, but these are some of the more common ways we disconnect emotionally or spiritually. Knowing how we can become disconnected does not solve the problem, but it can be enlightening. Sometimes we are simply unaware of the process of disconnection we have begun to experience. Not understanding what is going on can discourage and isolate us further.

So what happens when we begin to disconnect from Christians or churches, or both? Where do people who leave go? Where do people go who feel that they want or need to leave church or ministry but not their faith? Some of you may be there now. For the rest, we will learn the answer to that in the next chapter.

CHAPTER SIX

ESCAPE TO THE
VIRTUAL CHURCH

CHURCH—N.
*all Christians considered
as a single body*

"The Church is a workshop, not a dormitory."

ALEXANDER MACLAREN (1826–1910)

Escape from church! Though to some of us that may seem a strange concept, to many it is an appealing thought. This doesn't mean they hate church but that church can be the source of unwanted stress or problems. If church brings stress of any kind—relational, emotional, or spiritual—it is not strange that a desire to escape this source of distress might be planted in us. There was more than one time in my own life in the church when I envisioned what it would be like to simply be somewhere else, without any of the worries or stresses that church brought into my life. Furthermore, this isn't something new to the church.

The writer of Hebrews says, "And let us consider how we may spur one another on toward love and good deeds. Let us not give up meeting together, as some are in the habit of doing, but let us encourage one another—and all the more as you see the Day approaching" (Hebrews 10:24–25). Even in the early church, the temptation to forsake the fellowship of the local church was present, and it had to be warned against.

We have already talked about some of the reasons that cause people to begin to disconnect from church, but we have yet to talk about where they would go when they disconnected. When people make a decision to leave the church, where do they go? What do they substitute for church, if indeed they substitute anything at all? Statistics show us that most people, when they make a decision to disconnect from church, do not seek to disconnect from God.

MEDIA CHURCH

The Barna Group, a church polling organization, tells us that 96 percent of all evangelicals have been exposed to Christian media, ranging from 84 percent who listen to Christian radio to two-thirds who have watched Christian television or read a Christian book. Three-quarters of all churched adults (78 percent) supplemented their church experience with exposure to Christian media. Among adults who have what George Barna described as an "active faith" (that is, they read the Bible, attended a church service, and prayed during the past week), a group representing 30 percent of adults, 93 percent used one or more of the Christian media during the past month. About 132 million adults have been to a church service, compared to 141 million who have used Christian media.[12] In fact, a nationwide survey by the Ventura, California–based organization reports that a greater number of adults experience the Christian faith through Christian media than attend Christian churches.

Barna points out that "Increasing numbers of people are involved in informal discussion groups regarding faith matters, participate in faith forums and in-home worship activities, or use the Internet for faith exploration and communication. . . . Traditional Christian activities such as evangelism, worship, and discipleship may happen outside of a church building for many people—including millions of people who have no interest or intention of visiting a church."[13]

The media church, or what has been referred to as "the virtual church," was never designed to be a substitute for church. It is simply an arm of the church, an extension of ministry beyond the physical borders of a local assembly or group. It can be an extremely effective tool for teaching and evangelism. Even one-third of those who describe themselves as either atheists or agnostics (37 percent) admitted to listening, watching, or reading something related to the Christian faith.[14] Much good is happening through the virtual church.

The very fact that you are reading this book at the moment is evidence that the media church, or the virtual church, is touching you in some way. The printed word, the radio waves, and the television shows can be powerful tools of the church for the witness and encouragement of believers as well as nonbelievers. Many Christians listen to Christian radio programs as they drive to work or at their offices. Many Christians read Christian books from their favorite authors who help to illuminate subjects that the readers have been confused about.

It is not my desire to put down or ridicule the idea of the virtual church or attack Christian media as usurping the role of the church today. I believe that those involved in those ministries would be saddened at the very thought of being used as a substitute for a local church. That said, we would be terribly naive if we believed that many people do not use the virtual church for that very purpose.

In a real church, you must deal with real people in unscripted, unedited, often messy interaction. The virtual church allows you to be taught, entertained, and encouraged safely in the confines of your own home or vehicle. If you do meet with other believers, chances are they are believers of your own choosing. Church is often a drive away. Virtual church can be held at your own convenience, in your own home. Real church meets at the same place and time every week in a specific location. The virtual church is usually far more polished than real church—only the best music, the best speakers, and a built-in time limit to the message! Who could ask for anything more?

To attend real church, you must get up at a certain time on a weekend, the only time most of us have to rest. Trying to get the family ready and on time can be a monumental task at times. Even if you want to go, chances are there are some in the family who would rather sleep in on any given Sunday. Parking may be a problem, and, to add to the stress, you may have a responsibility that you have committed to in church. You don't get to be "ministered to" because you have to fulfill a job or responsibility. Even when you are truly enjoying your ministry or service, it can be draining at times. In real church, if someone or some activity has offended you, you have to face that person or situation every week.

These and more inconveniences can be remedied through the simple process of switching your allegiance to the virtual church: Everyone can sleep in; you don't have to drive anywhere; you don't have to do anything but relax, listen to your radio, watch television, or read your book. There is no one to remind you of some personal offense or whose personality you are offended by. You choose the time of the service, the speaker, and even the music! There is no offering plate to deal with (the radio or television preachers will ask for money, but there won't be a plate coming your way). You won't have to sit through a boring sermon (not all sermons are boring by the way!). Everything is smoother, better, more polished, and convenient in the virtual church. That's not hyperbole, it's just fact.

Having said that, why would anyone have any objection to a Christian dropping out of a local church and becoming a part of the virtual church? You don't have to leave your relationship with God behind; you can still get good teaching to help you grow in your Christian faith (often better than you can get at your local church). You certainly don't leave the family of God by leaving a local church, and you can still engage in most Christian activities (prayer,

Bible reading, witnessing, discipling) apart from the local church.

The problem comes in our understanding of the church itself. Often, because our understanding of the true nature of the church is incomplete, we feel safe in jettisoning it and moving on without it. We reason, correctly, that since we are children of God and our eternal destiny is secure, God will not reject us just because we don't go to church. That is true. But we need to ask ourselves an essential question: Is a local extension of the church part of God's plan for us? If so, just how will our fellowship with God be affected if we decide to unilaterally pull out of it? How will we be affected spiritually? Can we grow spiritually while neglecting something God has designed us for?

How would our relationship with God be affected if we decided to just pull out of our marriages or our parenting relationships? If we decided we liked our spouses but would find life more convenient without actually having to live in close contact with them, how would God view that? If we find we loved our children but discovered that they often caused us much trouble, discomfort, or stress, would God consider it acceptable if we just decided to put some distance between them and us? We would still be in relationship—just at a distance.

If we decide to pull out of Rotary or the Elks or Shriners, there will be no great effect on our family or relationship with God, and some look at church as just another human organization. Although the church is indeed filled with weak and sometimes difficult people, the Bible makes it clear that church is not a human invention. It was not invented by the apostle Paul or the early church to help organize our faith into some sort of religious structure.

As Charles Colson wrote in his book *Loving God*, "Biblically the church is an organism not an organization—movement, not a monument. It is not a part of the community; it is a whole new community. It is not an orderly gathering; it is a new order with new values, often in sharp conflict with the values of the surrounding society."[15]

C. S. Lewis, the late Christian philosopher and writer, points out that "The New Testament does not envisage solitary religion; some kind of regular assembly for worship and instruction is everywhere taken for granted in the Epistles. So we must be regular practicing members of the church. Of course we differ in temperament. Some. . .find it more natural to approach God in solitude; but we must go to church as well. For the church is not a human society of people united by their common affinities, but the Body of Christ, in which all members, however different (and he rejoices in their differences and by no means wishes to iron them out) must share the common life, complementing and helping one another *precisely by their differences.*"[16]

Lewis admits that at first it was difficult for him to envision going to church. "When I first became a Christian. . .I thought that I could do it on my own, by retiring to my rooms and reading theology, and I wouldn't go to the churches and gospel halls. . . . I disliked very much their hymns, which I considered to be fifth-rate poems set to sixth-rate music. But as I went on I saw the great merit of it. I came up against different people of quite different outlooks and different education, and then gradually my conceit just began peeling off. I realized that their hymns (which were just sixth-rate music) were, nevertheless, being sung with devotion and benefit by an old saint in elastic-side boots in the opposite pew, and then you realize that you aren't fit to clean those boots."[17]

WHAT IS CHURCH—AND WHO INVENTED IT?

If man invented the institution of church, then it is safe to disregard it, because it would then be merely an attempt to organize people into some semblance of coherence and common purpose around shared religious convictions and moral values. Attendance and participation would be purely voluntary. There are many clubs or service groups that are merely human inventions to accommodate common values and goals.

However, as Colson pointed out, church is not an organization, though outwardly it can appear that way. It is an organism precisely because it is a living body, the body of Christ.

"The church is more than a unified body," writes Dr. Robert Saucy in *The Church in God's Program*. "It is the body of a Person. The unity of the members is based not on a mutual relationship with the group, but in their vital relationship to the Head of the Body, Christ Himself."[18] The church is Christ's body, and that is a powerful statement. To deny involvement with some group is one thing; to withdraw from involvement with Christ's body is quite another.

The church was not created by a meeting of the apostles when Jesus left; instead, it was created by an act of the Holy Spirit of God on the day of Pentecost. Jesus spoke of creating the church in Matthew 16:18: "And I tell you that you are Peter, and on this rock I will build my church, and the gates of Hades will not overcome it." The church was still future when Jesus spoke to Peter here, but it was definitely part of His future purpose. And it was *His* purpose, mind you, not Peter's or the disciples'. On the day of Pentecost, in the Book of Acts, the believers who had been waiting for the baptism of the Holy Spirit that Jesus had promised (Acts 1:5) suddenly experienced it (Acts 2). Later, Paul the Apostle makes clear that the body of Christ, the church, was begun by that historic baptism of the Holy Spirit. In short, the church was God's idea.

"The body is a unit, though it is made up of many parts; and though all its parts are many, they form one body. So it is with Christ. For we were all baptized by one Spirit into one body— whether Jews or Greeks, slave or free—and we were all given the one Spirit to drink" (1 Corinthians 12:12–13). Speaking later of the body of Christ, the church, Paul writes, "But in fact God has arranged the parts in the body, every one of them, just as he wanted them to be" (1 Corinthians 12:18).

Note the words "arranged the parts in the body." This assumes that arms and legs won't be disconnected from the torso and head, but that the pieces are in intimate relationship with the other parts. The church is not to be a deformed body but a complete one with all the parts where they should be.

When a person becomes a Christian, he or she is placed into this body, not by church polity or group vote but by an act of the Holy Spirit of God, and becomes a vital and necessary part of it. In fact, God arranges just where each person should be and what role each person should have.

"When Christians say the Christ-life is in them," writes C. S. Lewis, "they do not mean simply something mental or moral. When they speak of being 'in Christ' or of Christ being 'in them,' this is not simply a way of saying that they are thinking about Christ or copying Him. They mean that Christ is actually operating through them; that the whole mass of Christians is the physical organism through which Christ acts—that we are His fingers and muscles, the cells of His body."[19]

George Barna writes that, despite the gaudy numbers of people reached via the Christian media, "In essence, Christianity is about relationships, a life-changing relationship with Jesus Christ that is fostered through supportive relationships with other Christians. The Christian media are helpful in focusing people's attention on things that matter. The focus is greatly enhanced when impersonal media presentations are made practical through supportive community. Unless there is a degree of personal accountability upheld through loving and focused relationships, Christianity becomes only an intellectual faith, and Christians run the danger of becoming modern-day Pharisees. The people factor must always be incorporated if Christianity is to be a genuine expression of God's intent."[20]

IF IT DOESN'T WORK, WHY BOTHER?

God's intent! That's what the church is. But I can already hear some who have criticism of the church in general or their church or denomination in particular. "The church doesn't work! It doesn't perfectly represent Christ to the world." Indeed, you can often find more agreeable people outside the church than in it! "Some of the activities that have occurred in church, in Jesus' name, are simply shameful." I humbly agree with that assessment at times. There are embarrassing moments and activities that take place in churches all too frequently. Having been in three churches over the past thirty years of my Christian life, attending regularly, I have my own memory gallery of incidents I would just as soon forget.

Moral failures, blatant hypocrisy, selfish conceit, anger, and unbridled ambition have reared their ugly heads in church. There is no denying this, but does the presence of imperfect people and less-than-perfect activities mean that church isn't "working"? I propose to you that the presence of such people and such activity means that the church is working as well as it ever has. As someone once said, "Some folks would close the churches because there still is sin—would they also stop medical research because there still are diseases?"

C. S. Lewis once addressed this issue creatively. He wrote, "Take the case of a sour old maid who is a Christian, but cantankerous. On the other hand, take some pleasant and popular fellow, but who has never been to church. Who knows how much more cantankerous the old maid might be if she were not a Christian, and how much more likeable the nice fellow might be if he were a Christian? You can't judge Christianity simply by comparing the product in these two people; you would need to know what kind of raw material Christ was working with in both cases."[21]

The New Testament is terribly frank and honest about the failures and shortcomings of New Testament Christians and their churches. Yet, it never records a church that "doesn't work" even though it recorded their frailties, weaknesses, and frequent mistakes. Even though the Corinthian church was filled with problems, God still claimed it as His church. In Revelation 2–3, Christ, speaking to a number of early churches, recognizes faulty and anemic churches as belonging to Him.

The reason we should still bother with the church is because the church is still God's plan for each believer, and it is still His body. *We can never fulfill our spiritual destiny if we take ourselves out of the church, for we were created for this fellowship.* We were divinely designed to function in this sometimes messy, awkward, and problematic church. Learning to live with each other's faults and weaknesses is one of the most important life lessons any human being will ever have. In fact, we face tremendous danger when we begin to place distance between us and the church.

THE DANGERS OF ISOLATION

Solomon noticed that some people had a tendency to withdraw unto themselves. In his God-given wisdom, he wrote, "He who separates himself seeks his own desire, he quarrels against all sound wisdom" (NASB). Although escape can seem like the best solution in difficult times, it does reveal a hidden selfishness. People want to be free from problems, stress, and pain, and they think that they can find this freedom in escape and isolation.

What we have not often considered is whether or not God intends us to go through just such a painful experience for His own purposes. As strange as it may sound, problems with others in the church is not a surprise or some kind of divine confusion; it is part of His plan for us to grow in Him. Pleasant experiences, happy moments, and always-supportive people would be a wonderful way to live, but it would not do much to strengthen our faith or character. In fact, just the opposite is often used to test our character. The very problems we seek to avoid are the very means of our growing in Christ.

True Christian love is not a mushy, sentimental feeling; it is a deliberate act in full view and knowledge of others' failings and shortcomings. It loves not because people are so lovable but in spite of the fact that they are frequently not. This is the way God loves us, and this is the way He wants us to learn to love one another. The imperfect church is the perfect place for Christians to learn the lessons of love. We could never learn to imitate our beloved Lord if we had only a Garden of Eden experience where everything was wonderful and easy.

When we choose to remove ourselves from His church, as believers we are choosing to forego one of the most important parts of our spiritual development. We do so at our own risk. I say this as a person who has experienced firsthand the difficult people and hypocrisy that the church can be accused of at times. But there are a number of dangers found in the idea of isolation—or spiritual cocooning.

We don't learn how to forgive and deal with people in need of God's grace through us.

"Therefore, as God's chosen people, holy and dearly loved, clothe yourselves with compassion, kindness, humility, gentleness and patience," writes the apostle Paul. "Bear with each other and forgive whatever grievances you may have against one another. Forgive as the Lord forgave you. And over all these virtues put on love, which binds them all together in perfect unity. Let the peace of Christ rule in your hearts, since as members of one body you were called to peace" (Colossians 3:12–15).

"Grievances against one another" are simply assumed. The church is not a magical place of happiness where perfect people interact with each other in perfect unity. It is the body of Christ, where saved but not yet perfected Christians learn how to live, work, and love those whose actions can at times put them sorely to the test.

Forgiveness is not an optional piece of equipment for the Christian; nor is it something that every Christian is born again with. Forgiveness is a choice for all Christians, one they will inevitably be faced with from time to time. When we have been offended (and we will) in church or ministry, we need to practice something that is foreign to our old sin nature but is part of our new spiritual nature. It will not be natural, and we can very easily choose not to forgive but to harbor ill feelings toward others. However, forgiveness is our calling: to forgive as God has forgiven us.

When we isolate ourselves from the sharp edges of church

life—from the uncomfortable process of looking fully at some-one's faults, cruelty, or ignorance, and choosing to forgive instead of retaliating in kind—we don't grow. Period. We remain AWOL (military term for Absent Without Leave) from the painful process of growing up. Forgiveness is part of life in the body of Christ. It demands that we humble ourselves before those who have offended us. This is why Paul links our forgiveness to Christ's: "Get rid of all bitterness, rage and anger, brawling and slander, along with every form of malice. Be kind and compassionate to one another, forgiving each other, just as in Christ God forgave you" (Ephesians 4:31–32).

People who have committed themselves to church fellowship have had to learn to forgive and to become kinder, more compassionate, and more patient. There were situations that encouraged cultivating those virtues in them. Choosing forgiveness helped to shape their godly character. Those who isolate themselves often become hypercritical, unforgiving, and impatient. It is not because they are bad people; it is because they were never forced to face the imperfections of others and allow God to love those difficult people through them. Painful situations are often God's means of developing character.

So many in church need a touch of God's grace. They know they have failed, hurt someone's feelings, made dumb statements, and made themselves odious to others. Only when someone reaches out to them in Christ's name and says, "I forgive you. . .I still love you," will they come to truly experience in a practical way, through the lives of other Christians, the grace of God in their lives.

Phillips Brooks (1835–1893) wrote, "In what strange quarries and stoneyards the stones for the celestial wall are being hewn! Out of the hillsides of humiliated pride; deep in the darkness of crushed despair; in the fretting and dusty atmosphere of little cares; in the hard cruel contacts that man has with man; wherever souls are being tried and ripened, in whatever commonplace and homely ways—there God is hewing out the pillars for His temple."[22]

*We don't have to learn how to give up our own desires
to show preference to one another.*

The church is where the unconventional, the foolish, and the illogical approaches to life are shown to be the wisdom of God. In our world we are encouraged to get all we can, watch out for number one, make sure that we are happy first, and then worry about anyone else. Because there is a constant revolution going on in people's lives, the church is an uncomfortable place at times. The life Christ called us to live in the church is so unnatural to our old natures that we sometimes rebel against it. Thus rebellion and obedience exist side by side in the church; in fact, rebellion and obedience exist side by side within each of us moment by moment. This will cause not only internal but external conflict.

In what other place but the church would these words be greeted with acceptance and true conviction? "Do nothing out of selfish ambition or vain conceit, but in humility consider others better than yourselves" (Philippians 2:3). There is tremendous resistance in us to truly carrying out this body-of-Christ life command. We may agree with it or think it a noble thought, but to actually begin to consider someone else's desires and wishes as *more important* than our own is a revolutionary thought. Yet, knowing how difficult an idea it is, God goes even further: "Each of you should look not only to your own interests, but also to the interests of others" (Philippians 2:4). "Be devoted to one another in brotherly love. Honor one another above yourselves" (Romans 12:10).

Diane and Thelma both have offered to host the next women's tea. Diane knows that her house is larger and more elegant than Thelma's smaller house. Her friends at church have already said as much, siding with her against Thelma. What will Diane do? Should she push her advantage and explain why she should host the women's tea, making it a much more enjoyable experience for everyone, or should she allow Thelma to host the tea? Diane loves to host meetings in her home and believes that Thelma is not nearly as well liked or respected as she is, so it wouldn't take much for her to get the coveted opportunity. What will Diane do?

Paul is a well-educated, young, ambitious, and goal-oriented member of the deacon board. Tom is the older, uneducated, and often timid chairman of the board. Even though Tom is a godly man, Paul knows he has better ideas. He is sure that if he were the chairman, the church would make much better progress. It wouldn't take much to sway the board members to his point of view because he is far more articulate and convincing than Tom. What will Paul do?

In the church, the operational rules are from a kingdom that is aimed toward a higher goal than self-realization and fulfillment. Although Tom and Diane may indeed make selfish decisions, if God is working in their lives, there will at least be a struggle. And often the unselfish decision is made, even though it is difficult and seemingly illogical.

When someone is gracious, kind, compassionate, wise, and loving, this may be easier. But to think of anyone as more important than ourselves simply goes against the grain of our basic sinful human nature. As Billy Graham has said, "Being a Christian is more than just an instantaneous conversion—it is a daily process whereby you grow to be more and more like Christ."[23]

If we need to get in physical shape, we are unlikely to make much progress sitting safely inside our homes on our comfortable couches. On the other hand, if we are in a gym, surrounded by exercise equipment and people working hard at the same task, we are surrounded by encouraging reminders of our need to exercise. The church is our "spiritual gym," where Christlikeness is being developed in us.

*We don't have someone who knows us well enough
to tell us the truth—even if it hurts.*

I was in an elders' meeting early in my pastoral ministry,

listening to the complaints of some of our members being voiced by some of our elders. The words were painful. One of my elders—a good friend—articulated a complaint of some he had spoken to. "Dan, some people feel that you are aloof."

Stung by this absurd accusation, I shot back, "Well, do *you* think I am aloof?" I really only meant this as a rhetorical question, a question designed to highlight the ridiculous nature of the question.

But, to my surprise, this godly man hesitantly and reluctantly said, "Yes, Dan, sometimes I think you are aloof."

Though this caused me pain and sadness, it was an insight into an area that I had been totally blinded to. As a protective device to keep me from pain, I had become aloof at times, especially toward those I considered hostile. But it was hindering my ministry and my growth as a Christian. Ephesians 4:15 reminds us that we are to speak the truth in love. Solomon reminds us in Proverbs 27:17 that "Iron sharpens iron, so one man sharpens another." Many other verses testify to the truth that I need others' input into my life to make me stronger. This is why God has put us each into the church. The very stresses we often want to avoid—the personality conflicts, hurt feelings, and misunderstandings—are opportunities for our greater growth and the growth of the whole body.

Those who don't know me can't see my weaknesses; they can't help me, warn me, or notice when I am harboring a destructive habit, idea, or thought. My wife, Annette, knows me better than anyone, and, as a result, God uses her to show me areas of weaknesses I can't see. I depend on her, and yet others can see things about me that Annette cannot. That is what the church is designed for: to help each of us become stronger by bringing all our gifts and insights to bear on each of us.

Will it hurt when people are painfully honest with me? Yes, but so is the surgery that cuts out a cancer, the painful adjustment that brings a broken limb back into alignment, or the application of healing ointment to an open and painful wound. When I isolate myself, when I choose a safe virtual church over a real church of flesh and blood sinners, my weaknesses stay put; in fact, they may fester and grow worse. In a strange sense, the isolation I can choose through committing myself only to a virtual or media church can actually strengthen and solidify my weaknesses.

Some may say that they have Christian friends outside of church, and that is true. And some of them can serve to help us in these very ways. Yet here we are in danger of trying to create our own little churches, built safely around our idiosyncrasies and personal preferences. We need all the members of a body—not just our hand-picked choices. Imagine a hand made up of all thumbs or a head with no eyes or nose, but five ears. I have found that we tend to pick our friends carefully, choosing those who are like us to spend time with. These people, though well meaning, may have the same weaknesses we do. It is not that they are unwilling to help us; but, at times they may be unable to help. In a church, God brings along people who are *not* like us and who can see clearly the areas of our weaknesses. The church is really a unique design for fostering growth in all its individual members.

We limit our abilities to grow in knowledge and wisdom.

This does not mean that you can only gain knowledge or wisdom in a church. God can help us gain knowledge and wisdom anywhere, but the truth is that our own experiences and wisdom are limited. Being an author, I certainly advocate the reading of good Christian books to help you grow spiritually, and listening to good speakers on the radio and television can help immensely. But there is also a built-in drawback.

Writers or speakers may correctly articulate scriptural truths or principles, but they don't know us personally. Each one of us needs Scripture and wisdom applied to our peculiar situations. This is something difficult for those who know us well but even more difficult for those we have never met and likely never will.

I have spoken at retreats and many churches, and I assure you that I am careful about the wisdom I try to dispense. I am only too aware that I frequently have a limited perspective of the people

I am speaking to. It would take a long time to get to know them well enough to know what their true needs are. I have learned to be guarded in my counsel with those I don't know well.

As a pastoral counselor, I have had people come to me for counseling for a particular reason. It doesn't take long for me to realize from talking to them and observing them in church that their needs actually are in other areas—ones they may be effectively blind to. Because I know them, I am able to address not only their "felt needs" but also the deeper issues they are not even aware of yet. But this only comes with time and experiences with them. When I remain a stranger to others and hide myself, my problems remain firmly attached to me. As some people avoid visits to the doctor to avoid any bad news, so some Christians can avoid real fellowship in the church to avoid bad news. Yet, as with a physical condition, avoiding the problem only makes it worse.

There are others who, because they know us well, can give us great insight into our difficulties and our problems. This is one of the great strengths of church fellowship. When we dare to let others get to know us, we make ourselves available for healing and growth. God uses others to sharpen and strengthen us.

We leave the church weakened because we are a necessary part.

When we forsake the church for a simpler virtual church setting, in a strange way we actually contribute to the very thing we often dislike and criticize about church. How much stronger and healthier the church would be, both locally and universally, if all the Christians who have left fellowship in the church were to bring their gifts, talents, and presence back? The Bible makes it clear God endows us with spiritual gifts and special abilities when we become a Christian. This makes the body stronger and healthier (1 Corinthians 12; Romans 12:6–8).

One of the greatest needs we have is the need to be a useful, helpful part of something bigger than ourselves. There is a joy to be found in serving others in a significant way that is simply not found in any form of self-fulfillment. Helping others calls out the best in us, because it allows us to serve others and not just ourselves. Of course, the virtual church can give opportunities for service in various ways but rarely in the way God has designed the local church to work. In the church, we invest in people we know and spend a lot of time with face-to-face. Service often can be difficult and require a sacrifice of time and resources from us, but instead of that being a negative, it becomes a delightful positive. We discover that we truly do make a difference. The knowledge that God can use us in His kingdom is a reward all by itself.

The virtual church, including some parachurch ministries, often can allow us to participate in wonderful and exciting ministries close to and far from home in various ways. These should not be minimized or slighted; they are a wonderful extension of the church's ministries. But when we desert the local church ministry we definitely leave it weakened.

There are those I have taught who have gone on to teach others what I taught them. There have been those I have led to Christ who have gone on to lead others to Christ. There have been those I have comforted who have learned how to comfort others. Like a pebble thrown into a still pond, the ripples begin to branch out in all directions from the initial point of contact. That is what God intended. Now reverse this process. Remove the point of contact, remove the personal investment in others. Hundreds, perhaps thousands, of people who were otherwise helped suddenly have not been. One person truly does affect so many others.

George Bailey, in the movie *It's a Wonderful Life,* learned this lesson as he was shown what his family's and friends' lives would have been like if he had never been born. I wonder whether this movie might not reflect in a parable the effect of one solitary person in a church. I was deeply impacted in my own life by an engineer; several pastors; an elderly, mentally retarded man; and many others along the way. Each one of them, in their own way, contributed to making me who I am. Had any one of them not been available, for any reason, I would not be who I am today. I would be less—less knowledgeable, less wise, and less compassionate. Though I am far from perfect, I thank God that I had many people in the church to impact my life.

Those who leave the church often don't understand what a void they leave behind them. Because the void is not often seen or no one even seems to notice, they feel they have done little harm in leaving. But the Bible makes it clear that every part of the body of Christ is necessary to the healthy functioning of the whole.

Early sailors used to fall prey to scurvy because they failed to take along any fruits or vegetables that contained vitamin C on their long voyages. They did not understand the importance of this essential vitamin to their overall health. Even though they had plenty of food and were not hungry, their bodies nevertheless displayed the sickness that comes when just one essential element is missing. The church today is missing many essential parts that it desperately needs. No wonder it looks sickly at times.

We leave ourselves vulnerable.

There have been numerous times when a member of a church I was pastoring would bring literature to me for my inspection. It would be from some group the person had come in contact with. Several times I was able to point out that the group was actually part of a cult, and I would demonstrate to them from the Scriptures the erroneous teaching and the background to the group. Many people in churches all over the country have the same ability to do this. I was not the only person in our church who could offer this help; we had many gifted teachers. God has gifted certain people in churches to be able to *discern* between scriptural truth and error more easily than others.

Unfortunately, when people separate themselves from solid teaching and a local fellowship, they can become targets of cults who aim for those who have a nominal knowledge of Scripture but have a desire to please God. I have come across those who have been victimized by these heretical groups who realized that, if they had been a part of a healthy Christian fellowship, they would not have been as vulnerable.

Some of those who are part of a virtual or media church may receive very fine instruction and be quite well protected against heresy, but there are many who desert the church who do not take advantage of these opportunities. They are alone and adrift.

As a singles pastor, I learned firsthand that the fellowship these singles experienced encouraged many to remain pure and faithful to Christ who otherwise might have been sorely tempted to follow this world in sexual immorality. The fellowship these singles had with each other was a constant source of affirmation that they were not alone. This gave them courage and strength to take difficult moral stands. The virtual or media church can offer great information and resources, but it cannot replace good friends to talk with, people who promise to pray with you every week, or a group of people who know and love you who can give you strength in your difficult days.

Beyond scriptural needs, we also all need encouragement, hope, kindness, sympathy, and many other things we cannot get on our own. We can be scripturally sound and emotionally vulnerable because we have chosen to isolate ourselves from those God intended to minister to us.

We retain all our sharp edges.

As a young boy, I was always amazed at the smooth, shiny rocks I would find in souvenir shops. Growing up in the country, I had never seen rocks like those in the country. I thought they were special rocks that came from a very special place. I used to go looking for those kinds of rocks on my hikes, but, alas, I never found any.

One day I learned the truth. The rocks had been made, not found. A friend of mine had a rock tumbler, into which he would place some rather ordinary rocks and mix in some sand. The tumbler would go around and around, rubbing the rocks together. The sand mixed in with the tumbling rocks produced the marvelous smooth surfaces I so coveted. Gradually, the constant sanding and the perpetual contact with other rocks with sharp edges served to smooth out the rocks. There is perhaps no better illustration of the reality of church. Each of us comes into God's kingdom with a generous assortment of "sharp edges." All of our weaknesses make us sharp, dangerous at some points, weak at others, and generally rather like everyone else in this world.

One day God interrupts our lives and joins us to His body, the church. Here we are surrounded with people just like us: people with sharp edges. Through misunderstandings, difficulties, sufferings, persecutions, and other sands of difficulty, the sharp edges are slowly and gradually rubbed off us. That is, if we stay in the tumbler. We can take ourselves out if we want; it might feel safer at times to do just that. We do not see the bigger picture, so leaving doesn't seem like it would hurt us at all. After all, who would voluntarily submit themselves to this kind of activity? Only those who wanted to allow God to make them into something very special— something that not only others but even they themselves would have to agree is far better than anything they had envisioned they would ever become.

I don't want to leave the impression that church is nothing but misery and difficulty and that we are constantly being "sanded." There are long periods of extreme joy, extreme happiness, and feelings of knowing that you are truly and genuinely loved. Deep and lasting friendships are made and nurtured over the years. Yet, the reality is that real life is not always fun and happy—not even in the church. God does not haphazardly throw us into a tumbler; He carefully puts us in particular situations that He knows will strengthen us the way we most need to be strengthened and will help smooth out our rough edges. We will help smooth out others' sharp edges as they help to smooth out ours, but the sand of difficulty is balanced with the lubricant of love.

The same people who can cause you consternation one moment can bless you when you are sick or in need in some way. We learn that people are a collection of strengths and weaknesses. We will be exposed to both in the church. We need both. As we learn to overlook the weaknesses of others, we gain patience; as others help us in our need, we learn humility.

Though the virtual church is a positive addition to the ministry of the church, it simply can't take its place. Isolating ourselves from the church's weaknesses both weakens the church and ourselves. We were not simply made *for* the church. If we are truly abiding in Christ, we *are* the church.

But this begs the questions: What is the church? What is real fellowship? Does the church really just not work for some Christians, or is there another answer? I propose that the church, with all its faults, is not really the problem and, therefore, escaping it is not the solution. What we really need to understand is what fellowship and friendship really are, so let's take a look!

CHAPTER SEVEN

FRIENDSHIP VS. FELLOWSHIP:

What's the Big Difference?

> FRIENDSHIP—N.
> *friendly feeling or*
> *attitude; friendliness*
>
> FELLOWSHIP—N.
> *a group of people with*
> *the same interests;*
> *company; brotherhood*

"Those early believers
in Jerusalem shared everything.
That was true fellowship.
It had a marked effect on the world,
and as a result,
many persons were brought to Christ."

JOHN MACARTHUR, *Body Dynamic*

Debbie and Lisa had been close friends for many years. When Debbie became a Christian, she maintained her friendship with Lisa, who was not a Christian. Debbie was attending a local church, where she had very high expectations for the kind of people she would meet there. She admired so many of the Christians she met; in fact, they had been influential in her decision to become a Christian.

Lately, however, she has begun to wonder about some of these "wonderful" people at church. She has discovered, to her dismay, that a few that she has gotten to know well are petty, calculating, and downright annoying. It is stressful for her to be around them, and she can't help wondering if she wouldn't be better off just spending time with Lisa. She's wondering if Christian fellowship is all it's cracked up to be.

There are people in every church who are really tough to get along with. Their personalities grate on us, their way of thinking confuses us, and their actions can at times infuriate us. When we compare these people to some of our non-Christian friends, the result isn't encouraging. At times we just can't help wondering, *Why bother anymore? Why spend time with other Christians who can cause us stress and annoyance when there are other more congenial people we might spend time with?* It is difficult to argue with this kind of logic. Surely some have slowly wandered away from the church in search of easier and less demanding relationships.

When the Bible talks about the idea of fellowship, many Christians get confused. "Fellowship" seems to be little more than spiritual jargon for the word "friendship." It doesn't really seem all that different. Each of us enjoys spending time with those we have things in common with, so what's the big deal about fellowship? Is there really any significant difference between fellowship in the church and friendships with non-Christians in our world?

In his book *Dare to Live Now,* Bruce Larson talks about the need each of us has for fellowship, and he describes its human counterfeit. "The neighborhood bar is possibly the best counterfeit there is to the fellowship Christ wants to give His church. It's an imitation, dispensing liquor instead of grace, escape rather than reality. But it is a permissive, accepting, and inclusive fellowship. It is unshockable; it is democratic. You can tell people secrets and they usually don't tell others, or want to. The bar flourishes not because most people are alcoholics, but because

God has put into the human heart the desire to know and be known, to love and be loved, and so many seek a counterfeit at the price of a few beers."[24]

It is no surprise that the *Cheers* TV show, set in a bar, was such a hit for so long. Even the theme song was enticing, with the words "Sometimes you want to go where everybody knows your name."

I can remember times when I would come home from church as a pastor, frustrated after having to deal with a particularly annoying or cantankerous member of the church. I would go out and begin to water the dry spots on my lawn to relax. Presently, I would see a neighbor, and we would begin to engage in some small talk. Before long we'd be having a good, relaxing, mutually enjoyable conversation. I couldn't help comparing him with some of the Christians I had to deal with that day. It made me begin to compare friendships with healthy non-Christians to fellowship with some of those inside the church. It wasn't until much later that I began to realize that therein lay my problem. I wanted a stress-free church experience and relationships without cost, without problems, without difficulties.

An unspoken expectation of mine was that church would be a place where all my friendships would be with healthy "normal" Christians and where I would be fed and nourished spiritually. I would minister to those who would always appreciate what I did and said and who would always be making progress spiritually and emotionally. The people at church would invariably be encouraging, helpful, and considerate—in short, they would be perfect and friendly at all times! When things didn't always work out that way, I couldn't help weighing the advantages of "fellowship."

Eventually, I found myself identifying with the words of Charles Spurgeon, the great preacher of the last century when he wrote, "We want to stay off the rough roads of life, and our primary objective is to secure a peaceful retreat from the world. . . . The real danger in spiritual laziness is that we do not want to be stirred up—all we want to hear about is a spiritual retirement from the world."[25]

We don't want to be "stirred up." I couldn't have said it better. In a human friendship, if someone treats you shabbily, you are free to ignore him or her and find a new friend—someone who will treat you better. Furthermore, you can find a friend based on your own choosing, someone who has your likes and dislikes—in short, someone who is a lot like you.

The idea of friendship and fellowship certainly overlap at many points, but there is actually a distinct difference between human friendships with nonbelievers and fellowship in the body of Christ, which is the church. In fact, the more closely you look at the two, the more pronounced the differences become. Fellowship with another Christian is far deeper in breadth and purpose than simple human friendships with non-Christians, as wonderful as they may be. Fellowship goes beyond just trying to find someone with whom you are compatible and share common interests.

I have always been amazed at how a church brings together people with such diverse backgrounds and personalities who can find common ground in their mutual lives together in Christ. Fellowship does not require us to be completely compatible in every way with others or to share all their likes or dislikes before we can enter into a close relationship with them.

Some of my wife's and my closest friendships in the church are with those whom we share precious little in common, except for our fellowship together in Christ. Yet, this fellowship binds us together deeper than relationships with nonbelievers we have far more in common with on other levels.

"Church Fellowship is more than a demonstration of unity," writes Dr. Robert Saucy. "It is one way God has ordained for the believer both to *give himself* (italics added) to the Lord and fellow believers, and to get from them that which is necessary for spiritual edification. . .the frequent commands to mutual admonition and encouragement (1 Thessalonians 4:18, 5:11; Romans 1:12) cannot be accomplished in isolation."[26]

This is the unique and wonderful aspect of fellowship that separates it from common friendship: giving to others for their growth in Christ and receiving from them for our own growth in Christ. This is what makes fellowship unique. The Greek word for fellowship in the New Testament is the word *koinonia*. Dr. Saucy writes that the word *koinonia* "Indicates 'fellowship or a sharing with someone or in something, a participation.' It represents the relationship of unity, both of believers with Christ and with each other."[27]

We are not simply giving human friendship and companionship to others, encouraging them in their life pursuits and holding them up in life's pains; we are actively involved in helping them to grow in their spiritual lives with Christ and His church. The focus of our fellowship is on Christ and His church, not merely our shared interests.

This leads us to begin to examine a number of specific differences between the biblical idea of fellowship and the human (though not unbiblical) idea of friendship. I am not denigrating friendships; they are also God ordained and important. Still, there are significant differences that we need to address. To some people, living together outside of marriage is quite similar to being married. And truthfully there are many similarities, but the differences are stark and significant. In the same way, fellowship and friendship are similar, but there remain stark and significant differences.

Friendship is based on common likes and dislikes;
fellowship is based on a common identity.

When I think back on many of my human friendships over the years, I can easily point to the similarities we shared: a love of sports, certain music, outdoor activity, adventure, and other common interests and values. These interests are actually what brought us together—the basis of our friendships.

We search out people with common interests and values. At work we will be drawn toward those for whom we feel an affinity in some way. Our conversations will naturally drift into areas of shared interests. We may be a part of a cycling club, drama troupe, political cause, or sports team. We may join a group of knitters, artists, writers, or quilters. Even in these groups we will form closer friendships with those who are more like us in personality.

There is nothing wrong with any of this. Fellowship was never meant to take the place of our friendships with people in our world or to cloister ourselves away from those who are not like us spiritually. It is not a sin to want to be with someone with your shared likes and dislikes.

However, in fellowship a different process is at work. God places us in His body, the church, and that is our common identity. We share a relationship with Christ that is often the sole point of commonality among us. There are certainly points of disagreement and conflict at church, but with the degree of differences represented, it is only amazing that there are not more!

In the churches I have attended, I have worked closely with stockbrokers, engineers, computer technicians, realtors, software writers, salespeople, marketers, nurses, doctors, lawyers, contractors, firefighters, police officers, and many others.

We have prayed together, ministered together, laughed and cried together, and gone on vacation together, and yet we were dissimilar in personalities and personal preferences. I was a writer, yet precious few of my closest associates shared my passion for writing. I love classic black-and-white movies from the 30s, 40s, and 50s, and I found myself strangely alone in this interest (good thing my wife likes them, too!). I was a diehard USC football fan, and I found them in short supply in our churches (but bless that faithful remnant!). In short, I spent most of my time with people who shared few, if any, of my personal likes or dislikes.

What we had in common was a faith in Jesus Christ so strong and abiding that personal differences were laid aside. It was not important that everyone was like me, because the glue that held us together was not personal preferences but a common spiritual identity. We had all become children of God by His amazing grace. We had entered into a relationship with God and each other that was eternal and irrevocable.

This is really not all that strange if you think about it. My wife, Annette, and I have three children we love with all our hearts. Of my previously mentioned likes and dislikes, I can safely say that my children do not share all of my passions. My wife is a home economist, who loves sewing, cooking, and the home arts. To say our daughters share her passion would be stretching it. Our children are not similar to us in all our likes or dislikes or even most of them.

Though our personalities differ, what binds us together is a shared identity: We are a family, the Schaeffer family. Regardless of how we may change over the years, that identity and our relationship will never change. It is irrevocable. We have our differences, and at times those differences cause stress, but we never stop being family. That is the tie that binds. In the same way, the tie that binds Christians together is not their likes or dislikes but a common identity—a common relationship to God. This identity is stronger than any particular like or passion or interest could ever be. It is so important that we can overlook differences and often must.

Friendships can be very selective;
fellowship reaches out to those not like us.

When I was in high school, I became a Christian through a church's ministry in the town. I soon joined the church and became a part of the youth group. I was shy, introverted, and by practice a loner.

But, as God began to work in my heart and I realized my place in this new organism called the church, I began to notice a subtle but distinct change taking place in my heart. I began to consider for the very first time reaching out to those who were not like me. Though I had friends in the group who were very much like me, I began to see others differently than ever before, and I began to care about them.

So I began to reach out to those who were not like me and found that our common faith bridged the gaps between our differences. I should also mention that for a good period of time I did *not* reach out to others. It took the Holy Spirit of God. He taught me to understand the revolutionary idea of fellowship.

One of the stern warnings found in the Book of James is against favoritism. It is tempting to favor some people over others because of what they like, dislike, have, or don't have. The warning is specifically against favoritism in the context of the church.

> *My brethren, do not hold your faith in our glorious*
> *Lord Jesus Christ with an attitude of personal favoritism.*
> *For if a man comes into your assembly with a gold ring and*
> *dressed in fine clothes, and there also comes in a poor man*
> *in dirty clothes, and you pay special attention to the one*
> *who is wearing the fine clothes, and say, "You sit here in a*
> *good place," and you say to the poor man, "You stand over*
> *there, or sit down by my footstool," have you not made dis-*
> *tinctions among yourselves, and become judges with evil*
> *motives? . . . If, however, you are fulfilling the royal law*
> *according to the Scripture, "YOU SHALL LOVE YOUR NEIGH-*
> *BOR AS YOURSELF," you are doing well. But if you show*
> *partiality, you are committing sin and are convicted by the*
> *law as transgressors (James 2:1–4, 8–9 NASB).*

Fellowship takes friendship into a different realm; it reaches out to those who are not like us. In the beginning of the early church, all the Christians were Jewish. It simply never occurred to the Jews that Gentiles would ever become part of the church. Jews did not have dealings with Gentiles if it was at all possible. They did not let them in their houses, did not spend time together unless absolutely necessary, and the thought of worshipping with them was simply not entertained.

When God opened the church to the Gentiles, it was a terrible shock that caused a great deal of consternation for awhile. God used Peter in this unexpected enterprise, dealing with his prejudices first (Acts 10–11) and then with the early church's prejudice. Soon Jews and Gentiles, longtime enemies, were fellowshipping in the same congregation. Picture modern-day Palestinians and Israelis coming together to love each other and worship together and you will have a pretty good picture of the cultural miracle that took place. That miracle is called fellowship. The Jews and Gentiles had nothing in common, except their common relationship to Christ and His church, and yet that was such a strong bond that they not only were able but were willing to put everything else aside.

In a more recent miracle, my family was visiting Colorado Springs, Colorado, one week and stopped in at a local church on Sunday morning. There happened to be a missionary to Arabic peoples speaking that Sunday. He reminded us of the war between Iraq and Iran, which was a particularly long and cruel one. Animosity was still strong between the two countries and peoples (as it is today). Yet, he shared how, at a recent Christian retreat, Iranian and Iraqi Christians gathered outside to sing praises to Jesus together! This is something simple friendship could not accomplish; it is amazing, astounding, and the miracle of the fellowship to which God has called His family.

Friendships can be temporary; fellowship is permanent.

One of my earliest friends was a little boy named Kelly, who was an important part of my childhood. Having just moved into a new neighborhood, I had no friends and was extremely sad and lonely. One day while I was hanging out in my front yard, Kelly came over and asked me if I wanted to wrestle. I was taken aback. Here was a kid I didn't even know who wanted to begin a fight. My world was going from bad to worse! I said no and started to walk away.

Then, sensing I had misunderstood, he said, "No, I don't mean like a real fight—just *wrestling*—for fun!" The look in his eyes told me he wasn't a bully, he just liked to wrestle! So I agreed. We had a great wrestling match on the front lawn, and I got a best friend for the next few years of my life. We did everything together, but one day I had to move and leave Kelly behind. I never saw him again. I don't know whether Kelly ever became a Christian, so I don't know if I will ever see him again in this life or in the next. Even the best of human friendships are temporary if our friends are not Christians. This is one of the sad distinctions between friendship and fellowship.

Here is where we come across a glaring difference between friendships with those who are not Christians and fellowship with other believers. The relationship we enter into with Christ and with His church is a permanent, eternal one. Our shared belief in Christ and His work for us on the cross is the glue that binds us together as the eternal family of God (John 6:47; Ephesians 2:19–22). True Christian fellowship cannot end, any more than my children can one day stop being my children.

My children and I can disagree with one another. We can hurt each other's feelings or get on each other's nerves. We can even get so angry that we choose isolation from one another for a period of time. But we are always family; nothing can ever change that. In the same way, we can get into disagreements with other believers—even to the point that distance comes between us—yet our common destiny is together, not apart. One day, in heaven, all our disagreements and differences will be forgotten.

Something that God made to last forever should not be quickly jettisoned by those of us in His church. Occasionally, a Slavic Baptist church that meets in one of our buildings joins us on Sunday morning for our service and we have fellowship, even though some of them don't speak English. I also have had the precious privilege of meeting Christians who came to visit our country from faraway places like Senegal, Switzerland, Indonesia, Russia, and other places. I was able to enter into fellowship with them in a wonderful way, despite cultural, language, and geographical divides between us. Though I saw them and met them only briefly, I know we will meet again. When we part, this is our common confession. Is there any other relationship we can have with people that is so permanent?

Friendship is optional; fellowship is not.

The nature of a friendship is that there comes a time when two people begin to get on each other's nerves. It doesn't matter how much you love one another or how much you have in common; there will always come a time when one is annoying to the other. If your friendship means a lot to you, you will try to overlook the differences. But there are times when you realize that the person you once called friend is simply no longer the person you knew. Or, at times, you have changed but your friend has not. The things that you had in common are no longer enough to bridge the gaps of the growing differences.

Many years ago, a man in our church with whom I had always been on good terms suddenly began to question my leadership. Tension developed between us. It was tempting to write this man off and ignore him; but I couldn't. As a Christian, it simply wasn't an option. He was family. We had a disagreement, and the serious nature of Christian fellowship demanded that I seek to reconcile with him.

When people talk about the Christians they have met in church who are less than what they think a Christian should be, they overlook something important. The church is full of Christians *in process.* They are not perfect and still make mistakes! Being a Christian is like being a football player; there are many different stages of development and expertise.

There are peewee football players for the youngest, Pop Warner football players for the elementary kids, high-school football players for the teenagers, and college football for those young men in the prime of life. There are also the professional football players—the Marshall Faulks, Rich Gannons, and Randy Mosses. All of these boys and men are bona fide football players, yet each plays the game at a decidedly different level of expertise, maturity, and experience.

In the same way, in any church there are Christians who are at decidedly different levels of spiritual maturity and experience. To judge Christians or a church by some who are still immature is not fair or realistic.

Some Christians will definitely get on your nerves. They will be immature, selfish, judgmental, and a variety of other characteristics that are less than desirable. Yet these same people can be capable of great good and effective ministry at times. In any case, we don't have the option of just writing them off. Fellowship is not optional.

We choose our friends; God chooses our fellowship.

We think we know what we need in a friend, which is why we go about trying to find the "right kind" of friends. It is a natural assumption we make all the time. Since we are looking primarily for friendship, companionship, and shared likes and dislikes, it isn't too hard to find friends along the way in life.

We choose our friends carefully, but have you ever asked yourself why? Isn't it because we don't want to get hurt, bothered, betrayed, annoyed, or inconvenienced by those we are planning to spend a great deal of time with? What we are really doing is trying to create a bubble of security around our lives to protect us from the kind of messy problems that a bad relationship can cause and also making sure our lives are immersed in those things we find pleasant.

We want lives we can control. The reason we want control is to be able to avoid the problems and enhance the pleasures of life whenever and wherever possible. It is a noble goal and a worthy pursuit. However, my understanding of Scripture and my personal experience lead me to tell you that you likely do not have a prayer of living such a life.

Fellowship is not just a way to avoid loneliness in the church;

it has a *purpose*. We are members of one body, each of us having a separate and important purpose within the church (Romans 12). We *think* we know what we need is a friend, but God is the One who *knows* that what we need is fellowship. Fellowship is the means by which God will strengthen our lives, mature us, challenge us to greater growth and development, and use us to do the same in others' lives. He is not just in the business of growing His church corporately; He is growing each one of us individually.

He often brings people into our lives to impact us in ways we never imagined—or wanted! I love to spend time in fellowship with bright, articulate, ambitious Christians who are growth oriented and are serious about their Christian walk. I have been blessed with many such relationships through fellowship. However, those relationships do not challenge me to grow in certain areas; in fact, if I'm not careful, they can keep me from growth.

I remember God bringing into my ministry someone who was—how do I put this—difficult to love? He was not nasty, or mean, or vindictive; he was just different. He was socially crippled, mentally challenged, and one of the most faithful members of my ministry. He was not hesitant to speak his mind, even when it had nothing whatever to do with the subject at hand (this was especially exciting during group discussions). He was not the epitome of normal, healthy, and attractive. But he loved me. He also sincerely loved God in his own special way.

I learned a great deal from this brother and many others like him. There were lessons I learned about compassion and patience that I would never have learned without him. He highlighted that I had a problem with favoritism when it came to ministry. He was a person that no matter how much I invested in him, the return would be slight to none. He would never be a leader, a mover, or a shaker. Yet, he craved attention—mine most of all. God knew I needed to minister to this young man, and that he, in turn, needed to minister to me. It was not a choice I would have made or a relationship I would have chosen.

Gradually, I have come to the conclusion that fellowship in a church is not in the slightest bit haphazard. People don't just "happen" to end up at one church in one town instead of another. The Holy Spirit of God knows precisely what He is doing in the corporate life of each church, as well as each individual believer in it. As God has moved me from one church to another over the years, in each place I have found people whom God has used to mold and shape my life, strengthen my weaknesses, and challenge me to higher living for Christ. Ironically, I have discovered that few of these people would have been natural choices as friends. We traveled in different circles, with different passions and interests. Yet I have always seen God at work in my relationships.

Some of these relationships are difficult and trying, but I have learned not to try to escape them. There is usually some important lesson or truth that I will learn in these relationships, and most of them are a joy and a pleasure to be a part of. We may choose our friends, but I thank God that He chooses our fellowship. "But now God has placed the members, each one of them, in the body, just as He desired" (1 Corinthians 12:18 NASB). Each Christian has something unique and special to offer us.

God alone knows what each church and each person in His church needs, and He provides it for us. He does that through the miracle that is known as fellowship.

Friendship places us in a unique relationship with a person;
fellowship places us in a unique relationship with a family.

When you have a truly good friend, you seek to do things together. You want to go places together, experience things together, and try new activities together. You want to share your joys and sorrows with this person. What makes this relationship unique is that this person feels the same about you. You are in an exclusive relationship. This does not mean you can't have other friends. You do, but none that holds this special honored status in your life.

The deepest example of friendship is in marriage. Annette is my best friend in the world. We have a very special, exclusive, and precious relationship. When I come home from work, I tell Annette my joys and struggles, and I listen to hers. When she succeeds, I rejoice; when I succeed, she is my greatest cheerleader. When she is hurting, she comes to me for consolation; when I am in pain, she is the one I seek. In the greatest of all situations, my wife and I not only share a best friend relationship, but we also share fellowship in His church together.

Even when your best friend is not your spouse, you place that friend in a special category among all the people you know. Although this is a marvelous experience, fellowship in the church is different. In the church the unique relationship you enter is not with a single human being but with a family. Our common relationship with Jesus places us in a family relationship with each other.

Not long ago my family and I visited Disneyland, where we decided to watch a parade on Main Street. My wife and I sat down and noticed another couple sitting at a table next to us. In the course of the next few minutes, we struck up a casual conversation. Before long, however, we soon realized that we were not just casual acquaintances but brothers and sisters in Christ. There, on Main Street USA, in Disneyland, we ran into family. We immediately shared a common bond that was unique from any other kind of relationship.

Recently a marvelous, gracious, and intelligent man, Rene Mbongo, came to visit our church in Santa Barbara, California. He is an African who works in Senegal and had come to the United States to improve his English skills—so necessary when doing business internationally. He had met a couple in our church who were out of the country, doing research on a book, and their instant fellowship in Christ had prompted them to sponsor him in America for a period of time while he immersed himself in English.

At first I could barely understand him; yet his face glowed when he talked about Jesus Christ and his love for Him. He would join us before the service for prayer. In his broken English, I still remember being thrilled that this man was my brother in Christ.

He so impacted our church that when he left many of us had

lunch together to say good-bye. It was a bittersweet parting—bitter because we had come to love each other and knew he was leaving and sweet because no part of God's family is ever separated forever. We all hope to see Rene again in this life, but we are family forever. Friendship places you in a unique relationship to someone, but fellowship places you in a unique relationship to an entire family. Furthermore, our fellowship extends backward to include believers of past ages and forward to believers of future ages. One day we will all be together forever. That reunion will be something!

It is tempting for many to bail out of fellowship at the church when it becomes less than pleasant, feeling that they can find the relationships they need or want outside of church just as easily as inside. The truth, if you are a Christian, is that you can't! Fellowship was meant to fill a very real spiritual need that God knew we had; it wasn't just offered as an optional extra to our Christian faith. There is indeed a wide gulf between fellowship and friendship, and though both are necessary, they are not interchangeable.

I wish for you good friendships, but much more, I pray that you enter (or reenter) the fellowship of the church. Whether you know it or not, you are needed. Whether you know it or not, you are missed. Don't be naive; everything won't always be peachy. At times you'll need to work through problems with people to exercise your Christian character. But please, for our sake and yours, don't be a stranger!

Chapter Eight

Shepherd's Defection:

Leading the Flock Astray

> AMBITION—N.
> *the drive to succeed,*
> *or to gain fame, power, wealth*

"Personal ambition and empire building are hindering the spread of the gospel."

John R. Stott

We have spoken of different factors that cause people to defect in their hearts and eventually literally defect from the church and service. I would be remiss if I didn't admit that we pastors, leaders, and Christian personalities also have been the cause for some defections—maybe more than we'd like to admit.

Within the last few years, we have seen many prominent Christian leaders, musicians, pastors, and Christian personalities fall into moral sin and disgrace. Certainly these tragic failures cause some to feel the church is corrupt, bankrupt, and no longer worth participating in. However, when I speak in this chapter of a shepherd's defection, I am really speaking of those leaders who have not fallen into immorality or had a conspicuous lapse of integrity, because frankly they are a tiny minority.

There are other ways, besides moral failure, that a shepherd or leader can provoke defections from those who follow them. Painful experience has taught us that someone can be saying all the right things and doing all the right things, yet doing them for the wrong reason. Not all sin is sexual sin. There are tremendous pressures that many Christian pastors and leaders of ministries struggle with today, and I personally believe that most of them surround the area of personal ambition (which does not make them unique, by the way).

Years ago I sat in a restaurant in Laguna Hills, California, with some pastors in our denomination as we were discussing the role of the pastor today. One pastor shared that he felt today's pastors are expected to be CEOs, great organizers, fund-raisers, speakers, strategists, and leaders who can deliver growth and corporate health. In short, many churches are searching for leaders who can deliver observable and tangible results. We agreed with his assessment, since we had all felt this pressure ourselves in our own ministries. But I remember saying, "Yes, I think that's true, but I struggle with that because when I got the call to ministry, it was not to be a CEO. If I had thought that being a pastor was being a CEO, I would never have wanted to be one."

Eugene Petersen, in his book *The Contemplative Pastor*, remarked that "American religion is conspicuous for its messianically pretentious energy, its embarrassingly banal prose, and its impatiently hustling ambition. None of these marks is remotely biblical. None is faintly in evidence in the gospel story. All of them are thoroughly documented diseases of the spirit. Pastors are in great danger of being undetected carriers of the very disease we are charged to diagnose and heal."[28]

Having been infected with this disease myself (and frequently tempted by it), I can speak firsthand of its dangers. I remember that when I first began a church in southern California, I was consumed with numbers and statistics. After the first few shaky months of our church's existence, a member of the church asked to meet with me. He casually offered me a copy of a book on church growth, with the clear implication that I still had a lot to learn. He was right; of course, I did. But most pastors put a great deal of pressure on themselves to succeed, and when others put additional pressure on them, it just fuels the spread of the disease. The disease consists of the need to measure ourselves against others and come out ahead or at least look respectable.

If we are church planters, we want to have our churches grow at a rate that is impressive. I remember attending meetings with other church planters where we were called to give reports on our church's progress. The only progress anyone mentioned was numbers, attendance, and conversions. You don't have to be brilliant to figure out how you will be measured.

If you are a musician, you might be tempted to measure yourself by the sales of your records or the number of people at your concerts. A parachurch organization might measure itself by how many converts a person had, how many new supporters they gained, or how many new ministries were started. A missions organization might be tempted to keep up with other missions that are planting new churches, reaching more new people, or sending out the most new missionaries.

A denomination might want to plant twenty new denominational churches, increase attendance by 10 percent over last year, or see its financial picture improve by $300,000. It might seek to measure itself by the average growth per church in its denomination. There are a variety of different measurements, but it all comes down to bigger and better—always, bigger and better. As a result, the pressure to perform can be relentless.

It surprises people to learn how much their pastors, leaders, or favorite Christian personalities are just like them. Making ministry a vocation does not suddenly transform all selfish thoughts or attitudes.

- Do you like to receive special attention for the work you do?
- Do you like to have a lot of money (be honest now)?

- Do you like to be praised?
- Do you like to hide your weaknesses and parade your strengths?
- Do you like to get your own way?
- Do you like having the last word?

Guess what? So do they!

- Do you have career ambitions?
- Do you ever measure yourself by your peers?
- Do you ever feel competitive around your peers?
- Do you want to be recognized as a success rather than as a conspicuous failure?

Guess what? So do they!

People hold pastors and Christian leaders to a very high standard, and rightly so, but they still fail. This doesn't mean they don't love God and want to serve Him. It means they are real people, just like everyone else, and they can defect from sincere service to Christ just like anyone else.

HELD TO A HIGH STANDARD

Pastors, leaders, or Christian personalities feel two often-competing pressures: (1) an internal pressure to succeed, which can be manifested in a desire to please God and use their gifts and talents effectively for Christ's kingdom, as well as a personal desire to be seen as successful; and (2) an external pressure from their ministry peers, their church members, or fans if they are musicians.

The Bible holds pastors and Christian leaders to a high standard (1 Timothy 3; Titus 1; James 3:1), but the standard is not results oriented; it deals with character, godliness, and spiritual maturity. These standards are truly high enough without adding layers of other expectations.

It is so tempting to fall into the trap of wanting to make a name for yourself in ministry, to be the one others look up to and admire. This temptation is just as intense for Christian leaders as it is for anyone in any other vocation. I have felt many times the pressure to produce results.

Well-known author and pastor Warren Wiersbe, in his book *The Integrity Crisis*, highlighted this pressure and how it has led to disastrous results:

> Once you make "getting results" your chief aim, there is no end to the mistakes you will make; and believe me, we made them. First you worry about numbers. Then you start substituting statistical records for spiritual reality, which is something like reading the recipe instead of eating the meal. How many attended? How many made decisions? How many joined? How much was given in the offering? All these things were more important than whether or not we glorified God in the meeting. Before long, the church ceased to be seen as people in an assembly: It became names and numbers in a file and, later, in a computer. People were not an end in themselves; they became a means to an end— getting a bigger crowd and getting more results. . . . This emphasis on statistics soon created an atmosphere of competition in the church. Who had the biggest church? Who had the biggest Sunday school? Unfortunately, the competition sometimes led to deception, until finally our contests were called off because of rain: The statistics were all wet.[29]

I say all these things to help those of you who are not in Christian leadership understand the pressures that many of your leaders face regularly. This does not excuse sin or justify wrong actions, but it helps to see the pressures that can lead a Christian leader to do things that might hurt your feelings, turn you off, or make you decide that you are better off without church. Each of us lives with our own pressures to perform in business and life, and if you are honest, you will admit they can bring out the worst in you sometimes.

Most of the Christian leaders I have met have a sincere love for God and truly want to serve Him with all their hearts. I also want to point out that churches do not grow because the pastors or leadership are pursuing some personal ambition but because God is working in a unique way through them. If you speak to them, you will often find them just as surprised by the explosive growth as anyone—and often a little intimidated by it.

But, like everyone else, Christian leaders, even the best of them, have motivations that at any point can be mixed. They are also human: frail, weak, and vulnerable to temptation. They are not immune to ambition and the desire for success. And, at times, these desires can overrule their better natures and cause them to speak and act in such a way as to leave hurt feelings, raw wounds, and lingering bitterness with church leadership and ultimately the church itself.

WHY ARE CHRISTIAN LEADERS DIFFERENT?

When a member of the church struggles with an issue of personal ambition, it can be an isolated event—at times not even affecting those within the church itself. But what happens when a pastor, elder, deacon, musician, missionary, or leader struggles with personal ambition in ministry? The answer is that it affects everyone around them—some directly and others indirectly, but all are affected in some way or another.

Furthermore, pastors, leaders, and musicians are typically smooth up front. They know what they are supposed to say and do and what they are supposed to avoid. They know what people expect from them. Good Christian leaders can become quite adept at controlling what others see of them. They can be polished in the pulpit and pious in the pew. They know when the camera is rolling and when it is not.

Years ago, when my children were little, I was working out of my house. On one particular day I was at home and trying to get some work done when my son was acting up. I was running out of patience. Finally, after several small incidents, I vented my anger, picking my son up and placing him firmly on the couch and yelling at him to stay put or he was going to get a spanking! Just then I looked up and noticed that our front door had been open and a woman from church was standing there watching all this with open mouth. She had never heard her pastor speak like that.

To say I was embarrassed is an understatement; after that it made me more careful of what I let other people see. Is that wrong? Of course, but I'm only human. I doubt I would have felt quite as embarrassed had I been a plumber. This is why pastors and leaders can become skilled at manipulating their own personal image. Unfortunately, this attitude can come back later to affect their ministries as well.

To a great extent, leaders control the direction, policies, and atmosphere of ministries. If they are tempted (which they will be) to use the church to further their own ambitions, to create their own empires, to begin the ministries and programs that they ultimately hope will bring them fame and honor (yes, Christian leaders can seek these things, too), how will this affect many in the church?

I know how difficult it can be for Christian leaders to separate their own personal ambitions from their spiritual calling. They can be almost clueless that they are working from any but the purest of motivations. They can justify almost any action they embark on or get others to undertake.

IN SEARCH OF AFFIRMATION

Everyone looks for affirmation that they are worthwhile, capable, important, effective, admired, and respected. Few of us can ignore the fact that those who succeed outwardly receive the lion's share of the honor and attention. In the secular world, awards and honors are habitually given to people who perform well in their fields. With recognition come perks like promotions, raises, bonuses, adulation, and admiration. Christian pastors, leaders, and personalities can desire these same kinds of recognition, yet they realize that their work is of a different type and nature, and their rewards will be given at another time and place by our Lord. On the other hand, it is tempting to get a few here and now as well.

Think about it, Christian leaders are not supposed to seek personal honor and recognition. In fact, no Christian is (Philippians 2:3; Romans 12:10; Proverbs 27:2). But the church's dirty little secret is that *at times we do!* Not always, because we are sensitive to our special calling and our unique reward system.

One year, my wife and I attended a pastors' conference. Just being together with so many other pastors and their wives was an encouragement. At the beginning of the session, to promote greater familiarity, the host encouraged all of us to introduce ourselves and tell what churches we pastor. Each of us did so, but there were several churches who had multiple staffs, where one pastor after another announced he was at "First Baptist Church of. . ." It was another silent witness to how big or little our churches were.

Later, when we all entered the dining hall and sat at tables with pastors we had never met, I found it almost comical how each pastor would dance around the questions we all were wondering about: namely, "How big is *your* church?" "How much has your church grown this year?" "How big is your budget?" "How large is your staff?" I was just as involved in this as anyone. At some tables I got congratulatory words on my church's growth; at other tables, with bigger ministries, my progress was not nearly as impressive to myself or others.

I would like to say that this is a new pressure, but I'm sure it has been around for a long time. "Pastors and churches in our hectic times are harassed by the temptation to seek size at any cost and to secure by inflation what they cannot gain by legitimate growth," writes A.W. Tozer. "Many a man of God is being subjected to cruel pressure by the ill-taught members of his flock who scorn his slow methods and demand quick results and a popular following regardless of quality."[30]

I would probably say that, while I agree with Tozer about the temptations, I'm not sure I would blame only the "cruel pressure by the ill-taught members of his flock." There is an ample amount of pressure found within the leaders themselves, derived from their own sin nature and their desire to be recognized as successes. Each of us struggles with what the apostle John identified as the common malady of man: "For everything in the world—the cravings of sinful man, the lust of his eyes and the boasting of what he has and does—comes not from the Father but from the world" (1 John 2:16). There is a little of the world left in all of us, pastors and leaders included.

I do not mean to paint a portrait of insecure pastors and leaders who are spending all their time trying to gain personal recognition. That would be insulting those who take great pain to deflect honor and glory back to Him who called us and who work and serve so humbly. I simply point out the pressure that Christian leaders are under to help explain why they do some things they do.

There are times when Christian leaders will begin to preach, lead, administer, organize, recruit, or sing—primarily, though not exclusively—for the affirmation they can receive from doing so. They will be tempted to use people to accomplish their own personal goals, which may or may not be for the good of the individuals or the churches. In the process of encouraging others, we can unwittingly begin to use others to accomplish our goals. They did not start out this way. To the contrary. However, over time, if leaders are not careful, they can be lulled into thinking that their spiritual vocations legitimize all their ambitions.

It is not hard for some of us to use the Scriptures or persuasion to get people to sign on to help do something. This, of course, is part of our God-given job: "equipping of the saints for the work of service" (Ephesians 4:11–12 NASB). We can make it sound so spiritual, because it is spiritual. But as we have seen, looks can be deceiving.

Christian leaders can get people excited about visions, dreams, or goals and inspiring them to try to achieve it all for the glory of God and the growth of the kingdom of God on earth. Who can argue with that kind of reasoning? Yet, sometimes, a corollary desire, sometimes a significant part of what we are trying to achieve, is perhaps far more carnal than spiritual. Even if the activity we are encouraging is a good thing, the truth is that we can be encouraging it for reasons not entirely spiritual. And there are few who dare to question our motivation when the cause seems so noble.

Although having a godly vision to help the poor, reach the masses, affect the culture with the gospel of Christ, and more, can be very good things, it is not uncommon for a good vision to become diluted over time. Soon it is *our* goal to do these things, *our* great ambition, *our* great calling, for which *we* ought to receive the credit. Of course this is not public information. Our own private ambitions (I can attest) can be something we would never feel free to share. We can learn to use a godly vision (which is good) to accomplish our own desires.

It sounds really tacky to say any of the following:

"I want to be the pastor of a large church so I can feel good about myself. So who's willing to canvas the neighborhoods, spend hours making calls, and do all the thankless behind-the-scenes work that it will take?"

"This program will not only change lives, it might well lead to my getting a more choice position one day! So, what do you say, will you be one of my helpers?"

"Unless the Christian Education program increases and we can start attracting more couples with children, the budget will continue to languish and I'll never get a raise. Who wants to sign up to be the preschool coordinator?"

"If I can get five more people to go on volunteer staff here, I can move on to the ministry I really want. Will you be one of the privileged five?"

"I can be the first person to really make a dent in this urban neighborhood, and people will recognize me for the unselfish person I am. I will be loved and adored by those I reach. So if you will just sacrifice some days and weekends to help me realize this goal, I'll be grateful!"

Yes, these appeals sound terrible, and no one would ever say them that way, but those of us in vocational ministry know it strikes a little too close to the truth to be comfortable. When we as leaders focus mainly on our ambitions and becoming worldly successes, we can fall prey to the temptation to use people. In fact, there are several ways that Christian leaders can unwittingly spur defections from the church.

USING PEOPLE INSTEAD OF LOVING PEOPLE

When we as leaders are focused mainly—or even mostly—on results, programs, or other external indicators of success, we can fall prey to the temptation to use people. The difference between helping people find their spiritual places of service and using people to accomplish our own ends often can't be detected. It is not uncommon to find someone who felt used by a church, pastor, or Christian ministry, which leads to frustration, hurt feelings, and eventually total defection from the church.

Some leaders are visionaries who can get people genuinely excited about following them and pouring their time, talents, and treasure into their ministries. But, at times, these people will pay a hidden cost if their

- Generosity is taken advantage of
- Hard work goes unrecognized and unrewarded as the leaders receive all the credit
- Ideas and thoughts are discounted because they conflict with the leaders'
- Time is taken advantage of, leaving them tired, discouraged, and seemingly on their own

- Needs go unmet because the pastors or leaders are too busy building their empires to notice the human toll it is taking

How many people have left churches, missions, or ministries because of the way they were treated by those who were ostensibly supposed to be shepherding them or modeling Christ before them? How many people have grown disillusioned with the church because some of its leaders treated them shabbily?

One week our church hosted a Christian singing group from a particular ministry. We had spoken with the ministry specifically about the issue of fund-raising before they came. We did not want our people bludgeoned with fund-raising appeals. We agreed to allow the students who were singing in the program to share their financial needs briefly within their musical presentation. Then came the day of the event. The kids put on a tremendous program and kept their word, giving a brief request to help them financially further their ministry.

But to our surprise, we discovered that the head of the organization was present with them. He took the microphone after the students finished and proceeded to go on a twenty-minute harangue for financial help, using every emotional tool in the book. Afterward, I heard quite a few comments from our people who felt used by this organization.

I was angry myself, but I must admit that I also have been guilty of using people instead of loving them. When I was a singles pastor, I was trying to "grow" our group and had a bumper crop of student leaders to help me. I had them doing a number of things—from planning activities, to making phone calls, to discipling others. They were also full-time students, and most of them had jobs. It was not hard to get them to sign on to be totally committed to the cause of Christ because they so loved the Lord. But in retrospect, I did not consider how I might not have been very considerate of their feelings or time.

I was so tunnel-visioned that the idea that someone might be laboring under a burden I had put on him or her never occurred to me. Years later I commented on this to one of my leaders and apologized to him. He admitted that he had indeed felt that way at times and greatly appreciated my apology. I can only wonder whom else in my zeal I might have hurt, whose feelings I might not have considered, whose time I might have taken advantage of.

A very wise man named Wally Norling, my mentor for years, developed a philosophy of ministry for pastors in our local denominational region. One of his enduring precepts was that people are to be loved and not used. He had also noticed how easy it was for pastors and Christian leaders to try to build their empires on the backs of others. He had noticed how many people felt used by their pastors.

When we view people as a means to our own end, we do not seek what's best for them, only how they can be used to help us. We don't stop to consider their true spiritual needs, their own limitations, their own feelings, their own pressures, unless they go out of their way to make them known. Tragically, most will not. We simply want something done, and we hope they will do it. Once they are in place and producing, it is tempting to move on to "fill some other hole," forgetting about the continual needs of those people.

There is a fine line between trying to get people involved in ministry and using people to promote your own ministry. At times, we can err on the self-promotion end. Jesus did not say, "They will know we are Christians by our programs," or "They will know we are Christians by our large churches and ministries." He said, "All men will know that you are my disciples, if you love one another" (John 13:35).

A.W. Tozer rightly said, "In an effort to get the work of the Lord done we often lose contact with the Lord of the work and quite literally wear our people out as well. I have heard more than one pastor boast that his church was a 'live' one, pointing to the printed calendar as a proof—something on every night and several meetings during the day. Of course this proves nothing except that the pastor and the church are being guided by a bad spiritual philosophy. A great many of these time-consuming activities are useless and others plain ridiculous."[31]

When I remember some of the work I had people so busily engaged in, I have to agree with Tozer. I wanted to show that we had a great program, and of course a great program is a busy program! So we were busy! Our activity calendar was my pride and joy. Something going on every week, and something big going on regularly. In retrospect, I'm not sure that all my ideas were necessary or that all our events were worth the burden put on our people. An easy way to hurt people and encourage defection is simply to be guilty of using people instead of loving them.

MISREPRESENTING TRUE DISCIPLESHIP

I had just preached my Easter sermon and walked to the back of the church, as is my habit, to greet those who were leaving. As I did, I spied a young man wandering toward the door. I greeted him and asked his name. As the service was ending behind us and the sweet songs of worship were echoing in the background, I engaged him in some small conversation. Soon I learned that this man had been involved in a legalistic Christian cult. Coming to church this morning had been far more difficult for him and his wife than I could possibly imagine; it was a return to the same kind of group that had burned them once.

We met a few days later at a Starbucks in our area, where he poured out his story. He and his wife had become Christians while young college students and became involved in a local church. The man who led the church encouraged a deeper commitment to Christ than was evidenced at many other churches, which was attractive to the young eager converts. Soon, however, the teaching became even more exclusive, and the meetings became more frequent. In fact, soon most of the nights and almost all day every Sunday were taken up by the church. A strict code of conduct was instituted and enforced by peer pressure and the leadership of one authoritarian man. No one had a personal life; the church and the authoritarian leader swallowed up their lives.

Having escaped the clutches of this tyrannical church and its tyrannical leader after thirteen years, the man shared, "I understand sin, but sin in the name of God is really sickening to me. When people open themselves up to God and get a heart full of pain, something's wrong there."

This all happened within the "safe" confines of a church and the guidance of a "shepherd." This man turned out to be a wolf in sheep's clothing, but he was for many years part of what would be called the organized church. Tragically, my friend has now left the faith.

This may be a more exaggerated example, but there are many cases where pastors and Christian leaders encourage or discourage activities that God or the Bible does not. It isn't hard to put people under a load of guilt to get them to do more and more and more.

There are some well-meaning pastors and leaders who have unwittingly misrepresented true discipleship. They have set up human ideas of what godliness looks like, going beyond what the Bible mentions. Through peer pressure, leaders can get others to believe that becoming a disciple is the same as becoming just like them!

I once attended a seminar given by a well-known speaker, famous around the country. He also happened to hail from the South and thus had a southern twang when he spoke. What I found fascinating was how so many of his followers also soon began speaking with a southern accent, even though they had grown up in California! To them, discipleship had come to mean more than just identifying with Christ; it meant identifying closely with the leader.

It is tempting for leaders, however, especially strong leaders, to believe that their own unique view of life and Scripture is the only truly acceptable viewpoint. If they don't listen to certain music, it is quickly communicated that it is certainly not spiritual for anyone else to. If they don't read certain books, it is certainly not spiritual for anyone else to. If they laugh at some jokes and not at others, well. . .you get the idea. Without meaning to, we can begin to have a cult following. True discipleship is not mimicking the personality of someone we admire spiritually; it is mimicking Jesus.

I remember having a leadership training class for a ministry I once had. I had each of my leaders get up and give a speech to acquaint them with public speaking, after which we would all listen and critique and encourage them. Because my gift was teaching, it just seemed natural that everyone ought to be able to get up and at least do a little bit of up-front speaking. After watching several of my "leaders" go through absolute agony when getting in front of people, I realized I was trying to teach pigs to fly. There was nothing wrong with those who were not good speakers; there was something wrong with me trying to make them into speakers. This had not been a necessary exercise for becoming a greater disciple of Jesus Christ; it had been unnecessary and painful for some.

Some disciples will never be up-front leaders; they will always be quiet, behind-the-scenes workers. Some disciples will never have great ministry vision; their viewpoint will always be more immediate. But these people are just as important as any pastor I have ever met. Their unique gifts and calling are perfectly fitted to His church. I regret making people feel inadequate by highlighting their weaknesses when I should have been helping to encourage them in their strengths. Fortunately, they were a very forgiving group!

Becoming true disciples of Jesus is seeking to follow Him in all our ways, to love Him with all our hearts, souls, minds, and strength (Deuteronomy 6:5; Mark 12:29–30). The goal is to be conformed to His image, not someone else's (Romans 8:29). Inevitably a part of our personalities will rub off on other people, and this is not a major problem. But if we aren't careful, we will begin to try to make people over into our own image, expecting them to think like us and respond like us.

Many people have had true discipleship misrepresented to them by well-meaning pastors and Christian leaders. They will inevitably become frustrated over time, and if the situation is not addressed or they become too disillusioned, they may well move on, deciding that to be a Christian in a church means becoming what they are not or cannot become.

REDEFINING SUCCESS

Kyle and Monica have been attending a small church plant for several years. They have labored diligently in the children's ministry, been involved in leadership in the church, and been heavy financial contributors. Their pastor has been following a cutting-edge, seeker-sensitive church model of church ministry, and though he has thrown his heart and soul into the work, there is not much to show for it. Each week they hope for more people and money to come in the doors. They want to reach people, but for some reason people haven't been knocking down the door to get in. They are beginning to get disillusioned. They came to know Christ through the ministry of the pastor and fully expected to have seen tremendous results by this time. The pastor made it clear that it was just a matter of time before they would begin to see success. But now they are exhausted and see no possible change in their church's fortunes. They are concluding that their church is a spiritual failure and they need to move on—or perhaps bail out of the church.

Jay and Sarah belong to a megachurch in the middle of a large suburb. They were initially attracted to the polished programs of the church, in which they became Christians, but now they are beginning to find themselves put off by them. At times the programs seem a little too polished, too glitzy, too Hollywood. They are beginning to feel isolated in the middle of the great crowd. The church doesn't seem spiritual anymore; it seems more like a giant company with great advertising and entertainment than a church. They are concluding that their church is a spiritual failure and they need to move on—or perhaps bail out of church.

There is a great debate within the church today on what constitutes success. On the one hand, some agree that when a church grows numerically and has many converts and programs, it must be doing something right; hence, it is successful. Conventional wisdom is that you can't argue with success. On the other hand, there are those who look with suspicion on anything big or polished, feeling that by its very nature it must be worldly and not truly spiritual.

I'm not sure either is completely right. There are times when God blesses leaders or church ministries in a unique way and many people respond. They did not start out to be successful in those particular terms, but it worked out that way. Yet, there are those who start out with the specific purpose of being "big" and succeed in doing so. Some of them (not all) are merely pursuing their private ambitions and manage to accomplish them. Are they also successful? Undoubtedly, but from what perspective?

There are also those who intend to be small and see bigness or large numbers as a sign that perhaps in some way they have compromised the message of Christ. To them, having a small ministry is proof of their success. As a result, success is an elusive concept for the Christian minister.

Perhaps Mother Teresa said it best when she said, "God has not called me to be successful; He has called me to be faithful." Unfortunately, most people, including many Christian leaders, define success as achieving what you set out to achieve. Yet, can we always guarantee that we had proper ambitions to begin with? Within every church, mission, ministry, and Christian organization there exists a definition of success. While most of them would agree with Mother Teresa's definition intellectually, there is often a different definition of success steering the ship.

Most leaders look at a ministry or church that is growing and popular with people and announce it a success. They may be quick to point out its weaknesses but secretly wish they were pastoring or leading that ministry. So from the pulpit or in the small groups, over and over, consciously and unconsciously, the idea of numerical success and bigness is being constantly communicated. Furthermore, the idea of multiplying ministry is not an unscriptural idea. There is nothing wrong with a growing ministry or the fact that some churches attract more than others. The problem resides in believing that if one church can do this, all churches can. If one pastor has done something amazing, it can be duplicated by other pastors.

The reason I bring this up is that so many pastors and leaders look at a successful model and seek to emulate it. Without thinking, they can be chasing a certain model of success without even asking if that is realistic. It is in the whole area of success that so many good Christian leaders have struggled. Tragically, those mistakes have had a negative impact on many Christians. Some of them have been discouraged to the point of defection.

By focusing on high-yield ministries—the ministries likely to attract the most people and affect the most people—leaders must be cautious that they do not ignore the low-yield ministries. Visiting the elderly shut-ins will never bring much numerical growth. Certain ministries to minorities will never pay for themselves. Yet, surely God cares about these people and wants His leaders to focus equally on them. The poor will not be able to help build large church buildings or pay for expensive programs, but the early church and her leaders were constantly concerned with them (Romans 15:26; Galatians 2:10; James 2:3–6).

People with chronic health problems, those in need of counseling, and many others can be overlooked if we define success the wrong way in ministry. It is so easy in ministry to lose our spiritual focus.

There are some who have been truly devastated by the actions of spiritual leaders within churches who took advantage of their flocks in horrible ways—from sexual abuse of the little children Jesus spoke about so powerfully (Mark 10:13–16) to sexual immorality with those they were charged to shepherd. Some have milked their members financially; others have abused their authority to the point of literally controlling the very lives of the sheep under their care. These are obvious examples of shepherds who have defected and given the church a well-deserved black eye.

Certainly some have become disillusioned with these sins and have defected from the church, but more commonly people get frustrated, disappointed, and discouraged with the less dramatic failures of the church's leaders.

Face it, many people have been hurt by those in Christian leadership. Often they either don't communicate their pain or they do and get little to no satisfactory result. They feel the easiest thing for them to do at that point is just leave, and they are right. It *is* the easiest thing to do. But being the easiest thing to do doesn't make it the right thing to do.

If we are going to leave a group just because we are slighted or offended in some way by those in leadership, we will forever be leaving groups. Furthermore, as Christians, we are commanded to be forbearing toward one another. Even leaders need to be forgiven—believe me, I know. We cannot be perfect 24/7. We will slip up; we will fail. At times it will be hard for us to admit it, if we ever do. Sometimes we are unaware we even have a problem.

But I thank God for all the gracious believers I have met who looked beyond my immaturity, ill-timed remarks, and awkward attempts at leading them somewhere they weren't even sure they wanted to go—just because I wanted them to. Their patience and prayer enabled me to keep growing, and I did. I learned and in the process became a more effective and, hopefully, more compassionate shepherd. The credit for that is due in a large part to those who were patiently praying for me even in the midst of my less-than-sterling efforts. As a result, their efforts have helped other congregations I have ministered to. They helped others by helping me.

I have learned that there really are no dragons to slay or empires to build. There is only Christ to serve and His sheep to shepherd. I try to be the most effective leader I can be, but I have learned to leave the results up to Him. If you have been hurt or discouraged by a Christian leader, don't abandon ship!

Christian leaders are not all the same; in fact, the one who let you down may one day be someone you can trust and depend on to lead you through your greatest struggles.

CHAPTER NINE

PLASTIC EVANGELISM

ARTIFICIAL—ADJ.
*in imitation of or as a substitute for
something natural; simulated*

"As for conforming outwardly,
and living your own life inwardly,
I do not think much of that."

HENRY DAVID THOREAU (1817–1862)

Sometimes we have good intentions for the things we do, but the results turn out rather badly. The story is told that during the firemen's strike of 1978, the British army had taken over emergency firefighting, and on January 14, they were called out by an elderly lady in south London to retrieve her cat from a tree. They arrived with impressive haste and soon discharged their duty. The lady was so grateful, she invited them all in for tea. Driving off later, with fond farewells completed, they ran over the cat!

At times, I fear, we have done something quite similar in our attempts to share our faith. With all the best intentions, we cause more problems than we solve. When we start to fake church within the church, it is but a small step to faking church *outside* the church.

Mark, while perusing the aisles of his local video rental shop, comes across a movie that he's not sure about. Should he watch this movie or not? As a Christian, he wants to be careful what he exposes himself and his family to. On the other hand, he has heard a great deal about this movie, and it stars his favorite actor. Everyone has been talking about it. He has pretty much decided to rent it, even though its rating clearly indicates there is material in the movie that he objects to. While looking at the back of the movie box, he suddenly spies Hal, his non-Christian neighbor, in the store. The decision is made: The movie goes back on the shelf. He doesn't want to be seen with a movie that might undermine his witness and his stand for godliness. *I'll just get the movie another time,* he decides.

Hypocrisy? You bet! Stupid? Right again! And for the record, Mark doesn't always get the movie another time, but he has. Chances are that you have struggled with the same thing from time to time. I know that I certainly have. Many debate the value of certain movies, songs, or books and whether they are appropriate for Christians to watch, listen to, or read, and although it is a worthwhile discussion, I will pass on it here. The problem I want to deal with is the artificial "witness" or example that we often feel the need to display for our non-Christian friends or neighbors.

Jim loves to joke. He loves finding and telling good jokes; in fact, he's famous for them. The problem is that Jim's conscience is beginning to bother him. Some of the jokes he tells would be offensive to certain groups, and he knows they aren't very kind. They are funny, and he doesn't really mean anything by them, so Jim has learned to be very careful where he tells certain jokes. He will never tell some of his more politically incorrect jokes to his non-Christian fellow workers for fear of their thinking less of his Christian faith and beliefs. So Jim has one set of jokes for his non-Christian friends and another set for his Christian friends. This enables him to maintain his Christian witness at work and in his neighborhood. Lately, Jim has begun to feel like a bit of a hypocrite.

Plastic evangelism is a strange sounding term for an even stranger activity. Plastic evangelism is nothing more than an artificial witness—a charade we can perform before others that does not truly represent our real spiritual condition or lifestyle. How did we get here? Each of us knows that there are times when we say things we don't mean, do things that aren't representative of how we really feel, and act in ways that are actually fake in order to impress the non-Christians around us. We are often torn between the tension we feel to be honest about ourselves and our struggles and the thought that our failures might be misunderstood and hinder our efforts to evangelize.

THE PRIME DIRECTIVE

Most Christians are aware of the passages of Scripture that encourage believers to keep their behavior beyond reproach. We are encouraged from the moment we are babies in the faith to always "be a good witness" to the non-Christians we know. The Scriptures are clear on this point.

"Live such good lives among the pagans that, though they accuse you of doing wrong, they may see your good deeds and glorify God on the day he visits us" (1 Peter 2:12). "But do this with gentleness and respect, keeping a clear conscience, so that those who speak maliciously against your good behavior in Christ may be ashamed of their slander. It is better, if it is God's will, to suffer for doing good than for doing evil" (1 Peter 3:15–17).

"You are the salt of the earth. But if the salt loses its saltiness, how can it be made salty again? It is no longer good for anything, except to be thrown out and trampled by men. You are the light of the world. A city on a hill cannot be hidden. Neither do people light a lamp and put it under a bowl. Instead they put it on its stand, and it gives light to everyone in the house. In the same way, let your light shine before men, that they may see your good deeds and praise your Father in heaven" (Matthew 5:13–16).

"Become blameless and pure, children of God without fault in a crooked and depraved generation, in which you shine like stars in the universe as you hold out the word of life" (Philippians 2:15–16).

As a result of these passages and the clear message that we are to be good witnesses of what Christ has done for and to us, many Christians feel a pressure to conform to an external code of conduct that represents the best of Christianity. We truly want to be witnesses for Christ to our neighbors, friends, and family.

We know there are certain sins that Christians are to assiduously avoid: immorality, substance abuse, abusive or coarse language, criminal activity, financial impropriety, and the like. In fact, Christians have become known for avoiding such activity and standing for morality and truth in an age when both are under attack. We are only too aware that some Christians have failed to live up to this code and have done tremendous damage to the cause of Christ.

A few years ago the Jim Bakker scandal was in the news. He was soon followed by a number of other public Christian figures whose sins were revealed to the public. What was usually discovered, however, was that the activities that they were guilty of had been going on in secret for quite some time. They knew the activities they were involved in were wrong, but they maintained a façade for the sake of their Christian reputations—not only for those in the church but those outside as well. Even though this behavior should be soundly condemned, we who condemn it should tread lightly. Most of us, if we were honest, would admit to feeling and giving in to the same type of pressure from time to time.

A DUMMY WITNESS

In the days of the old Soviet Union, the communists annually celebrated the Red Square parade, where the Soviet military exhibited their might by displaying their missiles and other weapons.

However, one of the amazing discoveries that was made after the downfall of the Soviet empire was that many of the missiles in the earlier parades were fakes! They were dummies, designed to be a gigantic bluff to the West. One such fake, the GR-1 (Global Missile), shown during a May 9, 1965, parade, prompted the United States to build an antimissile defense system worth billions of dollars. In fact, the Soviets had abandoned the GR-1 project long before the parade. Two other mobile ballistic missiles shown on the same day were also fakes. Their test launches had been a complete failure, as reported in the Russian magazine *Vlast* (Power).[32]

This story is amusing but no more so than our own attempts to hide our personal failures behind a "dummy" witness. Knowing the importance of having a good Christian witness, some of us have unwittingly felt compelled to improve our witness by taking shortcuts—just faking it. Since we have already spoken of how easy it is to deceive others and ourselves about our true spiritual condition, we should not be surprised that this attitude should find an outlet in our witness to non-Christians. Of course, here we do it for an ostensibly noble reason: We seek to portray a lifestyle, a morality, a spirituality, and a character that might not really represent our true condition *for the sake of impressing people with what God can do in our lives!* We are aware we are doing it, and we are usually uncomfortable with it, but we're just not sure what else to do. After all, isn't that what we're called to do?

A GOOD GOAL

Having a desire to reflect a compelling, winsome, effective witness for Jesus Christ is a worthy goal. We are instructed to seek to live our lives before others so that they will be attracted to the Jesus who has made such radical and wonderful changes in us. We have spent decades preaching about the importance of our public witness to our nonbelieving friends, family, and neighbors. To want others to see the changes that Christ has created in our hearts and lives is a good thing; it will hopefully be an inspiration for others to seek the same change through Christ.

Charles Haddon Spurgeon, the great English preacher, said, "A child of God should be a visible beatitude for joy and happiness, and a living doxology for gratitude and adoration." Gulp. While I don't disagree with the great preacher, I am the first to admit that I am not always a visible beatitude for joy and happiness and a living doxology for gratitude and adoration.

Yet, I am a witness wherever I go and to whomever I speak. Jesus said to His disciples, just before His ascension into heaven, "You will receive power when the Holy Spirit comes on you; *and you will be my witnesses* in Jerusalem, and in all Judea and Samaria, and *to the ends of the earth*" (Acts 1:8, author emphasis added). The "ends of the earth" part pretty much covers the places I've lived. Knowing that wherever I go I am a witness and knowing at the same time that I am not always filled with the Spirit and an example of the wonderful things Jesus has done in my life, I am tempted to fake it. My witness for Jesus may be well intentioned, and I may sincerely wish I was actually more spiritual, but often I am just pretending. I am acting out a part I neither feel nor truly represent.

I pretend to be a perfect husband.
I pretend to be a perfect parent.
I pretend to not be angry when I really am.
I pretend not to be offended when I'm furious.
I pretend that all my problems have been solved.
I pretend to be holy when my mind and heart are not.
I pretend that I'm not worried when I'm wracked with
     anxiety.
I pretend to be happy when I'm miserable.
I pretend to be confident when I'm confused.
I pretend to forgive when I haven't.

I'm not *always* pretending; I don't want to leave that impression. However, I pretend a lot of the time, especially if I think it might help nudge someone closer to God. I do this in front of others to leave a better impression of my Christian faith and my God. The fact that this is a plastic witness doesn't always stop me.

Many of us are encouraged and challenged by the apostle Paul when he describes his efforts at winning others to Christ.

"Though I am free and belong to no man, I make myself a slave to everyone, to win as many as possible. To the Jews I became like a Jew, to win the Jews. To those under the law I became like one under the law (though I myself am not under the law), so as to win those under the law. To those not having the law I became like one not having the law (though I am not free from God's law but am under Christ's law), so as to win those not having the law. To the weak I became weak, to win the weak. *I have become all things to all men so that by all possible means I might save some*" (1 Corinthians 9:19–22, author emphasis added).

It's hard to read a passage like this and not feel like we need to "become all things to all men," whether those things are true of us or not. Yet, Paul was not advocating that we pretend to be something we're not; he was only explaining that he used every honest circumstance at his disposal to present Christ to others. He did not pretend to be a Jew; he *was* a Jew! He simply used his Jewish background to build a bridge to his Jewish brethren. He was once under the law, so he knew what it was like to be under law and was able to speak effectively to that crowd. To the weak he became weak, because Paul knew what it was to be weak (2 Corinthians 12:7–10).

I was once working with some high school students, and to try to "become one of them," I tried to act like them. I used some of their lingo and generally acted immature. I really thought I was being "cross-cultural." It was a fool's errand! I was not a high school student, and my attempts to fake it were pathetic. When I stopped doing that and just talked to them normally, I got a much better hearing.

We know what is at stake spiritually, and we desperately want to help others receive eternal life, which comes only through Jesus

Christ. We likewise know that our lives are living, breathing billboards for Jesus. Second Corinthians 5:20 reminds us that we are ambassadors for Christ. It is indisputable that God wants us to have a powerful impact on our world through our lives and testimonies.

Just because our witness is plastic or artificial at times does not mean it is plastic all the time. There will be times when a real change in our lives will be the cause of others being drawn closer to Jesus. But the truth is that all of us who sincerely seek to follow Jesus will have moments of success and failure. Even if wanting to have a good testimony to nonbelievers is a good goal, the truth is, if we go about it the wrong way, we can do more damage than good.

PURSUED THE WRONG WAY

"God has a wonderful plan for your life."

"God wants to change your life."

"God can heal your marriage."

"God can put your family back together again."

"God can answer all your questions."

"God can help you not to be sad and lonely and depressed anymore."

Have you ever used any of these statements or heard them used by those sharing their faith? There is truth in each one of these statements. Yet, these statements are half-truths we have been trained to say because they are the official spiritual "language." Have you walked with God for a number of years and yet say these clichés almost wistfully, wishing they were true of your present experience?

I do believe that God has a wonderful plan for my life; I believe it with all my heart. Yet there are times when His plan for my life doesn't *feel* so wonderful. Been there? There have been times when I was sharing my faith with someone and I referred to the wonderful plan God had for that person's life, and I had to bite my lip. I knew that it was true, but at the moment I wasn't experiencing it.

How is my witness affected when parts of my life are clearly not wonderful? I know that God wants to change my life, but at times I admit that change comes so slowly as to be practically imperceptible. Certain areas of my life have been radically changed, but others, well, they are in process. How do you witness to this truth? "God can change *part* of your life. Look, He's changed *part* of mine!" That doesn't sound nearly as enticing, does it?

When we learn to share our testimonies (our stories of how we became Christians and what God has done in our lives since that moment), we are instructed to accentuate the positive. Of course there is nothing wrong with this, and it serves as a wonderful reminder of God's work in our lives. However, not everything in our lives is positive after we become Christians, is it? Sometimes our lives are anything but wonderful. We struggle with past sins, decisions, guilt, forgiveness, patience, faith, and many other things that are really quite normal. The hardest thing to admit to a non-Christian, however, is that we still struggle. We are afraid it might tarnish the gospel to them. We are afraid that if they found out the cold, hard truth, they might be turned off.

When we say God can heal your marriage and put your family back together again, we are not lying. *He can.* But He doesn't always, does He? He does not simply overrule our pettiness, bitterness, bad habits, or selfishness and zap us into kind, thoughtful, unselfish spouses. This makes it difficult for us at times when we try to witness for Christ. Being aware of the mistakes and failures we still struggle with, we are tempted to sugarcoat and minimize them so that the Christian life is still attractive to our non-Christian friends and family.

We know that God has all the answers to life, but the truth is that we don't. The answers exist, but they are not always in us, so we are tempted to fake it. We pretend that we have all the answers and that our questions and doubts have been laid to rest forever. God certainly uses His Word in the lives of people we share with, but each time we portray ourselves as something we aren't or as having something we don't, our integrity takes a hit. So does their understanding of what the Bible truly teaches. The results? We find ourselves becoming plastic, fake, and artificial. We stop being true witnesses and instead become salespeople. And deep down inside we know it.

WITNESSING TO THE WRONG POWER

When I was a young man and had just become a Christian, I desperately wanted to be a good witness for Christ. I read the passages that spoke of the fact that God is concerned not only with our outside activity (Matthew 23:25–28) but the inside of us—our hearts. I tried so hard to present a holy, pious, and moral exterior. Yet, when I would struggle with lust, as any adolescent young man will, I would be in such agony. I knew I was a fake but could never admit it. Yes, God was working in my life. He was making changes, but He wasn't done yet. How could I have a good witness if people knew the truth? I had no victory! So I lived a secret life.

It never occurred to me that the very struggle with lust was itself an act of monumental change, representing a new desire in my heart that had never been there before: a desire to be holy before God. I may not have won every battle or even most of them at first, but I was in every one of them. I wanted to change more than I wanted anything else. Yet, in the meantime, all I could think of was that I needed to "look better" or my faith might be negated.

It didn't occur to me that I was totally in love with Jesus because He had saved me from my sin and had begun a good work in me, even though I still wasn't the picture of perfection. *Maybe I am just different,* I thought. *Maybe to other people that won't be enough.* So I faked a pious morality that belied the sinful reality. Finally, God gradually changed my heart and mind, and I did gain victory in that area, but it took time. Ironically, one of my greatest motivations for misrepresenting myself was my belief that I was doing God a favor.

So many Christians are going through such turmoil in their lives because they are aware that their attempts at representing their faith are, at times, fake. The message of the gospel is still the power of God, yet we suspect that it won't have the same power unless our personal lives represent that truth 24/7. We remember that we are supposed to be more than conquerors "through him who loved us" (Romans 8:37). Ironically, before this verse, which we use so commonly to prop up our witness, Paul speaks of things we are conquerors of: trouble, hardship, persecution, famine, nakedness, danger, and sword. We are not conquerors because we win every victory in life, resist every temptation, and overcome every difficulty. We are victorious because of our relationship with Jesus, who is our Victor—the one who conquered death and every power to save us.

At the end of the Super Bowl, the victor not only gets a trophy, but each member of the team gets a ring. The ring isn't given just to the stars of the team but to every member, even if they didn't play. They are on the world champion team, even if they didn't contribute to the victory. That is how we are more than conquerors *through Him*. We conquer death and everything else through Him who has led the way and made us family. We don't have to be perfect to convey that message to others.

The danger in putting forth a false representation of our Christian lives is that we are not modeling the power of the resurrection in our lives but the power of deception to hide our moral and spiritual blemishes.

I think this is the reason that frequently in my past my own witness has been so anemic. There were times that I simply felt less than victorious in my Christian life and felt I had nothing to share. How was I all that different from the more socially healthy non-Christians I knew? My mistake was in believing that the important message was about how much I had changed, not about Him and what He had done for me, in spite of my present failures. A good goal pursued the wrong way can lead to a real problem.

A Real Problem

When we allow the way we witness to be fake, when we pretend holiness that does not exist, when we cover up weaknesses that are real, when we deny struggles that at times overwhelm us, we are entertaining some ideas that are ultimately harmful—to us personally, to the church, and to the reputation of our Lord as well.

We are often trying to impress our world with our lives, as if we are the sole exhibition for our faith. But the truth is that we are to be witnesses *of* Him and not just *for* Him. Our behavior, mistakes, and failures do not detract from His truth, His example, His death on the cross, or His resurrection. This does not mean, however, that our lifestyles have no impact on our sharing of the gospel; they do, but our lifestyles are not the gospel. The gospel has a power that is beyond our lifestyles and is able even to overcome the evident flaws in our own lives.

While we are being transformed, we are *primarily* witnesses to His mercy, forgiveness, and grace. He loves us not because we are so lovable but because He is love. We are sinners who (1) *were* saved from the penalty of sin, (2) who *are* being saved from the power of sin in our daily lives, and (3) who *will* one day *be saved* from the very presence of sin. Sometimes we get the last two confused. The fact that we are being saved from the power of sin means that there must be a struggle going on from which we need to be rescued. The Holy Spirit is doing things in us that will bring about change, but it sometimes feels as though He is a foreign presence in our lives.

Philip Yancey used the analogy of an organ transplant to describe this process. "After an organ transplant, doctors must use anti-rejection drugs to suppress the immune system or else the body will throw off the newly grafted member. I have come to see the Holy Spirit as something like that agent, a power living inside me that keeps me from throwing off the new identity God has implanted. My spiritual immune system needs daily reminders that God's presence belongs with me and is no foreign object."[33]

We have often forgotten that the change God intends to work in us has to first overcome our resistance to that change. This can take time, sometimes years. Part of us desperately wants to change. Part of us is terrified of the change. This constant tension makes drastic overnight change difficult. But when the change finally takes root, it usually stays put.

We don't always want to change. Sometimes we like gossiping, lying, lusting, hating, being proud, and hurting others. There are moments in our lives when those are the most natural responses to what we are encountering. We don't even have to think about it; it is a sinfully conditioned response. The people we were before we became Christians, the old sin nature that was in total and absolute control, can still exert pressure and intimidation.

When a child finally moves away from a domineering parent, the parent can, by a phone call, letter, or visit, still intimidate the child who has not yet established firm boundaries on the relationship. Such is our relationship with our old sin nature. Even when freedom has been achieved, or given, it must be maintained with great effort.

A PEOPLE IN PROCESS

Christianity is not the story of finished products here on earth; it is the story of a miraculous process that God has begun. It is not just hell from which God saves us; He is saving us from many present dangers: foolishness, selfishness, criticalness, maliciousness, bitterness, and a litany of other destructive and dangerous activities and ideas. We are a people in process. The process is as much a witness to Him in our lives as the finished product is.

No matter how much we have changed in some areas, there will always be others we need to change in. Yet, though we need change in many areas, that isn't all the truth. In certain areas we *have* been changed. These are real significant changes.

We love God when we used to ignore or even hate Him.

We have begun to love and depend upon God's Word, the Bible, instead of just trusting conventional wisdom.

We are beginning to love people we never did before, even those who treat us badly.

We are beginning to *want* to be holy, moral, and upright and not just do it because we think it is a social responsibility. Though we are still tempted by sin, our desire is to please God, even if it means denying ourselves pleasures we never did before.

We are able to admit things about ourselves we were never able to admit before. God's assessment of us is becoming the reality we embrace now.

We are becoming more patient, understanding, and caring. Even though we still get angry and can be impatient and thoughtless, the fact is that our character is slowly metamorphosing away from our old selves. We don't like ourselves when we get angry, impatient, and thoughtless, but we recognize it for what it is and ask God to help us with it.

We can point to these as proof of God's work in our lives. There are other areas in which God is still changing us. The changes are not all as noticeable; in fact, they may be almost imperceptible. But there is a process of change that each Christian seems to go through.

THE PROCESS OF CHANGE

Step 1: *We are suddenly open to change we hadn't considered before.* God is strengthening us to change our hearts and minds, a prelude to changing actions. Usually this is accomplished through reading the Bible and learning what God wants from us. We had not previously considered that we needed to change.

Step 2: *We seriously consider the need to change in a significant way.* This is something the Holy Spirit does in and through us. Now we know we need to change and it becomes a desire within us.

Step 3: *We ask God to help us change.* We are intimidated by the size of the project and know we need help. Prayer becomes one of our major weapons and sources of help.

Step 4: *We begin taking steps of faith to change.* We are now beginning to actually change some of our old habits, thoughts, and activities, though it feels strange and scary at first.

Step 5: *The change slowly begins to take hold in our lives.* Though we still fail occasionally, we begin to see progress and are encouraged by it.

Step 6: *Change is accomplished.* Though we are still subject to relapses, there is now a new habit or attitude or thought guiding our lives.

Friends, the truth is that we are somewhere in this process on a variety of different issues. We might be at Step 6 in issues of morality, which might be a quantum leap for us. On the other hand, we may only be at Step 1 in the area of substance abuse, or temper, or bitterness, or racism, or any number of other issues. We may be at Step 3 in the area of patience and at Step 4 in the area of greed.

This is what real change is like. So why don't we begin to be honest? Admitting a personal failure is not the same as admitting your faith is a failure, or your God is a failure, or your church is a failure.

Every one of Jesus' disciples failed Him in a very public way. At the end, each deserted Him, with some denying they even knew Him. And these were men who had been with Jesus day in and day out for several years! Nonbelievers saw these failures. Yet, it did not slow the spread of the gospel. The good news is not that Christians are perfect but that Jesus has saved us and is still saving us from our sins.

Our sins have been forgiven, but now the Holy Spirit who lives within us is challenging them. Each one needs first to be identified, admitted, and then slowly but surely evicted. With some sins this is easy. With others it takes longer. The New Testament church was full of failures. These weren't superspiritual saints; they were ordinary folks like you and me. They were constantly needing to be reminded to leave behind the old life and adopt the new one (Ephesians 4:22–24). We are no different.

WHAT THE WORLD NEEDS NOW

Maybe what others in our world would like to hear is a little more honesty. Maybe they'd find it refreshing to see a little more humility from us. Maybe if they knew the real nature of the Christian faith, that God comes in and deliberately makes changes in our hearts that cause us to begin to want to change our activities, they might be more interested.

Philip Yancey talks about a most difficult period in his life, a time of serious physical complications when he could not talk or walk. He could only lie in bed all day, barely able to move his arms and legs. His eyes did not focus. He could not feed himself and was incontinent. He had little idea of what was going on around him. As he said, "Resigned to my state, I could not imagine any improvement." Yet, he later outgrew that condition and saw it as a necessary transition time. What was that state? *Human infancy!*[34]

No one reaches adulthood without going through a period of immaturity, awkwardness, and helplessness. In the same way, no one reaches spiritual maturity without going through the same stage. To deny this reality is a mistake.

God can use our weaknesses for His purposes. Even our frailties, struggles, and failures can be used by Him to touch people. Though each of us has flaws, it is a misunderstanding to believe that we can't still be used as powerful witnesses for Jesus. The apostle Paul was a former murderer, King David was an adulterer, Abraham was a liar, Peter was a big mouth, Jonah was a bigot, Sarah was a doubter, and the list could go on and on. God has always used imperfect people to witness of His work.

This doesn't mean that we should not strive to change or to become more Christlike—only that we should stop trying to fake it because we think it would further the kingdom of God. Lies are not a good witness to the truth.

Let's begin to witness to the truth: God *is* changing us. Sometimes we cooperate and change comes quickly. Other times we resist, and change comes more slowly. But the greatest change that has taken place in us is in our relationship with God. We have peace where once we were enemies (Romans 5:1, 10). We love Him whom we once ignored. We now desperately want to please Him whom we once barely acknowledged.

We are not objects of perfection; we are the eternal objects of His grace. Yes, we are imperfect and full of flaws. Thankfully, the Holy Spirit of God is carefully revealing these to us; and as He does, we begin to work together to become more like our Lord and Savior.

We do not do God or His church any favors when we are fake witnesses. The truth is that none of us is all that good at acting. I'm afraid our world knows more of the truth about us than we think they do. They are also far more interested in our God and what He really does in our lives than we give them credit for.

Honesty, even a painful honesty, is still the best policy. In fact, I truly believe you will find the honest witness far more fulfilling. So shuck the plastic! Make your witness real! You'll be doing everyone a favor!

CHAPTER TEN

WHAT ABOUT SIN?

SIN—N.
an offense against God,
religion, or good morals

> "One reason sin flourishes is that
> it is treated like a cream puff
> instead of a rattlesnake."
>
> BILLY SUNDAY

Ultimately, because we have spent a great deal of time on the subject of faking church and how it is a subtle defection, in the mind of any intelligent reader will come the invariable question: *But what about sin?* Aren't there times when God makes it clear what He requires from us and we, in full knowledge of that information, turn our backs and go our own ways? Can't we defect from church and ministry just because we *want* to? Yep!

We are all tempted to use church for our own purposes and desires, despite what God created the church for. We have dealt a little with the idea that some people get involved in service for the wrong reasons, but the truth is that at times everyone comes to church for the wrong reasons.

Some people come to church initially, and actually primarily, because they want to do one or more of the following:

- Fulfill an obligation
- Repair their marriage
- Cure their loneliness
- Gain new friendships
- Fix their children
- Get inspiration
- Assuage their guilt
- Find new romances
- Network for business

We never complain about this, because we often advertise that church and faith will meet all those needs (except maybe the business networking). Come to church and you won't be lonely. Come to church, and we'll help you fix your marriage, your loneliness, your children. We'll help you find new friendships, give you inspiration for living, and help you deal with guilt. We just never think through the implications of this kind of advertising. As well intentioned as this may seem, we are turning the church into a spiritual Wal-Mart, where you can get everything you need under one roof. So people come, see if they can find what they are looking for, and then often depart with their "purchase," leaving us bewildered.

We discover to our chagrin that some of the people who responded to our advertisement were not interested in:

- Fixing their relationship with God
- Having their own weaknesses probed and examined in sermon or Scripture
- Giving up anything in their lives—only in adding something
- Being convicted of sin—only in being inspired for living
- Suffering
- Serving—only in being served

They have faked church by denying the church's real purpose and mission and substituting their own. We are told in Scripture that sin is a blindness (Matthew 15:12–14, 23:16–26), but we are also told that sin is a choice and that we freely make that choice (1 John 1:10; James 1:13–15). We may not understand all the implications of every sin we commit, but we know when we are doing something that isn't right or honest. Both our consciences and God's Holy Spirit reveal our sin to us.

When I was just a little boy, we lived on an old country road. One day my friend and I became involved in adolescent mischief as we were watching the cars drive by. Noticing all the shiny hubcaps passing by, we quickly devised a contest to see who could score the most hits. Now both of us inherently knew that this behavior was wrong. Yet, we didn't fully comprehend all the implications or the full danger of our sin.

Our rocks could have struck a window, seriously injuring someone or even causing death. The noise of a rock hitting a hubcap or another part of a car could distract a driver and cause an accident. We could have damaged the car itself. The number of problems we were potentially creating was staggering. Though we didn't think through all the implications of what we were doing, we knew throwing rocks at hubcaps was wrong. Fortunately, or unfortunately, we were caught when we were successful in hitting a car, but unsuccessful when the driver would stop the car and give us a tongue-lashing.

In the same way, some people try to come to church and to God on their own terms, knowing inherently that this is wrong. They seek to dictate the terms of their association with the God of the Universe, the Creator, the Holy One. They want to limit the One who created the Milky Way, the galaxies, the earth and all it contains, to those microchanges they will accept in their lives. It is utter madness and complete folly. The creation attempts to dictate terms to the Creator—with a straight face.

This is sin. It is the sin of ingratitude, the sin of dishonor, the sin of rebellion against the King of the Universe. Do we realize all these implications at the moment? No, but we do understand that it's wrong, regardless of what we might tell others or even ourselves.

CHURCH IS ABOUT GOD

Even though a church might have been advertising how to improve your marriage, find purpose in life, repair your relationships, and other benefits, everyone knows that the assumed power behind this change is God.

Church is about God. To come to church for purely selfish or self-centered motivations assumes God has no glory of His own, no divine authority over our lives, and no claim at all on us. Although God is a merciful, loving God who wants to meet all our needs, He is also the Lord of the heavens and the King of all creation. To treat Him contemptuously or as nothing more than a divine bellhop is sin of the worst degree. I know, because I've done it.

However, when you hear over and over how God will meet your needs, how He wants to change your life, how He loves you and accepts you just as you are (which, by the way, He does), you can begin to feel as if church is all about you. In fact, you can begin to think God's sole purpose for existence is to fix all your problems, meet all your needs, and generally make your life better! That He might have a purpose for your life different from your own can be a startling thought, especially if that purpose involves service, sacrifice, and even suffering.

We have spent so much time emphasizing the wonderful benefits of giving our lives to Christ and becoming involved in His church that we have at the same time minimized the cost of following Him. We have raised an entire generation of people, inside and outside of the church, who do not have a clear understanding of the call of God upon their lives. Their understanding of church is that it is a place where their needs get met, not that it is a place of service to the Most High God. Ironically, you can't find one instance when Jesus made following Him easy; in fact you find just the opposite in the following verses:

"Jesus replied, 'No one who puts his hand to the plow and looks back is fit for service in the kingdom of God' " (Luke 9:62).

"Then Jesus said to his disciples, 'If anyone would come after me, he must deny himself and take up his cross and follow me. For whoever wants to save his life will lose it, but whoever loses his life for me will find it' " (Matthew 16:24–25).

"And anyone who does not carry his cross and follow me cannot be my disciple" (Luke 14:27).

"In the same way, any of you who does not give up everything he has cannot be my disciple" (Luke 14:33).

Even though my original introduction into church stressed the importance of being Jesus' disciple no matter what the cost, years of involvement in the church and trying to get my needs met began to make me more comfortable with a different outlook. I became a judge of the church. There was no divine mystery, no waiting on God—just a careful analysis and evaluation each Sunday of what was good or bad.

- Worship was good, but preaching was bad.
- Preaching was good, but worship was bad.
- Sunday school was abysmal; the teacher was boring and used no illustrations.
- The bulletin contained not one but two typos!
- The announcements were too long.

The people who can be the most involved, the most indispensable, and the most committed in church are precisely the ones who can often feel that church and ministry have begun to feel like a grind.

We go to church because we know we should, and a part of us wants to. But at times a part of us really wants to:

- Sleep in
- Go out to a leisurely breakfast

- Take a stroll through the mall, a walk around the lake, a drive in the country
- See a movie
- Go out of town

There were times when I was pastor that I would be driving to church and see folks just out strolling around our community or walking their dogs. I admit that at times I envied them. At that moment I would be stressed, hoping that our Sunday school teachers would all show up, that the set-up crew was on the job, that our ancient sound system would last one more week, that the bulletins had been folded, and thinking about a myriad of other important details.

Church had become about me. I had undergone a slow metamorphosis from a disciple of Jesus who would gladly sacrifice and serve Him to a disciple of Jesus who was constantly trying to get God to do things for me.

Been there? Maybe you are there now. You serve, but without a lot of enthusiasm. You sacrifice, but not without some internal complaint. Church and ministry can begin to feel almost like a holy jail sentence.

In these moments of fatigue, regret, and discouragement, our old lives and lifestyles can come back with a vengeance. We're tired of:

- Serving others all the time
- Sacrificing all the time
- Having to be patient with undependable people
- Living with the hardships that faith and ministry put on us
- Preparing for church when others are sleeping in, skiing, surfing, or having fun
- Having Sunday mornings be a frenetic, hectic time

We'd like more time to indulge our favorite hobbies (or hobbies we'd like to have if we had the time). We'd like to be able to take off somewhere without worrying about our schedules, or ministries, or responsibilities at church. We'd like being able to take the money we tithe and buy a nicer car, or go on a nicer vacation, or just have more money to spend for fun. We'd like to once again feel like we are in control of our lives, instead of having them controlled by the church. Frankly, we're just tired of being at church. We aren't even toying with the idea of abandoning God or our faith, but the idea of abandoning the church can be tempting at times.

It wasn't by accident that Paul gave a reminder to the Galatian believers, "Let us not become weary in doing good, for at the proper time we will reap a harvest if we do not give up" (Galatians 6:9).

What is interesting is that just prior to that familiar announcement, Paul was reminding the Galatian church: "The one who sows to please his sinful nature, from that nature will reap destruction; the one who sows to please the Spirit, from the Spirit will reap eternal life" (Galatians 6:8).

The sinful nature is still alive and kicking! When it can't attack us in more dramatic and obvious ways, it fights back subtly, toying with our motivations. For every call of Christ to greater commitment, self-sacrifice, and service, we also hear another call from the one who tempted our Lord two thousand years ago. It whispers to us, "Give yourself a break! Think of yourself first once in awhile. Take care of number one. Why beat yourself up when life can be so much easier and more pleasant?"

And, that other voice is right! There is a much easier life to be lived. There are choices that will require far less of you and be wonderfully more enjoyable. There is a less demanding, less draining life to be experienced outside the walls of church and ministry. You *can* indulge yourself; life *can* be easier; you *can* have more money, time, and fun. But then again, that was always true, wasn't it? Jesus never said, "Come and follow me and I will make it really fun, easy, and profitable!" Besides, we will eventually find this "better" life growing old itself. There is only pleasure in sin for a season (Hebrews 11:25). Slowly the pleasure fades and you are left with nothing but gnawing emptiness.

We mustn't fool ourselves into believing, however, that the church or ministry is the culprit. The issue goes deeper than that. The church is founded on Jesus Christ. It is His words and His claims upon us that make our road harder than our nonbelieving neighbors'. It is also the struggle with our own selfish desires that invite defection.

OUR DUAL NATURE

Although the Scriptures make it clear that we have both an old nature and a new nature, the fleshly person and our spiritual person, sinful desires as well as spiritual desires, many believers are still relatively surprised by some of the feelings they thought were behind them. Paul says in Romans 6:6, "For we know that our old self was crucified with him so that the body of sin might be done away with, that we should no longer be slaves to sin." But that old nature had to be voluntarily set aside as well, as he reminds us in Ephesians 4:22: "You were taught, with regard to your former way of life, to put off your old self, which is being corrupted by its deceitful desires."

Many Christians have thought that our sinful, selfish, immoral, worldly desires would just slowly fade away into the sunset after a few years of being a Christian and growing in our faith. If we just prayed and read our Bibles, our inner desires would all change and serious temptation to return to the "good old days" would just go away.

We can eventually learn to resist these temptations and learn how God can strengthen us to do this (1 Corinthians 10:12–13), but this doesn't make them go away. After Satan failed to tempt Jesus to sin in the wilderness, he kept trying in many different ways (Mark 8:33; Hebrews 4:15). In fact, His last greatest temptation we can see in Jesus' agony in the Garden of Gethsemane. In the struggle, He literally sweated drops of blood (Luke 22:44).

An alcoholic who came to Christ, and in the power of his or her new life overcame alcoholism, can always be tempted to drink again. Even though that person overcame the slavery and addiction to alcohol for years, he or she at any time, in a moment of weakness or fatigue, can still succumb again.

People who were sexually promiscuous in the past and who through the Holy Spirit have overcome these sinful desires and activities, at some point in the future can still return to them. Even years in the future they can find themselves in situations in which returning to a sinful lifestyle is easier and more attractive at the moment than being faithful to Christ and His church.

A person who had always run from responsibility as a spouse, parent, child, or member of society, through the Holy Spirit and the encouragement of the church, can learn to challenge and change this destructive habit. But at some point in the future, when life again gets hard, there is a temptation to return to their old way of coping with stress and difficulty.

William Murray, son of the famous atheist Madelyn Murray O'Hair, in his book *The Church Is Not for Perfect People*, speaks of what he calls "transition Christians." He writes that "Transition Christians face an ongoing struggle with their past." One such person he calls Janet (not her real name) was a recent divorcee who had destroyed her marriage through a promiscuous lifestyle. She attended one of his crusades and met Christ. She started attending church and got involved in the singles ministry.

While there, she heard a sermon on the subject of being separated from the world and living for Christ. She was powerfully affected because that is precisely what she most wanted to do. But when the sermon was through, there was an announcement for the singles to sign up for the ski trip. This was a problem for Janet. The last time she had gone skiing with a group of couples, she had been involved sexually with several of the men.

Murray writes, "How could she go to (her pastor) and say, 'Pastor, I'm afraid to go on that trip because I might want to have sex with a man'?" Murray gave her some personal advice from his own struggle. "Since I've been saved, I've had to go through nearly every life experience that I went through before I was saved. Before I was saved, I had a child who got sick; after I was saved, I had a child who got sick. Before I was saved, I was tempted by alcohol; after I was saved, I was tempted by alcohol. Before I was saved, I was tempted by sex; after I was saved, I was tempted by sex." He urged her to go on the trip but to remember that this time she was going as a Christian. She went and had a wonderful, sin-free time.[35]

I propose that Murray is partly right. Not just new believers but all believers are "transition Christians." We are all in the process of transitioning from our old lives into new ones. It is a lifelong process. And, though we might forget this fact if we've been in church for awhile, we can always transition back.

There are several signs that a Christian is vulnerable to defecting from church and ministry and returning to the life left behind.

WE START TO DEFINE OUR FAITH IN TERMS OF LOSS RATHER THAN GAIN

Jesus did indeed call us to a life of sacrifice, service, and obedience, but there was more to the call than that. He who said we must deny ourselves, take up our crosses and follow Him also said, "I have come that they may have life, and have it to the full" (John 10:10). Paul, in Philippians 3, takes time to list all the things he had previously considered valuable, including his heritage, position, and even his zeal! But then he goes on to say, "But whatever was to my profit I now consider loss for the sake of Christ. What is more, I consider everything a loss compared to the surpassing greatness of knowing Christ Jesus my Lord, for whose sake I have lost all things. I consider them rubbish, that I may gain Christ" (Philippians 3:7–8).

What made his loss acceptable was what he had gained. Think about this for a minute. He was born in the right place to the right people. He had every birth advantage a Jew could have. He was a Roman citizen as well. He was an expert in the field of the Law, even among the Pharisees. He was a mover and a shaker and had the admiration of his peers and his community. When he became a Christian, he gave it all up. Listen to what he gained.

"Three times I was beaten with rods, once I was stoned, three times I was shipwrecked, I spent a night and a day in the open sea, I have been constantly on the move. I have been in danger from rivers, in danger from bandits, in danger from my own countrymen, in danger from Gentiles; in danger in the city, in danger in the country, in danger at sea; and in danger from false brothers. I have labored and toiled and have often gone without sleep; I have known hunger and thirst and have often gone without food; I have been cold and naked. Besides everything else, I face daily the pressure of my concern for all the churches. Who is weak, and I do not feel weak? Who is led into sin, and I do not inwardly burn?" (2 Corinthians 11:25–29). And I complain about too many church meetings and dull sermons!

When we read passages like this we can feel guilty when we're tempted to sleep in on Sunday morning instead of going and teaching the third-grade boys for one hour. Yet, we must not miss the point. It wasn't a love of sacrifice that drove Paul. It wasn't some sadomasochistic tendency within the apostle to enjoy suffering and pain. He explains his motivation. He had found Christ! One of my greatest tendencies is to miss the forest for the trees.

When I forget *whom* I serve, I lose sight of *why* I serve, and when I do that, I inevitably end up serving myself. In fact, I can become so focused on my sacrifices that I define my ministry in terms of loss rather than in terms of gain. I can even begin to feel quite sorry for myself.

- All I do is give.
- I show up when no one else does.
- I'm the only one who's really committed around here.
- I never get a break.
- No one appreciates what I do.

Now please don't think for a moment that any of the above statements is true. They were *never* true. They just *felt* that way sometimes. When I feel that my sacrifices are great, I have stopped focusing on Christ. When I feel that my service is too demanding, I have stopped focusing on Christ. When I see my sacrifice, my service, in light of what Christ sacrificed for me, I am humbled. When I remember what Christ has promised me for my pitiful labor and sacrifice—the forgiveness of all my sins, eternal life, a sin-free existence one day in heaven, adoption into His family, His presence to guide and direct me in life—I am reenergized. My service is one long "thank-you" for what He has done for me.

I decided a number of years ago that I was going to live my life in light of one all-consuming goal: to one day hear my heavenly Father say, "Well done, my good and faithful servant! . . . Come and share your master's happiness!" (Matthew 25:21). What I have had to give up or sacrifice in my life as a Christian does not begin to compare with what I have been given, even in this present life.

WHAT I FEEL BECOMES MORE IMPORTANT THAN WHAT I BELIEVE

There are moments when present pressures become more compelling than future promises. God says He will meet all my needs, but:

- I'm lonely, and God hasn't brought anyone into my life.
- I'm discouraged, and God hasn't made these feelings go away.
- God says He will provide for me, but I can't pay my bills and see no way out of my mess.

In times like this we begin to hear ourselves say things like, "I have to live in the real world. The life of faith just doesn't seem to be working for me. How can I adhere to principles like faith, honesty, truthfulness, and integrity when those who dismiss these principles are becoming wealthy, happy, and successful? Jesus said the meek shall inherit the earth, but they don't have it now! The ruthless, the ambitious, the movers and shakers have it now. The messages I hear at church and the things I read in the Bible contradict what I see in the 'real world.' "

If we have spouses, parents, friends, or children who are constantly ridiculing our faith or involvement at church and constantly pointing out how our faith actually hurts us; makes life more difficult for us; makes us appear fanatical; and costs us jobs, money, or fun, we might begin to believe it. We should also not be surprised. The most effective temptations will come to us when we are tired. Do not forget that Satan waited until Jesus had been fasting for forty days before Satan began his temptation.

It is tempting to just refer to this as weakness, but to have gained Christ, to have been forgiven of all our sins, to have had our Creator humble Himself to come to earth and die for us in the most humiliating way possible, to have been given eternal life and then to accuse Him of failing to hold up His end is nothing short of sin. Faithfulness to Him is not just appropriate, it is essential.

Jan has been a single in the church and struggled with loneliness for years. She has always been faithful to Christ and the church. She knows that she should not marry a nonbeliever, and therefore dating one is not an idea she would normally entertain. But she recently met Dave. He is a nice man who has treated her with kindness. They began dating, even though she had reservations, and they have been dating now for over a year. He is not a Christian; in fact, he is an agnostic. He has told Jan he has no intention of ever going to church with her or becoming a Christian. She has always believed that she should not marry a non-Christian, but Dave has asked her to marry him. There is no one else on the horizon, and she is desperately lonely.

All of a sudden Jan has competing loyalties. One is to her

Lord; the other is to herself. The Bible is clear about the fact that she should not be married to someone who does not share her faith (2 Corinthians 6:14–16). While I empathize with her situation, the truth is that a slow and dangerous idea has begun to emerge in her life—the idea that what she feels is really more important than what she believes. She is tired of living by faith. She wants answers to her prayers now, and if she doesn't get them, she will answer them herself.

Having a real, warm human being express love for you can be more compelling than a yet unfulfilled promise from God that He will "meet all your needs" (Philippians 4:19). The temptation to defect is real. But this time we know exactly what we are doing; our eyes are open. We know the issues; we know our options.

Jesus always praised those who could exercise faith in the face of circumstances that seemed to indicate the foolishness of the exercise. When Thomas, famous for his doubting of Jesus' resurrection, was finally face-to-face with the resurrected Jesus, our Lord instructed him to touch His hands and His side so that he could verify with his physical senses what he could not yet believe without them. "Thomas said to him, 'My Lord and my God!' Then Jesus told him, 'Because you have seen me, you have believed; blessed are those who have not seen and yet have believed' " (John 20:28–29).

If our feelings start to become more important than what we believe, we are in danger of defecting. But our defection won't be unwitting; it will be intentional. He does take it personally when we choose to disbelieve Him and rebel against His commands, however reluctantly.

SOMETHING ELSE BECOMES THE OBJECT OF OUR WORSHIP

Kevin has been trying to make a good life for his wife, Cheryl, and their two children. He is a bright, ambitious man who knows he can climb the corporate ladder. Kevin and Cheryl have been trying to reconcile the demands of his job with the demands of their faith. They have a nice house, drive a nice car, and are comfortable, but Kevin dreams bigger than that. He is sure that if he can just put in a lot of hours now, he can achieve his financial goals and then he will have more time (and money, he tells himself) to serve the Lord. He has been told what God wants from Him, and he has been reminded that you can't worship God and riches, but he tells himself he doesn't want to be rich, just comfortable.

So Kevin works long days and often on weekends. He tries to attend church, but it is hit and miss. He wants to get involved in church more, but he just doesn't have the time. Kevin knows the issues. He knows what God wants from him, but the truth is that he wants that job, that position of financial security, that position of accomplishment more than he wants to honor Christ or serve His church. He will never say it that way, but he knows it is true. Finally, he realizes that he has to make a choice: Either cut back at work or give up church altogether. Kevin gave up church. Several years later, the company gave up on Kevin.

Tom and Vanessa are avid athletes. Tom is involved with basketball and Vanessa with tennis. Athletics is their life. They have tournaments constantly, playing in several leagues. As a result, they rarely attend church anymore. Tom and Vanessa are Christians, but it just so happens that the church ministries and services coincide with their athletic pursuits. They have talked about this issue at length, but it always comes down to a choice. If they want to attend church and be involved in ministry, they will have to scale back their athletic schedule. Since they are both highly competitive, this is an extremely difficult thing to do. They pride themselves on not only their athletic ability but also their athletic condition. Frankly, to give all that up just to attend church and serve isn't an attractive option to them.

Worship is extreme devotion to a person or thing. One of the saddest defections is when a Christian chooses to worship something else more than God. This person's devotion to a cause, activity, person, or thing slowly dilutes his or her worship of God. Defection is the result.

In 1 Timothy 6:10, Paul warns Timothy of the danger of the love of money. After writing that people who want to get rich fall into temptation and a trap and many foolish and harmful desires that plunge men into ruin and destruction, he says something that is probably familiar to many of us. He writes, "For the love of money is a root of all kinds of evil. Some people, eager for money, have wandered from the faith and pierced themselves with many griefs."

Even though Paul is dealing here with money, I believe you can substitute many different desires in this verse. The love of security, the love of vanity, the love of pleasure, and many other things are also roots of evil. Notice what happens with such people: They don't just walk out of church one day; they wander away from the faith. It is slow, gradual, unsuspecting.

We don't just stop worshipping God; we slowly replace that worship with something different. Sometimes it is money or position, sometimes it is a relationship, sometimes it is popularity or acceptance, but though we once were devoted to God, now our devotion lies elsewhere. Because we aren't bowing down to a chubby little idol, praying to trees, or gazing at crystals, often we don't recognize it as worship. We break the first commandment—that we shall love the Lord our God with all our heart, soul, and strength and have no other God before Him—slowly, not all at once.

Maybe you have experienced this in your past. Maybe you are struggling with it right now. You know you made a choice, but did you make the right one?

There are many objects of worship; I have only listed a few. You don't need the list. Your objects of worship will probably come to mind fairly quickly. It may seem a very small thing in your mind, certainly not an object of worship. But are you sure? As C. S. Lewis once wrote, "It does not matter how small the sins are, providing that their cumulative effect is to edge the man away from the light and out into nothing. Murder is no better than cards if cards can do the trick."[36]

"To gain that which is worth having," someone once wrote, "it may be necessary to lose everything else." I remember when I was a brand-new Christian. As a young man, I had a newfound passion for Christ and a significant problem. Our youth group at church met on Sunday night for a time of fellowship and teaching. However, I was a Disney fan. Some of you might remember spending every Sunday evening watching *The Wonderful World of Disney*. The show was wholesome, fun, clean, and entertaining. It was not only a tradition for me; it was a passion. In my broken home, any flight into fancy or even fantasy was welcome respite. I longed for happy endings and warm, familiar traditions. I had few of my own. I *never* missed that show!

I felt terribly silly admitting that to anyone, but it was the truth. I can still remember the terrible struggle I underwent. I wanted desperately to go to the youth group and learn more about Jesus, and at the same time I desperately wanted to see Disney (this was before the age of VHS recorders). I literally had to make a choice. That was one of the hardest choices I ever made, but it forever changed the direction of my life. I chose the youth group. I wonder now what would have happened had I chosen to forego my growth in Christ to watch *The Wonderful World of Disney*.

It was not a choice between a good thing and a bad thing but a good thing and the best thing. The hardest choices usually are. I have had far more serious choices since then, but maybe none more pivotal. That youth group on Sunday evening changed my life. I was introduced to just who Jesus was and challenged to return His love with my service and worship. I did. Only God knew how hard the struggle was. He knows your struggle as well. This is where you will be tempted to defect. As wonderful a thing, person, or activity as it may be, if it steals or dilutes your worship from God or your service to His church, it is a sin.

There is an undeniable cost to following Jesus. We can defect from service and fellowship simply because we are weary of the cost of doing so. On the other hand, we can make a different choice. I have been blessed over the years by the faithful testimonies of average church folks faced with this perpetual struggle.

When they made the wrong choice initially and worshipped at other altars, leaving God and church behind, they were able and willing to correct. The Holy Spirit never stopped calling them back, and they soon began to realize that the pleasures of this world couldn't ultimately satisfy—something they needed to remember continually. They missed Jesus, and they returned to Him.

Lee Strobel, author of the book *The Case for Faith,* writes about the great preacher-evangelist Charles Templeton. At one time he pastored a large church in Toronto and helped found Youth for Christ in Canada. Then, abruptly, Templeton left the faith. Christians all over North America were shocked. Templeton went on to have a brilliant career as an editor of two of Canada's largest newspapers and ran once for prime minister. Strobel interviewed Templeton for his book and asked him about his denial of a belief in God. Templeton was unmoved about his departure and spoke calmly of why he could not accept the God of the Old Testament. Then Strobel asked him what he thought of Jesus. At this point Templeton bowed his head and wept. Through his sobs, he said, "I. . .miss. . .Him." [37]

He is the One who said, "Come to me, all you who are weary and burdened, and I will give you rest. Take my yoke upon you and learn from me, for I am gentle and humble in heart, and you will find rest for your souls. For my yoke is easy and my burden is light" (Matthew 11:28–30). This is the very verse that led me to Christ. He was the One I was hoping to find.

We will always be tempted to leave Him. We will be tempted to think church is all about us when it is all about Him. We will feel like leaving the church, abandoning our roles in the body of Christ. We will leave behind a body that is minus an eye, leg, arm, or finger and not realize at the moment the extent of what we are doing. We will grow tired of serving, sacrificing, and giving. When obedience ceases to be fun, we will be tempted to serve ourselves rather than Him. Mostly, we will be tempted to call our actions anything but sin.

You will be tempted to leave Him to find self-fulfillment somewhere else. You will know what you are doing. You will know it is wrong. Maybe you have already done it. Maybe it has been a long time since you've truly followed Jesus. Maybe you have spent a good part of your Christian life worshipping the wrong person or thing. That is the bad news. The good news is that it's never too late to start doing the right thing.

So, what will you do?

PART THREE

IDENTIFYING
THE SOLUTION

CHAPTER ELEVEN

COMING CLEAN

HONEST—ADJ.
frank and open

> "A spiritual community consists of people
> who have the integrity to come clean."
>
> LARRY CRABB[38]

When the Port Authority of New York and New Jersey ran a help-wanted ad for electricians with expertise at using Sontag connectors, it got 170 responses—even though there is *no such thing* as a Sontag connector. The Authority ran the ad to find out how many applicants falsify résumés.[39] We who are part of Christ's body, the church, need to understand that there is another Authority who checks spiritual résumés. He *will* expose the false résumés in time, unless He can convince us to do so voluntarily. What I urge now is that, fully aware of what we have done and are doing, we quickly come clean.

Sydney Harris has written that "honesty consists of the unwillingness to lie to others; maturity, which is equally hard to attain, consists of the unwillingness to lie to oneself."[40] Honesty and maturity are a difficult combination at times. Yet, this chapter is where all that we have discussed should naturally lead: how to begin the process of coming clean. Coming clean, confessing, admitting to the truth—however unpleasant it may be—is a voluntary process that God ordained and encouraged (Psalm 32:5; James 5:16; 1 John 1:9). We do not have to participate in this process, however; we can forego it. Many do. But most of us sincerely want to be honest before both God and others. Frankly, we're tired of the charade. It can be exhausting.

I have learned that it is possible, however, to listen to or read words that speak the truth about our true spiritual condition but remain safely detached from it. To my embarrassment, I must admit that I have at times made a science of it. I am much more comfortable being "enlightened" than being convicted. There are times when driving my car that I notice I am exceeding the speed limit. In those moments, I have been enlightened. Sadly, my enlightenment has not always resulted in my slowing down. If I am in a hurry, if I am sure there are no authorities around to catch me, I may be reluctant to feel the need for a change of behavior, especially if I'm in a hurry to get where I'm going.

There were certainly times in my past when I was enlightened about my spiritual deception, both personally and interpersonally, yet I made little effort to make a change in behavior. Like my escapades in driving, I am willing to risk "not getting caught" or at least "corrected" for awhile. As I have at times reached my destination without getting ticketed for speeding, I can also reach the conclusion that I may reach my personal goal or destination before getting spiritually "ticketed." And I have, many times. This is not a result of God's oversight of the issue but of His mercy and grace. He is a loving Father who first tries to get me to do the right thing of my own free will.

Coming clean is a scary thing; it challenges the spiritual myth we often create of and for ourselves. It might cost more than we're expecting. We're afraid that:

- Maybe we are unchangeable.
- We might discover more unpleasant truths about ourselves if we continue down this path.

- Everything spiritual we have done in the past will lose all its value.
- If we were honest about ourselves, we would no longer like ourselves.
- If we were honest with others, they would no longer feel the same about us.
- We would be giving up more than we would be gaining.
- God would no longer be able to use us.
- We might be called out of ministry.
- We would spend our remaining days wallowing in guilt.

It may never occur to us that there is any other way to live than the way we have been living. Unfortunately, when we deceive ourselves and others, we may ultimately seek to deceive even God. Even the attempt at deception creates a barrier between Him and us. God begins to feel distant to us. Church ministry begins to feel rote, mechanical. We can even throw ourselves into ministry with more zeal in the attempt to disguise our spiritual cover-up. Certainly God will see this spiritual activity and cut us some slack, we assure ourselves. But eventually this grows old.

Brent Curtis and John Eldredge wrote in their book *The Sacred Romance*, "There comes a place on our spiritual journey where renewed religious activity is of no use whatsoever. It is the place where God holds out His hand and asks us to give up our lovers and come and live with Him in a much more personal way. It is the place of relational intimacy that Satan lured Adam and Eve away from so long ago in the Garden of Eden. We are both drawn to it and fear it. Part of us would rather return to Scripture memorization, or Bible study, or service—anything that would save us from the unknowns of walking with God. We are partly convinced our life is elsewhere. We are deceived."[41] In coming clean, we are seeking to bridge the gap that has developed between God and us.

While we need to come clean, and it won't be easy, there is

some encouraging news about coming clean that you need to think about.

IT DOES NOT DEVALUE MINISTRY YOU HAVE BEEN INVOLVED IN

When we decide to come clean, we might be worried that all of our past ministries were worthless. After all, if we did a good thing for the wrong motivation, did we really do anything good in the first place? However, though we realize that we have at times been deceiving others about our true spiritual motivations and condition, that does not necessarily negate our past ministry. Who of us can claim to have had perfectly pure motivations for any ministry we have been involved in? As we have already seen, just because there is some insincerity or deception in our motivations, it doesn't mean that we weren't also genuinely motivated by a love for Christ and a desire to serve Him. Sin and obedience are in constant tension in each of our lives at any given moment. We might have been primarily motivated by an insincere desire, but we often still desired to do God's will. We were just doing it imperfectly, which, by the way, is the only way anyone does the will of God.

When Jesus called His twelve disciples, He almost immediately thrust them out into ministry. In fact, it amazed me how quickly He took men who certainly were not spiritual giants and gave them important kingdom tasks. Although these men vied continually for position and status in His inner circle, constantly displayed a lack of faith, and often let their ambitions run amuck, Jesus used them. He entrusted ministry to them, knowing that they were far from perfect and their motivations were not always pure, and at the end they all would abandon Him. Even three years later, at the end of His earthly ministry, in the upper room they were arguing about who was greatest among them. Yet it was to these men that He entrusted His church, His gospel, and His mission. God uses imperfect people; He always has. Amazingly,

He finds value in our imperfect ministry.

There are times when I have wanted to really "wow" people in the pulpit or during counseling or in a meeting. During those times I also wanted people to be challenged by God's Word and be prompted to further obedience and worship of Him. During the preaching, counseling, or leading, I was motivated by different ambitions. Yet, God used me to greatly challenge people and help them change. Although Paul makes it clear that one day our work will be judged (1 Corinthians 3:13), he also acknowledges that we are constantly at war with an internal foe: sin nature (Romans 7:14–25). Will only the results be judged, or will our struggles also be judged? I believe the latter. The struggles against sin are victories in themselves; it shows we are attempting to conquer the sin nature.

When I set out to wow the crowd, I never felt comfortable. I sincerely wanted to minister for Him alone. I was just amazed at how strong my sin nature and desire for personal attention could be. There would be moments in a sermon when I would truly be filled with His Spirit and be seeking to honor and glorify Him. Yet, in that same sermon, I might sense, through the way the congregation was responding, that they were impressed with me. I would instantly feel shame in it—but also joy. Sometimes I gave in; sometimes I resisted. God alone knows my true motivations. God is intimately acquainted with my weaknesses, and yet He entrusts ministry to me.

There has been only one person who had perfect motivations. Jesus, the perfect God/Man. There are no other perfect people with perfect motivations. They don't exist. They never have. Some of your favorite preachers, writers, singers, leaders, or missionaries have had numerous moments when their motivations for doing the ministry they were famous for were terribly diluted, insincere, and deceptive. Yet, their ministry, like yours, still has value. They struggled and wrestled, sometimes lost and sometimes won. In those times God was still able to use them for His service.

We offer to God an imperfect obedience because that is all we can muster. He knows that. We cannot be perfect in this life, so we can never minister, sing, lead, or witness with perfect motivations. Not ever. Period. Yet, knowing this, God still calls us to minister—imperfectly. And He still finds value in our ministry, however imperfect it may be.

My entire ministry has consisted of pure and impure motivations, surging back and forth in my heart like the ocean tide. This will *never* end in this life; yet, God still used me in amazing ways. When at times I wanted a position to further my spiritual résumé, He used me to encourage those who needed it. I was able to teach others things about God that helped them draw closer to Him and serve Him better. And you know what? That's exactly how He uses you. If every spiritual work of mine were written off my slate whenever I experienced improper motivations, every single work would have to be disregarded.

There never has been a time when I was not tempted to use my gifts and calling to a selfish end. But far from disqualifying my ministry, the fact that I was tempted often gave the ministry more value in God's eyes. I did not succumb to every temptation, but I struggled with the issue of obedience. God has used me to accomplish His will.

There is some encouraging news about coming clean: Your past is not a wash! Your work has not been wasted. Your ministry has not been without fruit. You have helped the kingdom of God, even in your weak moments, when you attempted to walk in obedience.

It Does Not Devalue the Progress You Have Made

At times, when I was made aware of my weaknesses and failures, I felt like I hadn't made any spiritual progress at all. I can recall moments in my life when my conscience and the Holy Spirit joined to convict me of less-than-sincere motivations. I would be devastated and, in my immaturity, would feel that not only had I not made any progress, but also I was going backward. It was terribly defeating and discouraging. Yet, in retrospect, the truth was just the opposite. I was making tremendous progress.

The more I became aware of how strong my sin nature still was, the more I understood the grace of God and the need for dependence upon the Holy Spirit for power over sin. Until that time I had felt that a good dose of willpower should suffice to keep me obedient to God. "Grace is the central invitation to life and the final word," says author Tim Hansel. "It's the beckoning nudge and the overwhelming, undeserved mercy that urges us to change and grow and then gives us the power to pull it off."[42]

We hide our spiritual blemishes because we think they should not be there. We disguise ourselves because we are sure we should look and act differently. There is truth in that, but the corresponding truth is that we are all in process. We are slowly being transformed into the image of Christ (Romans 12:2; 2 Corinthians 3:18). Saint Jerome said, "Every day we are changing, every day we are dying." We are changing into something we weren't before, dying to something we were before. This is the real life of every Christian.

Just for a moment, picture the process of transformation. To be transformed is to be changed from one form into another; yet, this process begins with the original form. In our case, that original form is a sinner desperately in need of God's grace and mercy. Our sin nature will never be completely subdued in this life, yet our new nature will empower a significant change. We will be transformed from the old nature into the image of Christ.

What does the image of Christ look like in a sinner? Look in the mirror! If you are in Christ, you are a new creature (2 Corinthians 5:17), but you are also an old creature. The good news is that the old creature is dying as the new creature is growing. As you make progress in this life, however, the old creature will linger; even in its death throes it will cling to you. You will perpetually struggle with truth, honesty, sincerity, and obedience.

C. S. Lewis wrote, "Fallen man is not simply an imperfect creature who needs improvement; he is a rebel who must lay down his arms. . . . This process of surrender—this movement full speed astern—is what Christians call repentance. Now repentance is no fun at all. It is something much harder than merely eating humble pie. It means unlearning all the self-conceit and self-will that we have been training ourselves into for thousands of years. It means killing part of yourself, undergoing a kind of death."[43]

If you are recognizing your own self-deception, interpersonal deception, and even divine deception, you are making tremendous spiritual progress. You are like a person who had just had eye surgery to repair blindness. At first your vision will be blurred. You will see only shadows, shades, and indistinct forms, but slowly your vision will improve and you will see more clearly. Though you will be saddened at the sin you now see so clearly, just remember when you were completely blind to it. God has always seen clearly what you are now only beginning to see, and He loves you anyway. It is His love that is opening your eyes—not just to your sin but to the immensity of His grace.

In recognizing and admitting that we have indeed been faking church, we are taking another step in our spiritual growth. You can certainly take steps backward if you want to, but you can also make tremendous strides forward. Furthermore, recognizing you have been faking church doesn't mean you haven't also been learning how to love more, how to serve more, how to obey more, and how to worship more.

Although at times we may be discouraged at the pace of our spiritual progress, we can always remember where we began and be assured that God is indeed finishing the good work He began in us (Philippians 1:6). Ironically, in those moments when God reveals unknown or unsuspected sin in our hearts, we have made the most progress. We are passing from one stage of spiritual growth to a much deeper one. "Repentance is not a fatal day when tears are shed," writes Ilion T. Jones, "but a natal day when, as a result of tears, a new life begins."[44]

IT IS NOT A CALL OUT OF MINISTRY
BUT A CALL TO RENEWAL WITHIN MINISTRY

Oswald Chambers wrote that self-knowledge is the first condition of repentance. Repentance is not simply an event that we involve ourselves in once to become Christians; it is a lifelong pursuit because there are always new things to repent of. To repent simply means to change our minds about our sins and then begin to change direction.

If you are involved in a ministry or service to Christ and His church and now realize that your service has been fake in many ways, God is not looking for your resignation. He is, in fact, looking for and preparing you for renewal. In a strange way, your ministry may look no different to others' eyes than it did before; only you and He will know the difference. Your repentance is often a private affair between you and God. Little might change on the outside, but your heart undergoes major spiritual surgery.

Whether you are a greeter, nursery worker, pastor, leader, teacher, missionary, worship leader, or in some other vital way a part of the church, God is not revealing the extent of your deception to cause you to leave ministry or the church or His service; it is to make your ministry real.

In an earlier chapter I spoke about the Sunday I had wanted to quit the pastoral ministry. I thought the church I had planted (and maybe God) no longer wanted me because of the trouble we had been experiencing. I expected them to ask me to leave the church.

After the sermon that day, I waited at the back of church to greet our people as they left. But on that fateful Sunday a young mother came up to me, and we began to talk. She shared how much this tiny church meant to her, how it had answered a prayer in her life, and how she was growing so much as a result. At the end of that discussion I experienced an epiphany. It was like a streak of lightning across my darkened spirit. I understood. God was showing me that I had made church all about me, and it was never meant to be all about me. It was about Him and people like that young mother.

Suddenly, I was filled with a warm love for this woman and all the rest of the people in my congregation. I no longer cared whether they were impressed with me, or if we'd ever be a large megachurch, or if I'd ever be a "successful" pastor. I no longer cared about all those personal ambitions that had been driving me for so long. They were suddenly so utterly worthless. I cared about that one woman and the small congregation. I suddenly felt a deep desire to shepherd and protect them. It almost seemed tragic. I realized what God had been trying to do in my life for the past three years, and now that I was there, I thought it was too late.

Only the expected request to leave the church never came. And I realized that God had never wanted to fire me—only to renew me. Yes, I had been a fake. Yes, I had been deceiving others and myself. Yes, I had even been using others. But no, He didn't want my resignation. He simply wanted me to become a real shepherd. It was the most pivotal day in my entire ministry. Coming clean wasn't a disaster; it was my salvation.

It Involves Entering a More Rewarding Fulfillment Than Self-Interests Could Ever Provide

If you are like me, you labor at times under the mistaken notion that if you just got your way, your life would be more fulfilling. You believe that God knows what you truly need, but you are fairly sure that He'll never give you what you really *want*. This is why we chase our own ambitions so desperately. We know God will give us what we need, but there are also a few things that we'd like to have, and we're fairly certain they aren't on God's "to do" list.

But we proceed on a false assumption. God is our creator. He is more intimately aware of how we are spiritually "wired" than anyone else is. He alone knows not only what we need but also what would truly bring us joy and happiness. Being omniscient means He knows all things, including all things about us.

When you chase your own personal ambitions, you probably never will be satisfied. No matter what progress you make, it will never be enough. A significant part of coming clean is trusting that if you quit chasing the things you think are important—namely, your own personal ambitions, your own desire for glory, your own self-interests—you can still find the true joy and happiness you seek.

The good news is that this is the *only* way you can find it. Curtis and Eldredge wrote, "We all want to be someone's hero or someone's beauty, to be in a relationship of heroic proportions. Contrary to legalistic forms of self-denial, we need to feel free to admit this without embarrassment. It is a core longing God Himself has placed within us and a deep part of our identity as men and women. It is in how we go about being heroes and beauties that is the issue."

They go on to say, "Most of us think of spiritual progress as requiring us to do more, even as our heart cries out to lay our burdens down. We renew our efforts at Bible study, Scripture memory, and Christian service, fearing that we will be discovered in our weakness and need. We try to use whatever small story we have been living in—competence, gifted speaking, service to others, and so on—to cross the chasm between living in the flesh and living spiritually, when only Christ can carry us to rest."[45]

I had been ministering in the small town of Rancho Santa Margarita, California, for over three years, pouring myself into the ministry, and I can honestly say it was frequently as stressful as it was fulfilling. I could not enjoy what God was doing through me and with me because I expected far more than I was seeing. I wanted bigger, more polished, more impressive. That's not what I got. So even though God was doing great things, I could not see them or really even enjoy them.

Yet, when God finally showed me what I had been chasing and what had been the source of my discontent, I was dramatically changed. Suddenly ministry took on a whole new meaning; people took on a whole new importance. Quite simply, I was finding joy in unexpected places and in unexpected ways. But, and this is important, unless I had come clean, I would have gone on missing the joy God had waiting for me. Coming clean allowed me to leave behind the unfulfilling pursuits of personal pleasure and glory for something I found infinitely more enjoyable. Enjoyment, fun, and pleasure are God's blessings, found in the places we often least expect.

Sometimes we think that what we need most to be fulfilled is a change of scenery, even with respect to our churches. It isn't. We need a change of focus. Each church is filled with people in genuine need, and being used of God to meet those needs is what we were designed for, what we were reborn for.

Coming clean involves believing that there is something more, something deeper, something far more meaningful than we have been chasing. Even ministry, when done for the wrong reasons, can become a grind, completely unfulfilling. Yet, that same ministry, when done with a changed heart, becomes a joy, a delight, and a true and genuine pleasure. Because you are no longer trying to please yourself or impress others, you are living for someone else, and Jesus wasn't kidding when He said that it is more blessed to give than to receive.

Did Mother Teresa have to drag herself to work every day, caring for those the world has no use for? Or did she find something so fulfilling that she couldn't leave it? The greatest blessing in life is not getting what you think you want out of it, even in ministry or the church. It is being used to make a real difference in someone's life, to be able to live without pretense and charades, to be able to understand the grace and goodness of our God who loves His imperfect children.

AND NOW. . .THE HARD QUESTIONS

There are hard questions that must be faced if we are to come clean: personal questions, private questions, uncomfortable questions. Are we willing to examine the *primary* reason we attend, serve, minister, lead, sing, preach, or help? Are we willing to look deeper and to admit the truth, even if we don't like what we find? Are we willing to see our service not through others' eyes or even our own but through His? Are we willing to entertain some unflattering truths about ourselves? This is the hard part.

I could spend more time listing all the benefits of coming clean, but at some point you've got to want to admit the truth because you are tired of the lie. In all true spiritual growth there is a price tag. I won't kid you, though; part of the price hurts. You need to know this. It is painful to admit that you aren't what you advertise yourself to be—even to yourself. It is nothing short of spiritual surgery, and the surgery is elective.

"The divine Surgeon," writes author and pastor Erwin Lutzer, "must be permitted to use His scalpel to cut, cleanse, and break, so healing can take place. In fact, such spiritual surgery is more painful than physical surgery. God doesn't use an anesthetic; He doesn't do His work while we are asleep. God can take any brokenhearted believer and make him or her a radiant, loving person. But when He performs such 'heart operations,' His children are wide awake."[46]

One of the hardest things in this world is to be willing to accept the truth about yourself, the real unvarnished truth. As I have exposed my own less-than-sterling motivations throughout this book, I'm sure the Holy Spirit and your conscience have begun to work in your heart as well. It is inevitable.

He will begin to point out the gaudy ornaments we have decorated ourselves with. The problem with decorations is that they are fastened to us unnaturally, like ornaments on a Christmas tree. But the Christian should resemble a fruit tree, not a Christmas tree. You don't decorate a fruit tree with fruit; it brings forth fruit naturally—first in the blossom, then in the fruit.

I won't pretend coming clean will be easy, but if you are willing to take the risk, the church is a pretty safe place to do it. "Everything in spiritual community is reversed from the world's order," writes psychologist Larry Crabb. "It is our weakness, not our competence, that moves others; our sorrows, not our blessings, that break down the barriers of fear and shame that keep us apart; our admitted failures, not our paraded successes, that bind us together in hope."[47]

You are not alone in needing to come clean. So does the person who sits next to you every Sunday, as well as the person preaching to you, and the singers, and the leaders, and everyone else. The church is a hospital where people are in varying stages of healing—even those who pretend that there's not a thing wrong with them! You are in good company.

There is nothing wrong with wanting to be spiritual or godly or even successful if it is in the right way. But when we try to portray a spirituality, godliness, or even success that isn't real, we are chasing rainbows. The greatest danger is not to our reputations but to our hearts. We fail to chase the right things, we fail to be moved by the right things, we fail to appreciate those things that are truly worthy.

A. W. Tozer once wrote:

> God may allow His servant to succeed when He has disciplined him to a point where he does not need to succeed to be happy. The man (or woman) who is elated by success and cast down by failure is still a carnal man. At best his fruit will have a worm in it. God will allow His servant to succeed when he has learned that success does not make him dearer to God or more valuable in the total scheme of things. We cannot buy God's favor with crowds or converts or new missionaries sent out or Bibles distributed. All these things can be accomplished without the help of the Holy Spirit. A good personality and a shrewd knowledge of human nature are all that any man needs to be a success in religious circles today. . . . We can afford to follow Him to failure. Faith dares to fail. The resurrection and the judgment will demonstrate before all worlds who won and who lost. We can wait.[48]

You may be a Sunday school teacher, Bible study leader, worship leader, performance artist, pastor, or the leader of a mission, denomination, or Christian organization. You may be a helper, someone who works behind the scenes, or even an infrequent attender at church. But no matter who you are, you need to come clean. You can do this in the wrong way or in the right way.

THE WRONG WAY AND
THE RIGHT WAY TO COME CLEAN

The wrong way to come clean is to discover the extent of your deception or defection and wallow in guilt. When your deception is discovered, you can be overwhelmed with sadness. This is appropriate. The facts are out and the truth is clear. You have failed. You have failed Him. To fail God, to misrepresent Him in any way, is one of the most painful experiences you can have.

In Scripture we have two examples of men who had inflated views of their own spirituality. They were self-deceived and then proceeded to try and deceive others. These two men faked it in serious ways. The first was the apostle Peter. As we alluded to earlier, Peter had convinced himself that he was spiritually much stronger and braver than he really was. Jesus knew better. When Jesus began to speak about His own imminent arrest at the Last Supper, He revealed that each and every disciple there would desert Him. Peter's inflated view of his own spiritual maturity demanded a retraction: "Even if all fall away on account of you, I never will," he protested proudly (Matthew 26:33).

We know the rest of the story. Peter, after Jesus' arrest, denies that he even knows Jesus (Matthew 26:69–75). Peter's deception is unraveled before his eyes. I can't even imagine what he felt when, as Luke's Gospel tells us, Jesus looked right at him in the midst of his denial (Luke 22:60–62).

Following Peter's failure, we read in Matthew 27 of Judas's betrayal. This famous apostle had already betrayed Jesus earlier to the Jewish authorities for thirty pieces of silver, but when he saw Jesus condemned by the Sanhedrin, he was "seized with remorse" (Matthew 27:3). He returned the money and admitted that he had sinned and betrayed innocent blood. But when he realized that his actions could not reverse the process of Jesus' death, his only solution was to commit suicide.

Often when we are confronted with our own failures, we wallow in guilt and despair. We attempt to punish ourselves for our failures. Sadness over sin and deception is normal, but it can go too far. In fact, this is to further fake church, for it is based on the assumption that we should be able to be perfect: perfectly faithful, perfectly loyal, perfectly honest, perfectly moral, perfectly everything. We come to believe that we should not fail. Wrong! Failure is inevitable. We should not *seek* to fail, but we must not come to believe we can avoid it. Jesus expected it or He would never have entrusted imperfect men and women with kingdom responsibilities.

Did Peter deny Christ? Yes. Did Judas deny Christ? Yes! Which was the greater betrayal? Peter denied even knowing the man he had promised to die for. Judas denied Jesus by selling Him out for money. They both failed badly. But Peter found that his Master was forgiving, understanding, a High Priest who could sympathize with weaknesses. He not only was welcomed back into fellowship by Jesus upon His resurrection, he was further entrusted with service (John 21:15–19). Judas also had an opportunity to receive forgiveness, but he chose a different path.

Coming clean should result not in our wallowing in guilt and attempts to punish ourselves, but in a renewed understanding of our true weakness and appreciation for the Lord's love, grace, and mercy toward us. We should note that Jesus never asked Peter to do any penance for his failure. Peter went back to fishing after Jesus' death and resurrection, but Jesus sought him out and reminded him that He had called him to a different task: "Feed my lambs" and "take care of my sheep."

Despite our sins, those of us who are His children can rest assured that "there is now no condemnation for those who are in

Christ Jesus" (Romans 8:1). Our sins of commission and omission have all been paid for, judged, and removed from us as far as the east is from the west (Psalm 103:12). Yes, we are fakes, but we are forgiven fakes. He forgives our lies, deceptions, and hypocrisy.

COMING CLEAN BEFORE OTHERS

As we come clean before God, it may be necessary to come clean before others as well. To come clean is to admit before others that we are indeed weak, prone to failure, and totally dependent upon the Holy Spirit for our strength. We not only need the help of the Holy Spirit, we need the help of others. We are not all we appear to be; we never have been. We aren't as spiritual, holy, selfless, confident, or faithful as we have appeared to be. And at times we have appeared to be these things on purpose, to impress others. We need others to help us, pray for us, and encourage us, which is precisely what God has created the church for.

Writer and editor Adam Holz admits:

> *Few things make me feel more vulnerable than admitting my weaknesses and then sitting quietly as others lift those needs before our Father. It's one thing to ask for a friend's counsel in a tough situation. But it's something else entirely to admit that I don't have all the resources I need to make life work, to confess that I'm not in control and don't know what to do. Genuine dependence on one another is easier to talk about than to practice. I often hear about the role of the Body of Christ, how different gifts have been given for the support of the members of the body. But in reality, it's so much easier to act as free agents than as interdependent team players. I can acknowledge the theoretical importance of others' support while working hard to live in functional independence. When I am willing to ask for and receive others' prayers, however, it opens the door to blessings I can't receive when I rely upon my*

energies and talents alone. I recognize—and actually begin to believe—that others want to undergird my life in times of weakness. I discover that it's good and right to experience the provision of the Body of Christ in reality, not just in theory.[49]

There are times and places when it might be most appropriate to come clean before a larger audience (such as acts of immorality within church, and or leadership, etc.). However, each of us can begin to come clean to one person or to a few close friends. It can be as simple as saying casually, "You know, I'm not all I appear to be at times. I *don't* have it all together. My spiritual life isn't perfect, even though it might appear that way from the way I act and talk sometimes. I'm learning to be more honest about myself and stop padding my spiritual résumé."

Once you have done this, it becomes easier the next time. Believe me, I know. People don't typically respond with judgment, they respond with tremendous grace and acceptance. Chances are, there will be a long conversation concerning how they "fake church" as well. It takes courage to come clean, and people admire that.

There is no specific way to come clean before others—no methodology, no rules or regulations. It is really just relearning to walk in the truth. It is making a commitment not to parade all your strengths and not to hide all your weaknesses anymore. It is being absolutely convinced that you are accepted, faults and all, by the Savior of your soul. The greatest motivation for change in the Christian life is not guilt or fear; it is love for Christ and gratitude at how He has forgiven you and loved you in spite of your failures.

COMING CLEAN BEFORE GOD

I have purposely left this until last, when in reality it should come first. But I wanted to make sure that the last thing you read in this chapter is the need to come clean before God. I hope I have convinced you of His attitude toward us, despite our failures, deceptions, and faults. He is never surprised by our sins, only our attempts to cover them.

Dorothy Sayers (1893–1957) once wrote, "Like the Father of the Prodigal Son, God can see repentance coming a great way off and is there to meet it, the repentance is the reconciliation."[50] There are no magic words of contrition or apology. In fact, at times words are totally unnecessary. We know now that He sees, He understands, He has seen all along. Chances are He has begun to show us even more than we suspected. Attitudes and motivations we were oblivious to before are now fresh in our minds. Incidents when we have been fake, plastic, or insincere have been paraded before our hearts and minds.

The reason I know this is because I have experienced this in my own heart, but I can come clean before God because I am absolutely convinced that He loves me with an intensity I cannot imagine. He is not mad at me; He is not punishing me; He is transforming me as He promised He would do. This is part of that transformation. It is uncomfortable at first, like new shoes, but eventually the old ones need to be replaced.

Coming clean before God is almost a misnomer. There is nothing God does not know about us, but the process of confession, of agreeing with Him, is spiritually renewing. We do not confess to inform God but to obey Him and remind ourselves. The process of coming clean before God removes all barriers, lies, deceptions—all those things that we have hidden behind. We can now approach God more openly and honestly—maybe for the first time. The personal relationship with God we've talked about for such a long time may actually become just that: personal, intimate.

"No amount of falls will really undo us if we keep on picking ourselves up each time," writes C. S. Lewis. "We shall of course be very muddy and tattered children by the time we reach home, but the bathrooms are all ready, the towels are put out, and the clean clothes are in the cupboard. The only fatal thing is to lose one's temper and give it up. It is when we notice the dirt that God is most present in us: It is the very sign of His presence."[51]

So why not come clean? You might as well get used to it. You'll have to do it again. In fact, it will become habitual after awhile, but you won't mind. You will always find forgiveness, acceptance, and love from Him. You will fail again and again, but each time you come clean, each time you know you are forgiven, your desires will slowly change. You will begin to love Him more than your reputation. You will start to want to please Him more than anything else. Gratitude will build within you a love for Him that makes you want to be real, even if that reality is not as impressive as your former spiritual façade. Faking it will bother you more than it used to. Then you will know, then you will understand. The change will have begun, and you will welcome it.

CHAPTER TWELVE

A COMMAND PERFORMANCE:
Giving the Performance of Your Life

SIMPLIFY—V.
to make simpler,
less complex

> "The only path to pleasure is in pleasing God."
>
> RICHARD OWEN ROBERTS

I was asked to speak at my daughter's high school baccalaureate. Because I have spoken at youth camps, conferences, Christian schools, and different churches, it is not intimidating or difficult for me to speak in front of people. So when I was asked to speak for ten minutes, you would not think that would be much of a problem.

In this particular situation, however, ten minutes was a lifetime! In truth, I dreaded it. I spent far more time worrying over and preparing that ten-minute message than I have preparing a thirty-five-minute sermon for church or a forty-five-minute message for a conference. The reason was the diversity of the audience. I knew that there would be not only Christians at the baccalaureate but also people of different faiths, other religious leaders, parents, and graduating seniors. To create a message that would speak to all of them and still honor God was a terribly difficult task.

The more diverse the audience, the more work it takes to keep their attention and get your point across. It can be mentally and emotionally exhausting. Who is the audience? Are they young couples with children, singles, college students, high school students, senior citizens? There are a great number of factors that must be taken into consideration.

What does this have to do with faking church? Faking church is ultimately a performance we give. We put on our masks, adjust our costumes, rehearse our lines, check our makeup, and then go out on stage. Whether our stage is a large one in front of many people or a small one in front of a few, the process is the same. But, as you have probably already learned, it takes a great deal of energy to choreograph our activities so that the right people will notice them.

When a celebrity is asked to perform before a king or queen, it is called a command performance. Even if others are in attendance as well, the main audience the performer is concentrating on is the royal one. They are the focus of the performance. Because of the royal nature of the audience at a command performance, the performers seek to give the performance of their lives. No matter who else is in attendance, if they haven't pleased the royalty, they have failed.

Since we were little children and first heard "Oh, look at that, isn't that adorable!" we have been playing to the crowd. Our audiences have been our families, friends, and acquaintances. We performed at school for our schoolmates, at home for our families, around our neighborhoods for our friends, and yes at church. As the years go on and we get older, our audiences expand and it takes more work to keep up the performance, to adjust it for everyone. Sometimes the pressure to perform gets overwhelming. We begin to long for a different, simpler life.

Jesus never applauded religious performances; He exposed

them. Frequently. He also never gave a religious performance Himself. Maybe this helps to explain some of His unpopularity with the religious rulers of His day. What everyone else was very comfortable doing, He detested. In fact, it is clear that Jesus' whole life was a command performance before His heavenly Father.

- Jesus did not come to impress us but to do the will of His Father (Hebrews 10:7–10). He played continually to an audience of One.

- Jesus said, "The world must learn that I love the Father and that I do exactly what my Father has commanded me" (John 14:31). Over and over Jesus referred to His Father in heaven.

- "My food," said Jesus, "is to do the will of him who sent me and to finish his work" (John 4:34).

- "I have come down from heaven not to do my will but to do the will of him who sent me" (John 6:38).

It is for this very same audience that we are called on to perform: our heavenly Father. Not to perform in the sense of pretending but to perform in the sense of seeking to please. You might feel this is an incredibly intimidating performance, but it is actually the easiest. Human audiences are frequently jealous, envious, critical, hostile, malicious, untrustworthy, and unkind. He, on the other hand, is perfect love. What others don't know about us, what we try so desperately to keep concealed, He sees. He has always seen it; yet, He loves us.

When our lives are lived to impress others, we are forgetting that the message we intend won't always get through. We learn some painful lessons.

People Can Misinterpret
Your Good and Selfless Activities

I remember one year a family in our church, unknown to anyone, was hurting financially. A woman in our church learned that this family had been living on credit cards for months. Concerned, she approached me. She wanted to know if we had any money in the church to help those who were in desperate financial straits. We did, and she excitedly called her friend to announce that the church was willing and able to help her. The reaction she got was totally unexpected. The woman became furious with her, making it very clear she hadn't wanted anyone to know about her family's situation and that she was insulted that help had even been offered. They could take care of themselves, she stated emphatically. The lady who had tried to help came to me totally bewildered.

One of the difficulties of living our lives for the response of other people is that the response will not always be an appropriate one. Even if we do something truly kind and noble, it can be completely misunderstood. We have grown up hearing about how we should be living to serve each other, but spiritually that is not the real goal, as laudable as it may seem. We are putting the cart before the horse.

"If you are going to live for the service of your fellowmen," warns Oswald Chambers, "you will certainly be pierced through with many sorrows, for you will meet with more base ingratitude from your fellowman than you would from a dog. You will meet with unkindness and two-facedness, and if your motive is love for your fellowmen, you will be exhausted in the battle of life. But if the mainspring of your service is love for God, no ingratitude, no sin, no devil, no angel, can hinder you from serving your fellowmen, no matter how they treat you. You can love your neighbor as yourself, not from pity, but from the true centering of yourself in God."[52]

Many Christians have been discouraged by the responses to

their attempts to be good or kind. If you aren't careful, you can lose heart in doing good things. On the other hand, even if people misunderstand your motivations, the good news is that God doesn't. You can be sure that He knows not only what you did but also why you did it. He alone knows that you were trying to help, even if the person you were trying to help doesn't.

When we choose to live our lives as command performances before our heavenly Father, we can know that our actions are fully understood and accepted. Even when they are imperfect, they are accepted. As A.W. Tozer said, "God expects of us only what He has Himself first supplied. He is quick to mark every simple effort to please Him and just as quick to overlook imperfections when He knows we meant to do His will."[53] From His perfect Son, Jesus, the heavenly Father expected perfect reactions, perfect obedience, perfect submission. He knows that this is impossible for us, but that doesn't mean that our feeble attempts don't bless Him.

When my children were young and I would give them a chore to do, they would soon report back to me, cheerfully, that they had completed it. In fact, they would drag me to the scene of the chore to get my reaction. Whether it had been to clean up an area, or put something away, or feed a pet, I would usually notice that it had not been done perfectly. But I would look at their young faces, so full of excitement, and hear myself saying, "Good job! You're a real helper-head" (a Schaefferism). They would giggle with glee. They wanted desperately to please me and had done their best. I accepted their efforts with great delight. The tasks might not have been done perfectly, but they were immature and could not do them perfectly yet. What was so pleasing was their attitude: They *wanted* to please me. That is what meant the most, and I accepted their service gladly. It was their love I was responding to and their hearts—not simply their actual performances.

That is how our heavenly Father responds to us as well. Do you think that everything you do has to be perfect before it will please God? God no more expects perfection from you than He expected sin from Jesus.

People Don't Always Appreciate What You Do!

Regardless of our motivations, whether sincere or diluted, when we do something kind for others, we are hurt or angry if they don't appreciate it. When we've made a sacrifice of some kind or have gone out of our way to do something for them and we get little or no thanks, we might think twice about doing it again.

A woman who lived in Washington, D.C., worked with her church among the homeless. They served the homeless meals on a regular basis. This woman had a very close friend she was always trying to get involved with the homeless ministry. The friend had resisted joining the ministry many times, but finally she agreed to give it a try. Afterward, as they were heading home, the woman who had invited her friend was understandably curious as to how her friend had liked the ministry experience.

"I didn't like it. I don't want to do it again," she said.

Her friend was surprised. "Why didn't you like it?" she asked.

"Because they didn't appreciate all the things we did for them."

The fact is that she was right. People in need don't always respond with gratitude. Why did the one woman enjoy working in the ministry even when others didn't appreciate it? Because before each meal she would pray the same prayer: "Oh, Lord, as You pass before me in this line today, may I treat You with love, respect, and kindness."

She was playing to an audience of One.

"Be careful not to do your 'acts of righteousness' before men, to be seen by them," Jesus said. "If you do, you will have no reward from your Father in heaven. So when you give to the needy, do not announce it with trumpets, as the hypocrites do in the synagogues and on the streets, to be honored by men. I tell you the truth, they have received their reward in full. But when you give to the needy, do not let your left hand know what your right hand is doing, so that your giving may be in secret. Then *your Father, who sees what is done in secret,* will reward you" (Matthew 6:1–6, author emphasis added).

God appreciates our service to Him. As imperfect as it may be, He appreciates it. Yet, He seeks a private showing. He does not pay any attention to our public performances, designed to call attention to ourselves. He is only interested in what we do for Him. Those who try to draw attention to their works, Jesus said, "have received their reward in full" (Matthew 6:16). The Pharisees of the first generation were shocked at this revelation and refused to believe it. Some of their spiritual descendants still struggle with it.

When we are seeking to please God by loving those who are unlovable, God appreciates it! When we are seeking to humble ourselves before others, when we could try to call attention to ourselves, it pleases God. An audience of One is infinitely more appreciative of our service than billions of people.

We struggle so much with appearance, wanting to please and impress others. But if we can shift our focus from pleasing others to pleasing Him, we can find far greater personal fulfillment. It is His reaction, His smile we are working for. And, truthfully, His comes much easier than theirs does.

People Aren't Always Worthy of Your Help or Service

Not long ago a man showed up at our church and asked to counsel with me. He did not attend our church, and I had never met him before. He seemed to be a sad fellow who had been going through some difficult times. He shared that he was a Christian and related some of his spiritual background, which helped to confirm the truthfulness of his story to me. Then, after I had talked with him about some struggles he was having in his life and we had prayed, he mentioned with embarrassment that he had a few physical needs as well. Could the church help? I could tell it was hard for him to ask.

He needed a room for the night—just one night—and a little money for food. I left the office and drove with him to get a room for the night at a local motel. On the way I noticed his gas gauge was on empty, so I told him to pull into a local gas station and I filled his tank. Then I gave money enough for food for several days. I was glad our church could help this man in need.

Later, as I was sharing this expenditure with the treasurer in our church, he asked the name of the man I helped. When I told him the name, he laughed. "Oh, he's a con. He did the same thing to me about eight years ago." Then he proceeded to tell me what this man probably had told me. I had been conned.

Face it: As much as we'd like to deny it, some people aren't worthy of help. They are lazy, or bitter, or unpleasant, or annoying, or ungrateful, or demanding. And that's *after* we have helped them! We can very quickly lose our motivation for serving these types of people. But I am reminded that Jesus never did.

"As he was going into a village, ten men who had leprosy met him. They stood at a distance and called out in a loud voice, 'Jesus, Master, have pity on us!' When he saw them, he said, 'Go, show yourselves to the priests.' And as they went, they were cleansed. One of them, when he saw he was healed, came back, praising God in a loud voice. He threw himself at Jesus' feet and thanked him—and he was a Samaritan. Jesus asked, 'Were not all ten cleansed? Where are the other nine? Was no one found to return and give praise to God except this foreigner?' Then he said to him, 'Rise and go; your faith has made you well' " (Luke 17:12–19). Nine were healed, yet only one showed any gratitude. Sound familiar?

Ingratitude! It is a mistake to believe that everyone that Jesus healed was a nice person or was grateful or worthy in some way. *None* of them were worthy. They were healed because Jesus felt compassion on them. Some of them were probably lazy, dishonest, malicious, gossipy, violent, backbiting, vindictive people. But He healed them. It was His Father's will. His Father loved them and He loved them. In the midst of their suffering, even the suffering some of them might have brought on themselves, He cared.

When we choose to play to an audience of One, we will be willing to serve those who either will not or cannot ever thank us or appreciate what we've done for them. He is the One we will be humbling ourselves before; He is the One we will be serving, caring for, sacrificing for. Unless we understand that, we will always struggle with motivation for our service to those whom we deem unworthy.

When we serve for the wrong reason, we begin to set ourselves up as judges. We determine who is really worthy of help or service and who is not. After all, we don't want to be wasting our time on people who aren't deserving. But when we are primarily serving Him, we see Him in every need that comes our way. Of course, we can neither meet every need nor give to every organization; we don't physically have the resources. But God brings people and opportunities into our sphere of influence. When we are focused on serving Him, we seek to meet those needs as if we were serving Jesus Himself (Matthew 25:26–30).

His Distressing Disguise

We are often tempted to minister where it will be most productive for us. In a world in which we are often judged by how much we can produce, the church can be just as competitive an environment as anywhere else. We want to see results. We want to pour our energies into activities that will demonstrate we are doing something significant. The only problem is that not all significant ministries can be judged that way. Some people we help (like the ones listed below) won't produce anything for the church in terms of healthy statistics, increased attendance, impressive changes in their condition, or financial giving.

- Lonely seniors at home or in a nursing facility
- The people who are irregular in church attendance
- The poor and disenfranchised
- The mentally retarded
- The terminally ill

Of course the list could go on, but you get the idea.

I recently went to visit a ninety-six-year-old woman named Elsie at a nursing home near us. She had been a part of our church many years before I arrived. A couple named Paul and Doris took me to visit her, and Paul served her communion. When we arrived, she was asleep, her head resting on a table. She was very ill, not even able to lift her head high enough to see my face. Several days later, she passed away. At that time I learned that another woman in our church, Cathy, had been visiting her regularly for many years.

Elsie had nothing to give. Though she was highly intelligent and had been a missionary teacher for years, she could also be crotchety, cranky, and opinionated. Yet, Cathy visited her regularly. Paul and Doris took communion to her. Why? There was little to be gained from visiting Elsie. She was not the beginning of a great ministry. She did not build up everyone's self-esteem. This act wouldn't pad any résumés or increase church attendance or fill the financial coffers. They did it because they love Jesus.

Their love for Jesus was translated into a love for Elsie. They did it for Him. They understood that in visiting Elsie, they were visiting Jesus. Our heavenly Father cares when people like Elsie are lonely, sad, in pain, hurting, or discouraged. It was love for their heavenly Father that motivated their love for Elsie. If our goal is to receive praise, attention, or reputation for the things we do, the Elsies of the world will be avoided. And, tragically, too often they are.

Years ago, in a church I pastored in southern California, a man named John McCullough became a part of our church. John was about sixty-two years old when he began to attend. He was also mentally retarded. John could be loud, inappropriate, and taxing, but he also could be tender, sympathetic, and very lovable. John never missed church; it was his whole life. At times he accosted our visitors, feeling his role was to be the official church greeter. He was a little deaf, so he spoke loudly! His hands were covered with scaly blemishes; his face sported perpetual stubble and nicks where his ninety-four-year-old mother routinely cut him shaving. He wore old black-rimmed glasses with lenses as thick as Coke bottles, and his Levis were cinched up around his belly button. At times he developed crushes on some of our ladies, and we had to inform him he couldn't keep giving them hugs and loitering around them all the time. Are you getting the picture?

But that church loved John and accepted him. They took him camping and on family outings or to movies, and they gave him and his mother gifts. When John developed cancer, they visited his hospital room and took comic books, balloons, calendars, and cards. When he went home to die, they were there—helping, watching, praying. An inordinate amount of time and energy was poured into John that could never be quantified. There would be precious little to be seen from this enormous investment. But everything done for John was done for Jesus, and that is the best kind of investment (Matthew 25:40).

Mother Teresa wrote that being happy in Jesus means. . .

Loving as He loves,
Helping as He helps,
Giving as He gives,
Serving as He serves,
Rescuing as He rescues,
Being with Him for all the twenty-four hours,
Touching Him in His distressing disguise. [54]

His distressing disguise. Unless we are focused on our audience of One when we serve others, we may very well miss "His distressing disguise." What about the man I helped? Do I regret it? No. He did need a place to stay, and he did need food and gas. What I did, I did for Jesus. God will deal with this man on his attitudes and behavior; my job is to love him, even when he is unlovely—the same way God loves me. I won't help him in the same way next time, but I will continue to try to help him.

Playing to an audience of One does not denigrate or deny healthy spiritual ambition; it simply turns it in a different direction. Can anyone honestly feel that Mother Teresa had no ambition? She was consumed with ambition. Her ambition was to love Jesus and to serve Him, and she did that through ministering to the untouchable, unproductive, unwanted people of India.

I don't want to leave the impression that having ambitious goals for church or ministry is wrong. There are many worthy spiritual ambitions. I want to address only one thing: If we are performing for the wrong audience, our ambitions have little ultimate value in God's eyes.

Pastor and author Erwin Lutzer rightly said, "Our generation has been taught to ask, What's in it for me? Will it give me pleasure? Profit? Security? Fulfillment? We are not necessarily opposed to God; we just fit Him in wherever He is able to help *us*. The idea that our wills should be subjected to His control, even when our personal ambitions are at stake, is not easy to accept. We can assent mentally to God's control, but in practice, we might still spend our lives pleasing ourselves."[55]

Shifting Focus

So how do we go about making the shift from faking it to sincere and genuine service? How do we begin to play to an audience of One? It's certainly not something we just go out and do without some considerable thought. For one thing, we aren't used to it. It requires a different frame of reference and time to think. But, as we think about it, there are some steps we will need to take to begin the journey.

Admit the Truth

I like to be complimented. I enjoy praise, awards, attention, and reputation. I try not to go looking for them, but I enjoy them when they come. I know I probably sound like a spiritual cad, but I don't think I'm all that different from anyone else. Furthermore, those things aren't bad in and of themselves.

After all, how can we tell if we're having an impact on others or really encouraging them or making a difference in their lives unless they tell us? And if we are having a positive impact, the result will be complimentary, positive, and affirming words from them.

On the dark side, we often desire a great spiritual reputation, whether we deserve it or not. At times we like to look good for the wrong reasons. We are willing to fake it to get what we want. We are willing to leave the wrong impression or even cause it, if the situation demands. The difficult part is admitting that.

It is only when all our pretense is stripped away, and we realize that even our righteousness and good deeds are inadequate to offer to a perfect and holy God, that we truly understand His love for us. No amount of good works or philanthropy can make God love us. No honors, awards, or reputation can impress God with our goodness. Isaiah the prophet, who understood God's holiness and people's unholiness, laments, "All of us have become like one who is unclean, and all our righteous acts are like filthy rags" (Isaiah 64:6). Yet, we discover that it is this holy God, who sees all our sin, all our evil, and yet loves us without reservation (Romans 5:8).

Without an admission of the truth about our condition, we cannot even hope to understand His love for us. Until we understand the extent of His love for us, we can't hope to truly serve Him out of pure hearts of gratitude. Our good works will be seen as little more than spiritual dues we pay to keep in good with God.

So there it is. Admitting the truth about the real condition of our hearts and motivations is essential to understanding the love of God. Entering the love of God is the key to genuine service. It is only when we are absolutely convinced that God loves us—with our self-centered goals, selfish ambitions, and desire for reputation—that we can be totally vulnerable and honest without fear. Bernard of Clairvaux said, "There are two reasons for loving

God: No one is more worthy of our love, and no one can return more in response to our love."[56]

When you don't feel the need to keep up a charade before God, you will begin to lose the need to keep it up before others. If you can begin here, there is great hope!

FACING THE HARD QUESTIONS

Bishop Fulton Sheen wrote, "Most of us do not like to look inside ourselves for the same reason we don't like to open a letter that has bad news."[57] To begin to change, really change, we will be forced to ask ourselves some hard questions—simple to ask, hard to answer, but ask them we must. "Self-knowledge is so critically important to us in our pursuit of God and His righteousness that we lie under heavy obligation to do immediately whatever is necessary to remove the disguise and permit our real selves to be known," wrote A. W. Tozer.[58]

These questions, of course, depend greatly on your particular situation. But I think they are general enough to be applied to all our different situations.

Why am I *really* doing the things that I'm doing?
    At church
    In ministry
    At home

Who am I really serving? Who am I really trying to impress?

Why did I leave?
    Church
    Ministry
    Service
    Fellowship

What was the real cause of my defection?
    Personally
    Interpersonally
    Before God

If I have stayed, why have I stayed?
    In church
    In ministry
    In service
    In fellowship

Yes, these are hard questions. No, you may not even know the real answers for awhile; it takes time. But yes, you need to ask them; yes, you need to wrestle with them; yes, it will be painful at times. God may reveal things to you that may make you sad or ashamed, if you are brave enough to risk the encounter. But as C. S. Lewis said, "The hardness of God is kinder than the softness of men, and His compulsion is our liberation."[59]

Oliver Wendell Holmes reminds us that "The great thing in this world is not so much where we stand, as in what direction we are moving."[60] These questions will move us in the right direction. They will get us to think as God thinks about the things that most concern Him.

"A man should never be ashamed to own he has been in the wrong," wrote Alexander Pope, because it is simply another way of saying "he is wiser today than he was yesterday."[61]

RENOVATE OUR AMBITIONS

As I have said earlier, I don't want to leave the impression that ambition or desire by itself is a bad thing or necessarily a sinful longing. God places within a man, a woman, or even a young person an intense desire to fulfill some ministry or service that God Himself has called them to.

While a young man, Joseph was given a dream of being a leader among his brothers, and David was called as a young shepherd to be the future king of Israel. Samuel was set aside to serve God as a judge in Israel. The prophets were called by God, as were the apostles and Paul.

God has called each of us to a certain and specific service for Him, and it should be our ambition to fulfill that service. To have a spiritual ambition is a wonderful thing. God has often placed our spiritual ambitions there for His purposes, even when our own motivations were less than pure at the time.

The fact remains that our ambitions need to be examined closely. Chances are, they are in need of renovation. Not demolition, renovation. Demolition destroys everything that has been built and starts over; renovation takes what has been built and improves on it. It is renovation that God is calling us to in this issue.

As a wallpaper hanger for over ten years, I was involved in many home renovations. I once hung wallpaper for a celebrity who had bought a nice, but definitely unassuming home in a suburban tract in southern California. If you looked at the home from the outside, it would seem identical to the other cookie-cutter homes on the block. But inside, ah, inside was another thing. Every wall was painted or wallpapered professionally, expensive furniture was everywhere, unique and valuable art decorated the walls. The house was absolutely transformed from a plain tract home to a veritable mansion on the inside. But the outside looked the same. Renovation!

Serving doesn't change—why we serve changes.

Leading doesn't change—why we lead changes.

Helping doesn't change—why we help changes.

It is impossible to admit the truth, answer the hard questions, or renovate your ambitions until you are confident that you are truly loved by God and accepted, forgiven, and precious to Him. But once you are confident of His love, your natural response will be intense gratitude and joy.

When I was a young Christian, I took all my carnal competitiveness and applied it to my faith. I didn't just want to be an ordinary disciple of Jesus; I wanted to be someone special! I thought of heaven and the kingdom of God and dreamed of being a person of some renown in heaven. I was like James and John, seeking a special place in heaven, special honor, special recognition. This might be why I was so focused on accomplishing great things in my faith.

Today, I no longer desire place or status in heaven. As I honestly look back upon my life and reflect upon my own sinfulness and inadequacies, even as a believer for some thirty years, I am ecstatic that I have been granted entrance into the gates of heaven at all (2 Peter 1:11). I am absolutely confident of my salvation and equally confident that only by His grace am I going. I will be honored to be a street sweeper in heaven. I will gladly take the lowest position available, not out of false modesty but because it is enough for me to just be there. To live with Him forever is enough. Nothing else matters anymore.

An understanding of His grace has revolutionized my ambition. It is a great joy to serve Him alone. Yes, in serving Him I serve others, but I receive my greatest joy from knowing that my attempts—however diluted or inadequate—please Him. It is my joy to serve Him.

BEGIN YOUR COMMAND PERFORMANCE

If Jesus were to return to earth and visit your home and ask you for help in some way, how would that make you feel? The Bible teaches that He *has* come to ask help of you. But He disguises His requests.

Maybe He asks you to just sit with him for awhile and keep Him company.

Maybe He asks you to come and visit Him because He is lonely.

Maybe He asks you to cook a meal for some of His friends.

Maybe He asks you to help Him fix a car.

Maybe He just wants to visit with you once a week to receive your worship.

Maybe He asks you to teach some children about Him.

Maybe He asks you to clean up a dirty house for Him.

Maybe He asks you to visit one of His friends in prison.

You know where I'm going with this, don't you? If Jesus were to really do this, we would consider it the greatest of honors. Yet, the truth is that He asks us these things every day. But when we are consumed with our own personal agendas, our own reputations, our own conveniences, we can miss it. Sadly, if we see no personal or vocational benefit to some of these activities, we can pass on them.

But giving a command performance means that we are playing to an audience of One. He alone is the beginning and end of our motivations.

Give me a pure heart—that I may see Thee,
A humble heart—that I may hear Thee,
A heart of love—that I may serve Thee,
A heart of faith—that I may abide in Thee.[62]

These words of Dag Hammarskjold reflect the heart of one who has learned the joy of a command performance.

Is this some magical formula that will guarantee sincerity and a true heart of ministry and service to Him? No, there is no formula. Furthermore, I hope I've made it clear by now that this will be a perpetual struggle.

But there is good news. Living for Christ, truly living to please Him in private as well as in public, in our hearts as well as in our words and deeds, is so much more fulfilling than trying to pad our résumés. There is joy in knowing we have served Christ in even the smallest of ways. Intimacy between us and God is built and nurtured as we seek to serve "for His eyes only."

Your witness for Christ should be very public, but much of your deepest and most meaningful service will be secret. If you've discovered that, maybe even in a small way, you've been faking church, it is almost always because you've been playing to the wrong audience. You have been called to give the performance of your lives—a command performance.

CHAPTER THIRTEEN

CHANGING COURSE

DECISION—N.
to make up one's mind,
or reach a decision,
about; determine

"There is a time when
we must firmly choose
the course we will follow,
or the relentless drift of events
will make the decision."

HERBERT V. PROCHNOW

I remember years ago watching the *Wide World of Sports* television program. At the beginning of each episode, the announcer would laud "the thrill of victory, and the agony of defeat." One of the opening scenes of the show became indelibly printed on my mind: an attempted ski jump. A ski jumper is racing down a jump in good form, until suddenly he falls and tumbles head over heels off the side of the jump, his arms and legs flailing wildly. This was all we ever saw. The conclusion I had always drawn was that he had lost his balance and fallen.

However the truth is somewhat different. What viewers were never told was that the skier *chose* to fall rather than finish his jump.

He never lost his balance; he instead made a choice. The reason, as he later explained, was that the jump surface had become too fast, and midway down the jump, he realized that if he completed the jump, he would land on the level ground, beyond the safe landing area. This could have been fatal. He made a decision to fall and suffered no more than a headache from the famous accident.

Making a change of course in life can also be a dramatic and sometimes painful undertaking. It is fearful to change course, but it is also dangerous to continue the way we are going. It is not a choice between safe and dangerous but between risk and risk. Each course holds dangers; each course holds pain.

We have spent much time dealing with the issue of faking church—its motivations and its consequences, both personally and for the church. But now we must choose. We are much like the skier heading down the jump, faced with a hard choice. If we change course, if we decide not to fake church anymore but to address our deception and our defection, it will hurt and it might be inconvenient or embarrassing. There is just no getting around that. On the other hand, if we don't make a change, we might be on an ultimate collision course with truth. That also will hurt, and the consequences could be far more severe.

Although I advocate changing course, I acknowledge that this will be different for every individual person. Some of us are involved in church but realize now that we have been faking our spiritual reputations and ministries at times. Others of us have possibly left fellowship and service. We haven't been to church in years, maybe decades. And there are some who became Christians but never got connected with church, service, or ministry at all, being "lone rangers" in their faith. Finally, there might be those who have been in church for years but realize that not only has their ministry and service been fake but so has their faith. They do not yet truly have a relationship with God; they have been faking church in the ultimate sense.

To each group there is a different encouragement, a different challenge. We must begin to change course from our present positions. "God judges a man," says James S. Stewart, "not by the point he has reached, but by the way he is facing; not by distance, but by direction."[63] Changing course involves intentionally facing in a new direction. We will begin with those who, like me, remain in church but realize that we have spiritually defected.

SPIRITUAL DEFECTORS

If you are presently involved in a church in a frequent or even infrequent way, and yet you realize that you have been faking your spiritual reputation and ministry at times, changing course does not involve a change of scenery. You do not have to return to church; you never left—at least not completely. What you have to return to is what our Lord called our "first love." Our Lord in the Book of Revelation left messages for churches still in existence in those days. The one that speaks particularly to our situation was to the church in Ephesus. It was a good church in a number of ways, yet Jesus pointed out its greatest flaw. "Yet I hold this against you: You have forsaken your first love. Remember the height from which you have fallen! Repent and do the things you did at first" (Revelation 2:4–5).

The love of God that had so characterized the Ephesian church at first had grown cool, and a love for other things, along with compromise and spiritual corruption, had taken root. Jesus called them back to their first love, their love for Him. Early in the life of the church, we discover that people were faking church, going through all the correct religious motions, looking extremely good externally, yet doing them for the wrong reasons. Note that they were not doing *bad* things; they were doing *good* things for the wrong motivation.

They had not left church, they had not abandoned service, they had not denied the faith. Just the opposite was true. From every external sign they were a healthy, dynamic church. They worked hard, they persevered, they did not tolerate wickedness,

they tested those who claimed to be apostles, they endured hardships for Jesus, and they did not grow weary in any of it. What
more could you ask for in a church from Christians? Many pastors
today would love to pastor such a group of Christians.

But Jesus looked beyond their résumés, beyond their programs, beyond their activities, and directly into their hearts. His
laserlike gaze exposed their greatest flaws immediately. They were
not doing it out of love for Him; some less noble motivation drove
them now.

I have a very special place in my heart for those of you who remain in church, who work so very hard, who have denied yourself
so much, who have sacrificed so greatly—often for many years.
And yet, as one of you, I remind you that God is calling you to
serve Him out of a love for Him.

For us a change of course involves going back into our Sunday school classes, into our pulpits, into our elder and deacon
boards, into our various positions of leadership, ministry, and
service with an entirely new mind-set—in fact, with new hearts.
Ironically, everything we have been doing will look precisely the
same as it did before. We will preach, teach, serve, help, bake,
build, sing, evangelize—just as we have for so long. All that will
change for us is the *reason* we are doing it. And yet, this will be a
change of eternal and lasting significance.

The change of course will be inward, private, hidden from all
eyes but His. An incredible metamorphosis will have taken place,
but to most eyes little will have changed.

Can you begin to see with new eyes? Can you begin to honestly assess the motivations that drive you in your ministry and
service in church? Yes, you served, taught, led, baked, built, sang,
and evangelized before, maybe for many years, but for you it will
never be the same again. It must not be. In repentance, in sorrow,
in sadness you have recognized that you have at times deceived
yourself and others about why you do what you do. You have mis-
led others as to your real spiritual condition. Now a corner has
been turned. Now you will see all those activities in a radically new

light. If the truth is that you aren't nearly as spiritual as you pretend you are, you will admit it—first to yourself, then to God, then to trusted others.

If your service has been motivated by less-than-sterling ambitions, you will not pack it up. You will ask God for a new heart, just like King David (Psalm 51:10). If a former murderer and adulterer can be accepted back into service, you can, too. If Peter, who denied even knowing Jesus, can be immediately put back into service, so can you. But it won't be the same service. Not to you. Your reason for serving, leading, teaching, baking, singing, and evangelizing will be totally different. You will be doing these things not to impress others or to pad your spiritual résumés but to please Him and Him alone. Your service to others will find its source in your love for Him, which found its source in His love for you.

It is a new audience you will be playing to. You will not deny your deception or defection, but you will not wallow in guilt over it either. The time has come to make a change and to walk in a new direction with a new heart.

The One you are serving is patient, kind, all loving, all merciful, all gracious, and knows that your best efforts will be imperfect. He won't be expecting perfection, but He will be expecting a change of heart. If you understand how much He loves you, how much He accepts you, this won't be hard; it will be freeing, refreshing, and life changing. This, for us, is the greatest change of direction. We cannot go back. We must not.

We will not seek to mislead or pad our spiritual résumés anymore. It won't be easy. We will have temptations, failures, setbacks, moments when we feel we aren't making any progress at all. But remember that just being in the battle is progress. Just fighting the fight, just knowing there is a struggle going on is progress. Yes, you will still fake it at times. No, you won't always have perfect motivations, but you will be aware of those moments now, maybe for the first time. And you will not feel comfortable with deception anymore. Now *it* will fit you uncomfortably. Like a dirty shirt you have cast aside, you may take it up now and again, when it seems convenient, but you will feel dirty in it and desire to remove it as quickly as you can.

This is a change of direction, a substantial course correction. It is a move from duty to devotion. What people think of our service will not be nearly as important to us as what He thinks of it. And joy will return. Joy unspeakable. To serve out of gratitude for His love is the most compelling, the most fulfilling, the most freeing motivation in life. Once we have experienced it, we will lose our appetite for anything else. We will have set a new course.

Billy Graham remarked that "a compass is narrow-minded— it always points to the magnetic north. It seems that is a very narrow view, but a compass is not broad-minded. If it were, all the ships at sea and all the planes in the air would be in danger. We must discipline ourselves, personally, to fight any deviation from the course Jesus set for us. We cannot be tolerant of any other course. To deviate is to sin."[64]

Jesus' greatest joy was to do the will of His Father. That was the course He set for His life, and He never deviated from it. That is now magnetic north to you. You will find true joy in no other direction. Yet, maybe you have slowly, reluctantly defected from fellowship and the church. It has been a long time since you were there or were involved. Your change of course will look different.

PHYSICAL DEFECTORS

As you have read this book, you may have been reminded, or maybe even learned for the first time, what church and fellowship is really all about. Yes, at a point in time you gave your life to Jesus, you committed to serve Him, you entered into ministry in some way, small or large. Maybe you served in church for many years and had fellowship with many. Some of you might have been heavily involved. You might have been pastors, missionaries, teachers, elders, deacons, youth pastors, or worship leaders. You weren't fringe attenders; you were committed. Your sacrifice was real, your involvement serious.

But you haven't been back in a long time. When you do visit, you have not been inclined to stay. The same problems exist, the same issues and feelings you faced before are still there. For you a course change involves first making a commitment that you will return to fellowship. You understand anew or have been reminded that you are a part of the body of Christ, designed by God to be intimately connected with the rest of the body.

Columnist Jonathan Rauch, a longtime atheist, has been heartened by a new phenomenon he has noticed in America that he calls "apatheism." Writing for the *Atlantic Monthly,* he points out that "It's not that people don't believe in God anymore—the majority will still say they believe. But statistics show that they're going to church less, and when they do go, it's more to socialize or enjoy a familiar ritual than to worship." As he observes, they're refraining from sharing their faith with their friends and neighbors. On the whole, Rauch observes, people are looking for comfort and reassurance, not for a God who asks anything of them.[65]

It is against this culture of "apatheism" that you should revolt. The church is not about you; it is about God. You have been reminded of that. It isn't about just meeting your needs; it is about taking the God-given gifts you have and offering them to Him in His church. It is about responding properly to the eternal love, eternal sacrifice, and eternal mercy He has shown to you. A. W. Tozer wrote, "Thank God you don't have to be flawless to be blessed! You need to have a big heart that desires and wants the will of God more than anything else in the world. You need also to have an eye single to His glory."[66] An eye single to His glory—what a wonderful phrase. It is the answer to "apatheism."

A change in course will look quite different for you. Instead of isolation from church and fellowship, now association is the new direction you will take. Instead of staying away from church, fellowship, commitment, and church life, you will make a concerted effort to reverse your direction.

This will be more than good intention; it will be resolve. I encourage you to seek a Bible-teaching, Christ-honoring church where God's grace is clearly understood. If you are comfortable in a high church with a more liturgical setting, fine; find a local Christ-honoring liturgical church (of which there are many) and return. If you are comfortable with a less formal setting, find a local church that you can be more comfortable in and begin attending.

You won't go in with an eye to judging the church, or the pastor, or the choir, or the worship music. You will go to associate with your fellow brothers and sisters in Christ. You are merely family that has returned home. It may be like attending a family reunion of brothers, sisters, cousins, aunts, and uncles you have never met; you will feel a little awkward at first. That's to be expected, but just remember that you *are* family!

This won't always be easy. Maybe you don't know what church to go to. Maybe you have put some other activity in place of church attendance and fellowship. Changing course for you involves reprioritizing your entire life. Your life *will* look different— radically different. Some things may have to be given up or given lower priority in your life.

Maybe past offenses or fears will tempt you to stay away, but this time you won't listen to them. There may be some false starts: You intend to go and then bail out. But the desire won't leave you, and you will eventually return. The change in heart and mind has already taken place; it is only a matter of time before the change of heart leads to a change in activity.

But you *will* change course—even when you don't feel like it, even if it is embarrassing, even if it is humbling. What you would not do for people you will do for Him. Once the decision has been made to do that, the result is inevitable.

Don't look for a perfect church; you'll never find one. You will not be going to simply meet your own needs but to honor God and to love and serve Him with all your heart, soul, and strength (Deuteronomy 6:5). You will not be seeking to throw your weight around or to impress others with your past résumé but to find a place to humbly serve Him with others who also love Him—imperfectly, just like you do. You will not be surprised or put off by the hypocrisy or sin you find in those you fellowship with, since you know those same sins can reside within you. But you will be surprised to find some whose hearts are so tender toward Him and toward others that you will wish you had come back sooner.

You will no longer convince yourself that you will be better off without church or will be able to grow closer to God without the "problems" of church. You will acknowledge that the church is the place where you will grow the strongest and that the problems of church give you the opportunity to grow in areas like forgiveness, patience, understanding, and compassion.

You will begin to ask God to give you a place to serve Him in the midst of His body, your local church. Maybe you will return to the ministry you left behind, or maybe God will put a brand-new passion in its place for service or ministry in a different place. The Lord's Day will have a new meaning in your heart and life. Service for Him will be new for you as well.

One of the greatest obstacles will be past hurts you endured at church. You may have been clinging to bitterness or unforgiveness. Yet this will no longer keep you from fellowship. If God can forgive all your sins, which are many, you can forgive the sins of those in the body of Christ who are still in the process of growth. This is how you will demonstrate your love for your God. This is the sacrifice you are willing to make for Him. You will realize that you cannot possibly grow spiritually while you are refusing to be a part of the very church that the Holy Spirit birthed you into and that you are so inextricably connected to. The church isn't something you go to join; it is something God has joined you to.

Pastor and author John Claypool once told the story of a thunderstorm that swept through southern Kentucky at the family farm where six generations of Claypools had lived. In the orchard, the wind blew over an old pear tree that had been there as long as anyone could remember. He recalls that his grandfather was grieved to lose the tree on which he had climbed as a boy and whose fruit he had enjoyed for so many years. A neighbor came by and said, "Doc, I'm really sorry to see your pear tree blown down."

"I'm sorry, too," said his grandfather. "It was a real part of my past."

"What are you going to do?" the neighbor asked.

Claypool's grandfather paused for a moment and then said, "I'm going to pick the fruit and burn what's left." He then went on to share that this is the wise way to deal with many things in our past. We need to learn their lessons, enjoy their pleasures, and then go on with the present and the future.

Some of your experiences at church might have been painful, but they weren't terminal. God had a purpose even in them. Maybe one day you will see it, or maybe you won't know it until this world is over, but it must not keep you from following Him fully. None of Jesus' original twelve disciples were perfect, and none of today's disciples are either. But God is calling you to return to fellowship and service.

Now I want to mention a group that might want to attend church but no longer can: the shut-ins. Certainly a physical inability to get to church is different than someone who has consciously chosen not to go. My only encouragement is that you seek to find a local church who might be willing to visit you and encourage you in your faith. For you the virtual church holds great encouragement. But there is nothing that takes the place of the flesh-and-blood church, and if you can become a part in any way at all, I encourage you to try.

"All heaven is waiting to help those who will discover the will of God and do it," writes J. Robert Ashcroft.[67] When you feel hesitant, unsure, or indecisive, you only need to ask God to give you the strength and resolve to do what He would have you do. He doesn't want to send you into misery but into joy and fulfillment in serving Him. The pleasure you will bring to your heavenly Father is greater than any earthly reward you could hope to receive. He knows how to convey His pleasure in your heart and mind as you do His will; you don't have to guess at it.

If you have left church, fellowship, and service, or any of these three, the call of Christ is to return. You are missed more than you know. And you are missing more than you know. You have felt the gentle call of the Holy Spirit to come back before, and you have resisted it. This time, obey the call. In the words of Abraham Lincoln, who knew well the nature of difficult decisions, "Having thus chosen our course, let us renew our trust in God and go forward without fear and with manly hearts."[68]

IGNORANT DEFECTION

Perhaps you truly do believe in God and have trusted in Jesus' work on your behalf, but you were abandoned at your spiritual birth. Someone led you to a knowledge of Jesus but you were never discipled, so your spiritual life was stunted. You never got to know the family God joined you to. Or perhaps church was such a foreign institution to you that you never truly understood its importance in your spiritual life. Maybe you felt you could get along quite well without it. Or maybe someone led you to a belief in Jesus but never made it clear that you were now not only a child of God but also a part of His church.

God is waiting to do wonderful things in your life and character through the church. There's a potential for you to grow in unexpected and very important ways. Fellowship with other Christians is not just a nice spiritual option; it is the very way God has designed us to grow spiritually. Your greatest course correction will be to enter the doors of a church—maybe for the first time or maybe for the first time with a commitment to becoming a real part. You may feel like a stranger, but if you are a believer in Jesus, you are family. You *do* belong there; it is your spiritual home.

Or maybe you have been a Christian for some time and have even attended church sporadically, but you have never committed yourself to ministry and service. Your greatest course correction will be to realize that you are not an atrophied member of the body of Christ. You are an important, pivotal part and you are needed. God has designed you for some special place of service in His kingdom, in His church.

Maybe you have tried to remain anonymous in churches you have attended, resisting all attempts to get any more involved. But now you realize that this is what God has put you into His church to do: to serve Him by serving others. You have been AWOL in His service. But you now know that God doesn't save us so that we can keep on living the same old life we did before but to become involved in His great new kingdom. There is a new world coming and a new kingdom that lives within us.

You don't have to be perfect to be in service in His church, and you don't have to be a Bible scholar. Many Christians in church aren't knowledgeable about the Bible. In finding a place to serve, you will be taking your place in God's kingdom and within His church. There you can learn more about the Bible, God's Word. You will also learn how to receive and give love to people—an immensely important lesson in life.

Serving God is the greatest joy a Christian can receive in this life. Don't cheat yourself out of this joy any longer! Find a church nearby, one that teaches and honors the Bible and honors Jesus Christ. Don't be a homeless Christian any longer. Everywhere I have traveled all over this country, I have found churches I could enter and immediately find sweet fellowship and people who loved God and were trying to serve Him the best way they knew how. Churches aren't hard to find.

I know how difficult this step might be to you. You might not have any tradition at church at all. It might be as strange to you as a blazing hot desert would be to an Eskimo. You have virtually no history in church. Maybe no one you know goes to church. If so, I know this is asking a lot. It will be hard, I won't deny it. To go from being an absolute stranger to church to entering one is a frightening proposition to some people. If you are afraid of what you will find, let me prepare you. You will find people who believe in God, who are trying to serve Him as well as they can, who fail at times, who get humbled, who make mistakes, and yet who love God. In short, you will fit right in, because they are just like you.

The songs may sound strange to you, the traditions of that particular church may be foreign to you at first, but the call to follow Christ leads you there. It is His church you are entering, and you are part of His church if you have trusted in Him.

This leads to one last group that I need to address. There may be some reading this book who have attended church periodically or have been an active part of a church for many years. You might have spent your entire life in church, or you might have attended hit and miss. But you may have recently come to the startling conclusion that you have been faking church in the ultimate way: You have never really placed your faith in Jesus Christ completely. You have always called yourself a Christian but in much the same way you called yourself a Democrat or a Republican or an Independent. It was, at the most, a cultural description.

But now the Holy Spirit of God is calling you to reexamine what you really believe about God. You have not made the connection between the incredible sacrifice that the eternal God of the universe made when He humbled Himself to become a baby in our world. When He lived on our earth and suffered for us. When He allowed Himself to be put on a cross it was so He could make the ultimate and final payment for sins. It was for you that Jesus came, and it was for you that Jesus died. His death was not an accident; it was His life deliberately given for you—to bring you into the kingdom of God.

It is not by your good works or your birth in a Christian family or nation that saves you from sin and opens up the gates of God's eternal kingdom to you; it is His grace. "For it is by grace you have been saved, through faith—and this not from yourselves, it is the gift of God—not by works, so that no one can boast. For we are God's workmanship, created in Christ Jesus to do good works, which God prepared in advance for us to do" (Ephesians 2:8–10).

You have understood religion a little, but now you are beginning to realize that you have missed having a relationship with Christ—the very thing God is seeking. You weren't intentionally faking your faith. You just never made the connection that God came to earth to enable you to enter a relationship with your heavenly Father (2 Corinthians 5:19).

You are the reason God became a man. You are the reason the holy, eternal God gave up His glory and His heavenly throne to humble Himself before us (Philippians 2:5–8). You are the reason He suffered human indignities. You are the reason He came to earth to die. It was His love for you that drove Him to the cross to take the punishment we deserved, which would allow God to forgive us all our sins—past, present, and future. And you are the one He is calling to, searching for, reaching out to. Your course correction is the most obvious: It will take you from death into life, from blindness into seeing, from enmity with God to friendship and peace with God.

This course correction is not something you have to do at church; it is something you can do right now. There is no magical formula for becoming a Christian. There simply comes a moment when you choose to believe that Jesus is truly the Son of God, that He died for your sins, and that He actually rose from the dead and is now offering to you forgiveness for sins, eternal life, and fellowship with Him forever. It is a moment of personal realization that God loves you personally and that His death was for you. It is in faith you accept this gift, and you place your trust in Him and what *He* has done for you for your eternal life. Do not trust in yourself and your own goodness. You can never respond to God's love unless you have experienced it through becoming His child.

Dwight Moody, an evangelist of the past generation, once said, "Seeking to perpetuate one's name on earth is like writing on the sand by the seashore; to be perpetual it must be written on eternal shores."[69] Make sure your name has been written on an eternal shore.

In reality, you have not found God; He has found you. Jesus came to seek and to save that which was lost. After you place your trust in Him, you become a part of the church all over the world and will now need to find a local church to begin to find your place in this exciting new life you have entered. Or, if you have been attending a church, realize that you are now a member of the church by spiritual rebirth.

This kind of a decision is difficult. "Jesus never met a disease He could not cure, a birth defect He could not reverse, a demon He could not exorcise," writes author Philip Yancey. "But He did meet skeptics He could not convince and sinners He could not convert. Forgiveness of sins requires an act of will on the receiver's part, and some who heard Jesus' strongest words about grace and forgiveness turned away unrepentant."[70]

Maybe that described you before but no longer. That is my hope and prayer. You can now enter the church being real—your faith is real, your relationship with God is real, your relationship with the church is real. Your whole life God has been calling to you, guiding you to Him.

"God leads us step by step, from event to event. Only afterwards, as we look back over the way we have come and reconsider certain important moments in our lives in the light of all that has followed them, or when we survey the whole progress of our lives, do we experience the feeling of having been led without knowing it, the feeling that God has mysteriously guided us," wrote Paul Tournier.[71]

God has mysteriously guided you to Him. And now He is guiding you into His church, of which you are now a part. He has made you a member of His church. Welcome!

Now, as I close this book, I want to emphasize that the best way to keep from faking church, from sliding back into deception and pretense and spiritual charades, is to live focused on a new reality.

ONE EYE ON ETERNITY

J. B. Phillips, a pastor and author of the last generation, responded once to critics of the church who complained that if Christianity was really a good religion, the world would be a much better place now than it is. "They make two mistakes," he points out. "In the first place Christianity—the real thing—has never been accepted on a large scale and has therefore never been in a position to control the 'state of the world,' though its influence has been far from negligible. In the second place, they misunderstood the nature of Christianity. It is not to be judged by its success or failure to reform the world which rejects it. It is a revelation of the true way of living, the way to know God, the way to live life of eternal quality."[72]

Living a life of eternal quality. That is what the church is truly called to do. We do not achieve this by being perfect (or pretending to be). To live a life of eternal quality is to live our lives with one eye on eternity. It is hard to make correct decisions as a Christian in this world unless we keep an eye on eternity at all times. Keeping one eye on eternity reminds us that a change is taking place within us—a change that will see fruition one day when we pass from this life to the next.

This life is not all there is. To try to create a false impression of our spiritual condition here on earth is a waste of time and energy. There is another world coming. We are "practicing" for this new world, growing and preparing for the next world here, in the church, the body of Christ He left behind as a witness. We were never left to become actors or actresses for Him but real, live, breathing examples of transformation from one life into another.

Change takes place slowly but surely. This is evidence that a new kingdom has come; a new world order has been established. C. S. Lewis writes, "A continual looking forward to the eternal world is not a form of escapism or wishful thinking, but one of the things a Christian is meant to do. It does not mean that we are to leave the present world as it is. If you read history, you will find that the Christians who did the most for the present world were just those who thought most of the next."[73]

Time is too short to spend faking church. Deception no longer becomes us. It is one of those things that, in the process of being transformed into the image of Christ (Romans 12:2; 2 Corinthians 3:18), must slowly detach itself from us. It no longer fits our new life. We have been remade for a new life of service in the body of Christ, the church.

*"In her voyage across the ocean of this world,
the church is like a great ship being pounded
by the waves of life's different stresses.
Our duty is not to abandon ship
but to keep her on her course."*

SAINT BONIFACE (680–754)[74]

Barbour Publishing, Inc., expresses its appreciation to all those who generously gave permission to reprint copyrighted material. Diligent effort has been made to identify, locate, contact, and secure permission to use copyrighted material. If any permissions or acknowledgments have been inadvertently omitted or if such permissions were not received by the time of publication, the publisher would sincerely appreciate receiving complete information so that correct credit can be given in future editions.

CHAPTER 2
1. *Draper's Book of Quotations for the Christian World* (Wheaton, Ill.: Tyndale, 1992), #6853.
2. Ibid., #7866.

CHAPTER 3
3. *Draper's*, #6296.
4. Philip Yancey, *Reaching for the Invisible God* (Harper Collins/Zondervan, 2000), 130. Used by permission of the Zondervan Corporation.

CHAPTER 4
5. *Draper's*, #7862.
6. Ibid., #7867.

CHAPTER 5
7. George Barna, *Grow Your Church from the Outside In* (Ventura, Calif.: Gospel Light/Regal Books, 2002). Used by permission of Light/Regal Books, Ventura, CA 93003.
8. Janette Gardner, "New Trend in Unchurched Christians," *Moody Magazine* (Gardner Littleton, March/April 2003).
9. Nathan Jones, "On My Heart," *Biola Connections* (Spring 2003), 17.
10. Yancey, 242–243.
11. Gary R. Habermas, *The Thomas Factor* (Broadman and Holman, 1999), 101–103.

CHAPTER 6
12. www.barna.org
13. Ibid.
14. Ibid.

15. Charles Colson, *Loving God* (Grand Rapids: Zondervan, 1987), 175.
16. C. S. Lewis, *Letters of C. S. Lewis* (Harcourt Brace Jovanovich, 1966), 224.
17. C. S. Lewis, *Answers to Questions on Christianity* (Grand Rapids, Mich.: Eerdman's, 1970), 61–62.
18. Dr. Robert Saucy, *The Church in God's Program* (Chicago: Moody 1972), 24. Used by permission.
19. *Draper's*, #1352.
20. www.barna.org
21. C. S. Lewis, *Answers to Questions on Christianity* (Grand Rapids, Mich.: Eerdman's, 1970), 59.
22. *Draper's*, #1401.
23. Ibid., #1269.

CHAPTER 7
24. Bruce Larson, *Dare to Live Now* (Grand Rapids: Zondervan, 1965), 110. Used by permission of the Zondervan Corporation.
25. Charles Spurgeon, "The Spiritually Lazy Saint," *Daily Devotions*, May 10.
26. Saucy, 102.
27. Ibid., 190.

CHAPTER 8
28. Eugene H. Petersen, *The Contemplative Pastor* (Grand Rapids: Eerdman's, 1993), 49. Used by permission.
29. Warren Wiersbe, *The Integrity Crisis* (Oliver Nelson, 1988), 44–46.
30. A.W. Tozer, *The Next Chapter After the Last* (Christian Publications, Inc., 1987), 7–8. Used by permission of Christian Publications, Inc., 800.233.4443, www.christianpublications.com.
31. *Draper's*, #115.

CHAPTER 9
32. "Displays of Soviet Weaponry Called Fake," Associated Press.
33. Yancey, 167.
34. Ibid., 213.

CHAPTER 10
35. William J. Murray, *The Church Is Not for Perfect People* (Eugene, Ore.: Harvest House, 1987), 48–49.
36. *Draper's*, #0324.
37. Joseph Stowell, from "I'd Rather Have Jesus," *Moody Magazine*, Jan/February 2001.

CHAPTER 11
38. Larry Crabb, *The Safest Place on Earth* (Thomas Nelson, 1999), 30. Reprinted by permission of Thomas Nelson, Inc. All rights reserved.
39. Peter LeVine, *Boardroom Reports*, July 15, 1993.

40. *Draper's,* #5873.
41. Brent Curtis and John Eldredge, *The Sacred Romance* (Nashville, Tenn.: Thomas Nelson, Inc., 1997), 137. Reprinted by permission of Thomas Nelson, Inc., All rights reserved.
42. *Draper's,* #5221.
43. Ibid., #9577.
44. Ibid., #9591.
45. Curtis and Eldredge, 168–170.
46. *Draper's,* #890.
47. Crabb, 32.
48. A.W. Tozer, *Born After Midnight* (Christian Publications, Inc., 1989), 59. Used by Permission of Christian Publications, Inc., 800.233.4443, www.christianpublications.com.
49. Adam R. Holz, "Without a Net," *Discipleship Journal,* Issue 137, Sept/Oct 2003, 8.
50. *Draper's,* #9582.
51. C. S. Lewis, *The Business of Heaven: Daily Readings,* January 1 (Inspirational Press, 1987), 296.

CHAPTER 12
52. *Draper's,* #10159.
53. Ibid., #4810.
54. Ibid., #6569.
55. Ibid., #5467.
56. Ibid., #7533.
57. Ibid., #10012.
58. Ibid., #10019.
59. Ibid., #4818.
60. Ibid., #1914.
61. C. S. Lewis, *Surprised by Joy: The Shape of My Earthly Life* (New York: Harcourt Brace Jovanovich, 1955), 228–229.
62. *Draper's,* #7458.

CHAPTER 13
63. *Draper's,* #4713.
64. Ibid., #9965.
65. Jonathan Rauch, "Let It Be," *Atlantic Monthly,* May 2003.
66. *Draper's,* #5442.
67. Ibid., #5373.
68. Ibid., #1918.
69. Ibid., #3860.
70. Philip Yancey, *The Jesus I Never Knew* (Grand Rapids: Zondervan, 1995), 174. Used by permission of the Zondervan Corporation.
71. *Draper's,* #5392.
72. Ibid., #1188.
73. C. S. Lewis, *Mere Christianity* (New York: Macmillan, 1952), 118.
74. *Draper's,* #1398.

ABOUT THE AUTHOR

Dan Schaeffer is a conference speaker and author of hundreds of magazine articles and seven books, including *In Search of the Real Spirit of Christmas*. He is co-pastor of Shoreline Community Church in Santa Barbara. Dan and his wife, Annette, have three children.

Visit Dan's web site at www.danschaeffer.com.